ECONOMIC RESTRUCTURING AND RURAL SUBSISTENCE IN MEXICO

TRANSFORMATION OF RURAL MEXICO SERIES, Number 2
EJIDO REFORM RESEARCH PROJECT
CENTER FOR U.S.-MEXICAN STUDIES
UNIVERSITY OF CALIFORNIA, SAN DIEGO

David Myhre, Series Editor

CO-PUBLISHED WITH THE UNITED NATIONS RESEARCH
INSTITUTE FOR SOCIAL DEVELOPMENT (UNRISD), GENEVA

PRINTED WITH THE ASSISTANCE
OF THE FORD FOUNDATION

ECONOMIC RESTRUCTURING AND RURAL SUBSISTENCE IN MEXICO: CORN AND THE CRISIS OF THE 1980s

edited by

CYNTHIA HEWITT DE ALCÁNTARA

TRANSFORMATION OF RURAL MEXICO, Number 2

**EJIDO REFORM RESEARCH PROJECT
CENTER FOR U.S.-MEXICAN STUDIES, UCSD**

**UNITED NATIONS RESEARCH INSTITUTE
FOR SOCIAL DEVELOPMENT (UNRISD)**

 CENTRO TEPOZTLÁN

Printed in the United States of America
by the Center for U.S.-Mexican Studies
University of California, San Diego

1994

Cover: Linoleum block print by Annika Nelson

ISBN 1-878367-19-6

Revised and updated edition of the original in Spanish:
Cynthia Hewitt de Alcántara, compiladora. *Reestructuración
económica y subsistencia rural: El maíz y la crisis de los
ochenta.* México, D.F.: El Colegio de México, con el
Instituto de Investigaciones de las Naciones Unidas para el
Desarrollo Social (UNRISD), y el Centro Tepoztlán, 1992.

NB: The information and analysis presented herein are the
responsibility of the authors.

TABLE OF CONTENTS

PREFACE

This book, and the seminar on which it is based, were conceived as elements of a dialogue on the future of the Mexican countryside. Rural Mexico, like the rest of Mexican society, is changing rapidly in response to a variety of circumstances, many of which are very imperfectly understood. It is clear, for example, that both the debt-related recession of the 1980s and the kind of macroeconomic policy implemented to deal with the crisis have changed the parameters of livelihood for a great many rural people. It is also clear that the more recently instituted restructuring of the economy, which includes participation in a North American Free Trade Agreement (NAFTA), has profound implications for agriculture, rural industry and other central elements of economic activity in the countryside. What is not at all evident is how these macroeconomic shifts make themselves felt in concrete local contexts and how, through the varied responses of different kinds of people, the nature of rural life is being altered.

This is too broad a question to be addressed without some effort to structure the dialogue. The approach of this book is therefore to focus upon a central element in the livelihood of most rural people, the production and consumption of maize, and upon a key component of macroeconomic policy reform, that which has been concerned with reducing the cost and increasing the efficiency of the maize provisioning system of the country. Within the latter one finds one of the most politically important points of conflicting interests in the Mexican economy: the contradiction between low-income producers and low-income consumers of maize. And in consequence, one has also traditionally found some of the most extensive areas of public subsidy, directed toward the agricultural sector on the one hand, and toward low-income consumers on the other.

The concerted effort to restructure the entire maize pricing and marketing system, which has gone forward in conjunction with a broad ranging agricultural policy reform, affects the economic options, as well as the levels of living, of many different kinds of people in the Mexican countryside, and it does so in complex ways. The initial frame of reference of large commercial farmers is of course distinguishable in important respects from that of small commercial farmers, semi-subsistence or subsistence cultivators, and the landless. Similarly, maize pricing and marketing reform is experienced differently by rural households according to the importance of various kinds of crops or activities in generating a total pool of income, and in relation to the idiosyncracies of local and regional markets.

Although this is obvious on an intuitive level, there is currently very little new material with which to document specific processes of change in the rural maize economy. While there is a continuous flow of information in newspapers and other public media on the incremental policy changes which gradually restructure the parameters of economic activity -- including the macroeconomic reforms of most immediate relevance to maize agriculture and to food policy -- this information is not often synthesized in a way which permits analysis of its probable impact on various categories of rural people.

As part of its program of international research on adjustment-related food policy, now completed, UNRISD therefore sponsored two projects in Mexico which, it was hoped, could provide useful new perspectives on the implications of economic restructuring for rural livelihood. The first project was carried out at the macroeconomic level and involved a detailed consideration of the course of maize pricing and marketing reform, explained within the context of the broader effort first to adjust the economy to the constraints of the post 1982 period and then to reorient it definitively toward a competitive free-market stance. This analysis is presented in a book entitled *De la milpa a los tortibonos: La reestructuración de la política alimentaria en México*, by Kirsten Appendini (El Colegio de México, 1992).

The second project moved from the macroeconomic terrain to the microeconomic, social and political. At a seminar held at the Centro Tepoztlán in early January 1990, a group of social scientists deeply involved in research on rural life -- and often engaged in governmental or non-governmental programs in support of rural livelihood -- considered the evolution of local survival strategies in particular communities or regions, in relation to the changing macro-economic context. Their ideas were discussed not only with colleagues working in different geographical settings, but also with seminar participants from various official institutions, economic research institutes and agencies of the United Nations.

A selection of the seminar papers appeared first in a book titled *Reestructuración económica y subsistencia rural: El maíz y la crisis de los ochenta*, co-published by UNRISD, El Colegio de México and the Centro Tepoztlán in 1992. The present English-language edition, jointly sponsored by the Center for U.S.-Mexican Studies of the University of California at San Diego, is shorter than the Spanish-language version and has been modified to include discussion of policy changes in the period 1990-1993.

It should perhaps be stressed that since none of the participants in the Tepoztlán seminar had been previously commissioned to orient his or her own longer-term work in the countryside around a rigorous effort to trace the effect of a specific policy reform, or group of reforms, on a particular group of people, this book should not be read as a treatise on "the impact of adjustment." It is a collection of reflections on various aspects of a central political and social issue: the changing parameters of maize production and consumption in the Mexican countryside during a period of prolonged economic crisis and macroeconomic redefinition. In some cases, the links between changing public policy and the adaptations of local people are direct and obvious. In others, contributors have attempted to provide the elements of structural analysis which are necessary for beginning to predict what the differential social impact of particular policies might be.

Local and regional-level perspectives are supplemented by chapters which provide both macroeconomic and macropolitical context, which question some of the central suppositions of the new policy framework and which propose alternatives. The frame of reference of contributors is broadly *campesinista*, if that term is taken to designate people who habitually work with civic organizations defending the interests of middle- and low-income rural people, and/or with official institutions charged with a similar mandate, and who are convinced of the need to ensure a viable future for small farmers. Like everyone else, they are searching for answers to complex questions in unstable times.

In closing, it is a pleasure to acknowledge the contributions of many individuals and institutions who made the Tepoztlán seminar -- and subsequent books in Spanish and English -- possible. Carlos Tello, then head of the Consultative Committee of the National Solidarity Program, provided early encouragement for the dialogue, as did the Director of the National Indian Institute, Arturo Warman. Don Víctor Urquidi issued an initial invitation to hold the seminar at the Centro Tepoztlán, an invitation graciously confirmed by the incoming President of the Center, Eduardo Terrazas. In the United Nations, Antonio Tapia (then Chief of the Joint Division of FAO/CEPAL for Mexico and the Caribbean) was most supportive of the project. In addition, the interest and concern of Rodolfo Stavenhagen of El Colegio de México, and Iván Restrepo, then Director of the Centro de Ecodesarrollo, is most gratefully acknowledged, as is the willingness of Carlos Bazdresch, Director of CIDE, Carlos Montañez, Director of the Research Division of the Rural Credit Bank, and Rafael Paniagua Ruiz of the Vice Ministry of Policies and Concertation of the Ministry of Agriculture and Water Resources, to engage in a useful and sometimes heated debate with participants of diverse persuasions.

Kirsten Appendini of the Center for Economic Research of El Colegio de México played a central role both in the organization of the seminar and in the consequent preparation of Spanish- and English-language versions of the book. Her intellectual insight and personal commitment to the project are reflected throughout the manuscript, not only in her own chapter but through dozens of consultations with contributors and editors.

Others whose contributions to the seminar should be noted include Ursula Oswald, Arturo Argueta, María Eugenia Gallart, Arnulfo Embriz, Laura Ruiz, Livia Ulloa, Francis Mestries, María del Carmen Cebada, Isabel Cruz, Emma Zapata and Josefina Aranda. Miguel Székely contributed a thought-provoking essay to conclude the Spanish-language edition of the book. Solon Barraclough, Jonathan Fox, Carole Appel Piña and Sergio Alcántara Ferrer provided very useful comments on the first draft of the manuscript.

Organization of the seminar was the responsibility of Irene Ruiz de Budavari at UNRISD and Adriana Arjona of the Centro Tepoztlán. Both deserve credit and thanks for the smooth functioning of the meeting. At UNRISD, Wendy Salvo and Josephine Yates provided indispensable administrative assistance. Fay Henderson de Díaz ably translated the majority of the chapters, first written in Spanish.

Finally, it is important to acknowledge that financial support for the UNRISD project was provided by the Office for Mexico and Central America of the Ford Foundation. Participants in the seminar are particularly grateful to José Gabriel López for his commitment to this program. Readers of the English-language version of the book will be grateful as well to Wayne Cornelius, Director of the Center for U.S.-Mexican Studies, and to David Myhre, Coordinator of the Center's Ejido Reform Research Project, without whose assistance and interest this book could not have been produced.

Cynthia Hewitt de Alcántara
Geneva, Switzerland

Chapter 1

INTRODUCTION: ECONOMIC RESTRUCTURING AND RURAL SUBSISTENCE IN MEXICO

Cynthia Hewitt de Alcántara

The twentieth century is coming to a close amidst efforts on the part of a great many countries to reform the rules which have structured economic and socio-political relations over the course of several generations. This is a voluntaristic attempt, unusual in the comprehensiveness of its scope and the conviction with which governments and peoples embrace the need for change. It is also, however, a process born of necessity. Previous models of socioeconomic organization have in varying degrees reached their limits and threaten to break down altogether if not fundamentally modified.

The economic crises of the 1970s, followed by the debt crisis of the 1980s, provided the immediate stimulus for change in most countries, and certainly in the case of Mexico. Fundamental shifts in world commodity and financial markets made it impossible for the Mexican government to meet its obligations to international creditors; and behind those obligations lay a complex structure of internal transactions, of both an economic and a political nature, which were then no longer viable. Conflicts of interest within Mexican society which had not been resolved, but could be assuaged through recourse to international borrowing, were forced into view -- just, it might be added, as they were in any number of other countries, including, most recently, the United States.

Among the major issues to be confronted, once the debt crisis erupted, was the structure of subsidies and programs which had developed over a number of decades to regulate the provisioning of corn in Mexico. Corn is both the single most important crop produced by Mexican farmers and the basic staple of most rural and urban diets; and as such, it plays a central role in the livelihood of the majority of the Mexican population. The precarious position of both low-income producers and low-income consumers has long constituted an argument for governmental intervention throughout the corn system. The centrality of that product in the national diet has also lent weight to repeated efforts to promote national self-sufficiency and to protect local corn producers from foreign competition.

ELEMENTS OF CONFLICT WITHIN THE CORN PROVISIONING SYSTEM: THE PRINCIPAL ACTORS AND THEIR INTERESTS

The network of conflicting interests underlying the corn provisioning system of the country is as complex and contradictory as Mexican society itself. To understand the issues at stake within this system, it is useful to begin by referring to the classic textbook confrontation between the general interest of all producers in ensuring relatively high grain prices and the opposing interest of all consumers in ensuring lower ones. While entirely valid at a certain level of generality, such a dictum does not reflect the situation of millions of families in the Mexican countryside, where the division between producers and consumers is often blurred. As in peasant societies around the world, the majority of all rural producers in Mexico buy and sell grain on a small scale throughout the year. As a result, they have an interest in obtaining an advantageous price for their production as well as a need to purchase grain at a low price when it is locally scarce, thus considerably complicating both the politics and the economics of national corn pricing policy.

Clear lines of producer pricing policy are further complicated by the extraordinary heterogeneity of the farm sector as a whole, marked over centuries by continuous struggles between small- and large-scale producers for control over land, water and other resources crucial to agricultural production. Conditions prevailing on larger commercial farms have differed so markedly from those in the peasant sector that the level of grain prices could not conceivably have the same economic significance for all producers.[1] An advantageous price for a commercial producer utilizing irrigation and averaging yields of two to three tons per hectare would be far from remunerative for a peasant family working a rainfed parcel which yielded less than one ton per hectare.

In this context, the setting of relatively low producer prices in order to ensure the provision of cheap food for a growing urban population has particularly unfavorable implications for the livelihood of smallholding producers. And given the intensity of pressure exercised on the government both by a poor urban constituency and by rural and urban employers, who have an interest in maintaining low wages, it is just such a policy which has ultimately prevailed. Throughout most of the 1970s, support prices for corn in fact tended to decline in relation to the costs of necessary inputs. Although in most cases the support price was high enough to assure profits for commercial producers, it has since the beginning of the 1970s been insufficient to allow peasant producers, cultivating corn principally for family consumption, to cover their costs.[2]

The relatively low level of return for corn farmers has, however, been offset to a certain degree when the latter have been able to obtain access to subsidized inputs and services provided by government agencies. For example, large-scale producers in irrigated areas benefitted over decades from ample subsidies applied to water, electricity, and fuel for agricultural machinery, as well as to the cost of fertilizers and other chemical inputs. Nevertheless, since the price of corn was usually less attractive than that of other crops, producers tended to utilize these subsidies for more remunerative ventures. In consequence, large-scale irrigated agriculture in most cases has not accounted for more than 25 percent of all commercial corn production in the country, and often it has provided considerably less.

Most of the marketed corn supply of Mexico is produced by medium and small-scale farmers, the majority of whom are *ejidatarios* (beneficiaries of the establishment of agrarian reform communities known as *ejidos*). Both the need to count on an increasing volume of the grain which the ejido sector produces and the obligation of the government to improve the standard of living in the countryside have worked over the years to ensure that a limited range of services and subsidies generally made available to larger producers would increasingly be offered to small and medium-scale farmers as well.

In the beginning, it was the better-endowed ejidos, located in irrigated areas, which gained access to subsidized official credit and to the agricultural inputs which could be acquired with credit. This relatively modern subsector of ejido-based agriculture, which began to take shape during the latter 1930s, came to provide as much as 25 percent of marketed corn output. In addition, during the 1960s and especially during the 1970s, government support was extended in a somewhat tentative fashion to smaller producers working unirrigated land -- first to those in areas with the most favorable conditions for corn production and subsequently to families cultivating grain on very small holdings in areas with unreliable climatic conditions.

It is important to stress the partial nature of this effort, as well as the differential significance which agricultural development programs and access to production subsidies could have in different rural contexts.

---

1. See Montañez Villafana (1988), who notes that the cost of producing a ton of corn can vary by a factor of 100 in different rural contexts (p. 679).

2. For a detailed analysis of the profitability of corn cultivation for various kinds of producers, see chapter 2 of Appendini (1992).

For example, even with the extension of state-sponsored credit programs to less productive areas, about 37 percent of all ejidos and other agrarian communities in Mexico still did not have access to official credit in 1988, 54 percent received no technical assistance, and only 70 percent applied chemical fertilizers, the subsidized input most commonly utilized in the rural sector (de la Mora Gómez 1990, p. 945).[3] The majority of all producers continued to live in backward areas where government investment in infrastructure of all kinds was extremely low.

Just as support price levels played a variable role depending on the type of producer, so too the benefits which could be derived from a range of other governmental subsidies for corn production differed among rural groups. Since more highly technified commercial farming operations (including the better-off stratum of ejidos) utilized more of these goods and services than their counterparts operating closer to the level of subsistence, they were of course the first to benefit substantially from production subsidies.[4] Nevertheless, it should not be forgotten that these subsidies were also of considerable importance for small-scale cultivators who managed to obtain access to them. No matter how modest the quantity received, it could represent a key element in the livelihood strategy of rural families and, in the best of circumstances, a potential instrument for rural development.

At the same time, however, delivery of these subsidized inputs could be, and often was, converted into a pretext for political control. Within the major public institutions charged with managing support programs for the agricultural sector, there was a complex play of interests linked to the implementation of economic policy and the exercise of political power, as well as to the promotion of rural development. In addition to constituting what might be considered a microcosm of struggle between factions within the broader society, these agencies were also bureaucratic entities with particular institutional interests to further.

The role played by state agencies in the process of agricultural development was shaped by the peculiarities of Mexican agrarian history and by variations in social structure throughout different regions of the Mexican countryside. In major areas of commercial agriculture, official institutions occupied key positions and could in fact exercise a form of monopoly control over important aspects of production within the ejido sector. As part of its subsidized credit program, for example, the National Rural Credit Bank (Banrural) -- or its predecessors -- furnished its clients with basic agricultural inputs and purchased their crops after the harvest in order to guarantee repayment of the debt. Such control over the entire production process, and over the sale of grain, which was instituted during the early post-revolutionary years as a measure to promote and protect the development of the ejido sector, lent itself over time to political manipulation and corruption. Organized ejido-based producers mounted strong protests against this trend, demanding greater participation in the management of their own production process; and beginning in the 1970s, they gradually gained the kind of control they sought.

Corn production in relatively developed areas was channeled through private grain dealers and governmental agencies toward industry and urban consumers. Within this context, both the active presence of Banrural and of the official marketing agency for basic staples (Conasupo) tended to assure that grain would be purchased from local producers at the support price or only slightly below it. Given the generally low level

---

3. Often these fertilizers are not properly applied, since the kind of technical assistance required to adapt general recommendations to the specific needs of local soils is not available. See the case of the Puebla Project analyzed in Chapter 3.

4. According to calculations by the Treasury Mininistry (SHCP), a producer who cultivated a hectare of land using traditional technology in 1983 received an average subsidy of 948 pesos (related exclusively to the use of fertilizers), while modern producers taking advantage of high subsidies for irrigation water and petroleum derivatives received 16,973 pesos (Kirsten Appendini, personal communication).

of the official price for corn, this supposed guarantee was not always perceived favorably by producers: it is obvious, as these producers noted, that the grain purchases of Banrural in better-off farming regions contributed to sustaining the prevailing cheap food policy of the government over many decades and that the major beneficiaries of this policy were urban consumers, businessmen and industrialists.

Nevertheless, it would be simplistic to characterize the role of government in corn marketing within these rural areas as totally adverse to local producer interests. Although support prices for corn were not high, when compared with average production costs, they were generally above prices prevailing on the world market. Conasupo, as the institution charged with regulating the market for basic food staples, protected the national corn market through exercising strict control over corn imports. This kept national industry from systematically importing corn as a way to reduce grain prices even further, and it ensured that commercial corn production in Mexico would not be completely undermined through unfair competition with the agricultural sector of the United States, where grain production was not only highly technified but also much more heavily subsidized than in Mexico.[5]

The presence of Conasupo and Banrural in the more developed areas of rural Mexico, as well as the gradual extension of their programs to other, poorer regions of the country, also provided small and medium-scale producers with some alternative to local power structures which could be extremely exploitative. For peasant families living in parts of the countryside which the state-managed institutions did not service, the prevailing support price for corn, no matter how low it might have been, was probably still considerably above the level they could hope to obtain from private merchants operating in their local markets.

In the poorest and most remote regions, where corn production is the central element in the livelihood of most families, the market has often been dominated in the past by moneylenders and oligopolistic mercantile interests -- a situation which in some measure persists today. The key figures within such traditional structures of power have been the local political boss (or *cacique*) and the intermediary (*acaparador*), whose functions were likely to be so closely intertwined that they could often be integrated within the sphere of control of a single individual or extended family. The cacique controlled the political resources of the village or the region and served as a broker managing relations between his local clientele and higher levels of the political system. The acaparador, on the other hand, channelled the flow of corn and other products from the community to the rest of the country and vice versa, under conditions which allowed him to buy cheaply and sell at high prices without having to confront a challenge from any serious competitor.[6]

Until a few years ago, a considerable proportion of all the corn which flowed from regional to national markets was subject to the kind of control described above. Grain sold in small lots (and at very low prices) to local merchants, from whom peasant families could then buy some basic consumers goods, was still cheaper than the grain delivered by better-off compatriots to the Ejido Bank. Thus while small and medium-sized producers located within the principal regions of commercial agriculture, where Banrural played a predominant rôle, could no doubt be characterized as a relatively captive clientele of state agencies, their counterparts in more backward areas formed the clientele of often exploitative private intermediaries. And if, for the former, it was necessary to struggle in order to ensure a greater measure of autonomy from governmental institutions,

---

5. It is important to stress the role which subsidies play in determining the price at which agricultural products are sold on the international market. Foreign grain is cheap in part because it is heavily subsidized. Thus while in Mexico, agricultural subsidies represented about 15 percent of the gross sectoral product in the period between 1983 and 1987, the figure for the United States was estimated to be approximately 38 percent (Salinas de Gortari 1988, p. 802). See also Warman (1988).

6. The principal social groups of rural Mexico are discussed in historical context in Esteva (1980).

improving the lot of the latter required the opposite: forming an alliance with state agencies in order to ensure protection from the abuses of local intermediaries.

CONASUPO AND THE MOBILIZATION OF RURAL PEOPLE TO IMPROVE CONDITIONS OF LOCAL PROVISIONING

The institution whose programs were most closely linked to the effort of small-scale producers to improve their living conditions was Conasupo, since in order to comply with its mandate to regulate the national grain market, that agency was often involved both in the purchase and storage of grain and in distribution to consumers. In coordination with the National Warehouse System (ANDSA), Conasupo purchased corn at the support price from producers and private intermediaries. Then, through its affiliate for retail sales (Diconsa), it provided some segments of the public with basic food staples, making use of its own network of retail outlets, as well as of private stores whose owners had obtained a concession to operate with Conasupo.

Until the mid-1970s, neither the grain reception centers of Conasupo in rural areas nor the network of retail outlets set up to reduce speculation on prices of basic consumers goods could be particularly useful in the struggle to counteract oligopolistic practices in regions of traditional agriculture. This was the case, first of all, because grain reception centers in the countryside required that producers deliver a certain minimum volume of corn of a standard quality, and the majority of all small farmers could not meet these demands. In addition, retail sales of grain to consumers were fundamentally circumscribed to urban areas, and to a few of the most developed rural regions of the country.

It was through formation of an alliance between certain reformist groups within the government, on the one hand, and peasant organizations on the other, that this structure began to undergo reform during the 1970s and thus to constitute a new element of competition in areas long controlled by caciques and intermediaries. In order to improve the terms on which grain could be sold to Conasupo, norms governing the purchase of corn were modified to allow for receipt of smaller quantities at the support price. At the same time, the agency inaugurated new programs (involving subsidies to reduce the cost of sacking and transporting grain) which facilitated the participation of small-scale corn producers. And efforts were made to establish a network of simple storehouses, controlled by local communities, where grain could be held for consumption or for later sale under advantageous marketing conditions. These community granaries also served as sales and distribution points for agricultural inputs and for a limited number of basic staples which Diconsa had previously provided only to the urban public at controlled and, in many instances, subsidized prices.[7]

Even in the face of tenacious opposition on the part of commercial and political interests affected by this initiative, the program to protect the livelihood of peasant families in backward areas continued to expand during the late 1970s and, furthermore, to foster innovative forms of community organization. Over time, a network of rural Diconsa stores, managed by thousands of local consumer cooperatives, was established. Members of each community provided a building for their store and contributed free labor, while Diconsa supplied these outlets with basic provisions at controlled prices. Subsidized grain was by far the most important commodity provided through these channels.

Organized participation by the community in the provisioning process was also extended upward, to the regional level of the system, through the formation of Regional Supply Committees made up of

---

7. For an excellent analysis of the problems of local grain markets and the efforts of Conasupo to resolve them, see Esteva (1979).

representatives from local supply councils. Although in principle these regional committees were responsible primarily for transmitting the opinions of local people to higher operational levels within the Diconsa bureaucracy, the establishment of such organizations in practice provided an unusual opportunity for the rural population to mobilize in pursuit of a broad range of goals.[8]

Mobilization for improving local provisioning conditions responded in many areas not only to the need to break the political and economic stranglehold of the traditional local elite, but also to the challenge of dealing with an inexorable monetization of rural subsistence and depletion of natural resources, even in remote regions devoted primarily to subsistence agriculture. By the 1970s, a growing proportion of all people in the Mexican countryside were net consumers of corn, and they demanded lower prices for purchased grain. It was in fact precisely the breadth of local interests brought into play during the mobilization for rural provisioning that lent the movement its particular political significance: local Diconsa committees contained deficit as well as surplus producers, and landless agricultural workers; and for the first time, women played a very active role in a process of community organization which was normally the province of men.

RURAL DEFICITS AND URBAN PRIORITIES: THE GROWING   IMPORTANCE OF FOREIGN GRAIN

Neither grain purchased and stored locally nor that accumulated at regional Conasupo warehouses was sufficient to satisfy the growing demand for subsidized corn in the countryside. The deficit in local markets could be attributed in part to declining production of basic grains for human consumption and to increasing population; but shortfalls were also encouraged by the structure of regional grain markets throughout much of rural Mexico. These markets are not generally designed to retain corn surpluses within the area of purchase, but to channel grain, whether through Conasupo or through private wholesalers, toward provincial cities and/or the national capital. The extraction of grain is encouraged both by the nature of existing warehousing infrastructure and by the fact that large private wholesalers have long enjoyed privileged access to federal permits for transporting grain over certain routes, thus creating an oligopoly which makes control over the better established rural and urban markets especially profitable.

White corn grown by the peasantry, and highly prized by urban consumers for its quality, tended in consequence to be channelled (generally through private dealers) from the countryside toward mills and *tortillerías* (mechanized small-scale tortilla-making shops) in the cities. The share of the total volume of corn which might be bought by Conasupo in both traditional and modern areas (a share which varied from 10 to 25 percent of the total volume of marketed corn production in Mexico) could be partially destined to provisioning programs for rural areas; but it was also delivered to urban mills and tortillerías at a price below its acquisition and transportation costs, as part of the effort to provide subsidized tortillas to urban consumers. Then, since the total amount available was often insufficient to meet the growing demand of rural and urban people, local white corn was supplemented with yellow corn, of lesser quality, imported as needed to regulate the national grain market.

Throughout the 1970s, the tortilla subsidy increased steadily. Not only was the coverage of the program extended from the national capital to other major cities throughout the country, and even to selected rural areas, but the real consumer price of this basic staple was also significantly reduced. In an inflationary period characterized by labor unrest, such a step defended the standard of living of the lower income population and contributed to the maintenance of national political stability. Nevertheless, the program

---

8. A detailed study of the rural program of Diconsa can be found in Fox (1992).

constituted an increasingly onerous charge against the federal budget and was open to a certain degree of misuse or corruption. The magnitude of the operation lent itself to diversions of subsidized grain from the tortilla subsector toward industries producing goods which were not subject to price control.

In sum, then, it became increasingly necessary to speak of a dual supply structure for corn within the Mexican food system. Since the efforts of the state to promote higher productivity had not reached the majority of all holdings and since decreasing priority was being given to corn production in the best agricultural areas of the country, national production stagnated; and to cover the widening deficit, purchases of foreign grain increased rapidly. Imported corn, which was cheaper than the national product for reasons explained above, helped keep the cost of consumer subsidy programs from rising still further, and thus constituted an essential component of the strategy to protect the purchasing power of lower income groups in both rural and urban areas. Yellow (imported) corn was not only utilized by flour milling and animal feed industries, but came to account for as much as 50 percent of the grain consumed by the tortilla industry in metropolitan Mexico City. It also appeared frequently in rural Diconsa stores, despite bitter complaints from peasant consumers about its quality.

THE PETROLEUM BOOM, AUSTERITY AND REFORM

The model of provisioning just described, with all the conflicting interests and elements of governmental support it implied, would have become increasingly difficult to sustain during the 1970s if it had not been for two developments. The first was a temporary and unusual abundance of capital within international financial markets, which could be drawn upon by the Mexican government in the form of loans. The second, toward the end of the decade, was an enormous increase in state revenues from petroleum exports. Both permitted the government to expand programs of support for large and small farmers, and for consumers, increasing subsidies throughout the corn provisioning system in an effort to improve the standard of living of low income groups and to reverse the trend toward growing dependence on imported grain.

Under the auspices of the Mexican Food System (SAM), inaugurated in 1980, planners defined a group (or "basket") of basic food products which should in principle be made available to low-income families at controlled prices, set with reference to the prevailing minimum wage. For certain products, of which corn was the most important, this level would be sustained through increased consumer subsidies; and at the same time, the retail program of Diconsa would be greatly expanded so that the "basket" of basic staple foods could be made available to a larger number of low-income consumers, whether in the countryside or in the cities.

In order to stimulate national production, annual subsidies assigned to the agricultural and livestock sector, which had increased from somewhat more than 13 billion pesos in 1970 to 29 billion in 1979, jumped to almost 49 billion pesos in 1981.[9] About 50 percent of the latter amount was destined to financing agricultural credit and the agricultural insurance program which was an integral part of the credit system. Although, as already noted, the largest producers received the greatest benefit from any subsidized credit program, the extraordinary increase in funds available to SAM during the short life of the program allowed for a considerable expansion of credit in peasant areas. Small-scale producers of corn also benefitted from exceptionally low prices for chemical fertilizers as well as from a new agricultural insurance program based on "shared risk", which took into account the disastrous effects of crop damage on subsistence livelihoods.[10] In 1981 there was also a significant increase in the real support price of corn.

9. Figures in constant (1977) pesos are from Gordillo (1990, p. 806).

10. See Austin and Esteva (1987) for a series of essays by participants in and analysts of the SAM.

Any evaluation of response by farmers to official programs designed to stimulate production must eventually confront the difficulties introduced by climatic factors -- most particularly in Mexico, where annual variations in climate are very pronounced. Nevertheless it would appear that incentives offered by the government through theSAM did stimulate increased production and yields of corn among peasant producers.[11] The issue is hotly contested, and tends to be debated within a context of polarized arguments and very partial information. In fact, global production figures conceal a series of complex changes within regions and sub-regions, and no doubt among different types of producers as well. The explanation of success or failure within any specific context would have to go well beyond a simple consideration of governmental macropolicies.

In any event, SAM had only a short time to implement its program of support for small-scale producers of grain. Two years after its inauguration, an abrupt change in the overall economic situation of Mexico eliminated the financial base on which the SAM program rested and, more broadly, the basis on which redistributive food policies had been implemented by the government throughout the 1970s. In 1982, oil prices plummeted on the international market, reaching a level only one-third their 1981 value and creating serious disequilibria in both the national budget and the balance of payments. At the same time, interest rates on short term loans, negotiated in European and American financial markets at the height of the oil boom, roughly tripled over the course of a few months. The financial position of the government of Mexico, already under great strain, was further undermined by capital flight.

Following a temporary default on payment of interest on the foreign debt, announced in August of 1982, virtually all the usual sources of international capital and credit dried up. The Mexican economy entered a period of deep recession, characterized by negative per capita growth rates in 1983 and 1986-1988, and by very low positive growth in 1984-1985 and 1989-1990. The recession implied a sharp reduction in wage levels and in the standard of living of many within both low- and middle-income groups.

Obviously, this was a time when public programs to alleviate the greatest distress caused by the crisis and to reinforce access to basic foodstuffs were especially needed. It was also, however, a moment when declining public revenues made the reduction of expenditures imperative. The Mexican government reaffirmed its commitment to meet its international financial obligations, thus committing a major proportion of the federal budget to debt servicing, and began a process of crisis management, oriented toward markedly reducing the level of subsidies and cutting back social services, selling off state-owned enterprises and postponing investment in the physical infrastructure of the country.

At the same time, macroeconomic policies followed by earlier governments were sharply reversed in the post-1982 period. The Mexican peso was allowed to devalue continually (until 1988), and internal interest rates rose to very high levels intended to offset inflation and reduce incentives for further capital flight. In the course of a few years, these measures were followed by the progressive opening of a highly protected economy to international competition (Ros and Lustig 1987).

Each of these elements of response to the crisis implied adjustments in areas of economic activity and sociopolitical organization of fundamental relevance to the production, marketing and consumption of corn. As the sharp decrease in governmental revenues and the progressive reduction of traditional levels of protection affected the capacity of the government to respond adequately to the demands of all groups within the provisioning system, conflicting economic and social interests grew stronger and more publicly visible.

---

11. The most systematic analysis of this point can be found in Andrade and Blanc (1987). The SAM programming model for the agricultural sector suggested that of all the principal crops in Mexico, it was corn which produced the best results for subsidies provided (Cartas and Bassoco 1987, p. 329).

As long as it had been possible to obtain international loans or count on high earnings from the sale of oil, there had been no need to affect the interests of commercial farmers who received the largest share of subsidies for agricultural inputs and credit, or to restrict the privileges of private grain merchants. It had not been necessary to reform governmental agencies providing support for agriculture or to put consumer subsidies on a sounder financial footing (in part through confronting a range of private interests with much to gain from an illicit use of subsidized corn).

As the decade advanced, these were to become major issues in the debate over the future configuration of the food system. The most immediate provisioning problem which arose at the outset of the economic crisis centered, however, around the central dilemma of any cheap food policy: if access to inexpensive staple food items is not assured through governmental subsidies, such access must, in the short run, be based either on lower producer prices or involve a growing dependence on cheap imports. In the longer run and with necessary reforms to the system, of course, consumer prices may also be reduced as a concomitant of increasing agricultural productivity and marketing efficiency.

At the onset of economic crisis, and despite the enormous political significance of such a step, it was imperative to reduce expenditures by the government on consumer subsidies for corn, wheat and sugar.[12] The most obvious way to proceed in the case of corn was immediately to increase the price paid by consumers of tortillas; and between 1982 and 1990, the price of this product rose precipitously, at a time when the diet of lower income groups in urban areas was in fact increasingly restricted to such basic foods such as corn, beans, and rice.[13] Nevertheless the fate of consumers was not abandoned entirely to the play of market forces. Although tortilla prices outside the capital were gradually allowed to rise until they reached the market rate, the price which could be charged within metropolitan Mexico City continued to be controlled. Thus at the end of 1990 a general subsidy of 25 percent of the cost of tortillas was still in effect within the confines of the capital city.[14]

At the same time, and as a precondition for eventually eliminating all general subsidies for the tortilla, an attempt was made to identify the neediest urban families so that steps could be taken to channel special compensatory subsidies exclusively to that group. In fact, however, it proved extremely difficult to work out a method which would permit valid definition of the poorest; and the experiment was laden with political pitfalls. Cheap tortillas were at one point delivered only through designated stores; then only in exchange for stamps obtained through certain kinds of outlets; then there was an attempt to utilize national household surveys to pinpoint the very low-income population. In a metropolitan area of some 16 to 18 million inhabitants, like Mexico City, many needy families were bound to be overlooked and many less needy ones included.[15]

---

12. Luiselli (1987, p. 340) notes that in 1982 the general subsidy for corn, wheat, and sugar consumption was 15 times more costly than all subsidies for the production of these three products.

13. As a study conducted by the National Consumers' Institute (INCO 1989) has shown, the progressive reduction of subsidies on a wide range of goods and services (such as transport), has meant that a decreasing proportion of the budget of low-income households can be allocated to the purchase of food. In consequence, it has become necessary to destine a relatively greater share of all expenditures on food to the least expensive staple products.

14. According to data provided by Appendini (1992, p. 205, the consumer price for a kilo of tortillas in metropolitan Mexico City, which was 11 pesos in 1982, rose to 275 pesos in 1989 and 750 pesos in the fall of 1990. Outside the capital, the same price, which was not subsidized, was 1,050 pesos in the fall of 1990.

15. Lustig (1990) suggests, after studying the effect of subsidies on food consumption, that "it can be argued that a general price subsidy on corn and its derivatives, beans, bread, rice, noodles, cooking oil and eggs, is justified from a distributive point of view. Such a subsidy [leads] to progressive redistribution of purchasing power. Thus eliminating some general price subsidies on basic foodstuffs may have been regressive compared with the past situation, despite the intended protection provided to the poorest through

The search for a politically acceptable and socially just method for delivering subsidies to particular groups of consumers continues. In the meantime, differences in geographical coverage of the subsidies which had been reduced during the 1970s have reappeared or been reinforced. Not only is there a tendency to give preferential treatment to consumers in Mexico City, when compared with counterparts in provincial cities, but there has also been a significant reduction in grain subsidies which were transferred during the 1980s to rural consumers through local Diconsa retail stores. At the end of 1990, the latter were selling a kilogram of white corn at 830 pesos, when the official price to the producer was 636 pesos per kilogram (Appendini, 1992, p. 213).

Until 1987, reduction in the level of subsidy to corn consumers was not matched by the kind of decreases in producer prices which would have transferred a part of the cost adjustment to the latter group. In fact, between 1983 and 1986 the support price for corn increased at a rate relatively equal to changes in the consumer price index. Nevertheless the support price lagged further and further behind increasing costs of production. While consumers were absorbing the impact of reduced subsidies for corn grain and tortillas, producers were also seriously affected by a reduction of subsidies for agricultural inputs and credit and by restrictions on agricultural support services imposed by the program of austerity.

Between 1983 and 1987, governmental subsidies to the agricultural sector decreased on average by 13 percent annually, after having increased by 12.5 percent per year during the 1970s (Gordillo 1990, p. 806); and the cost of many agricultural inputs rose sharply in response to the withdrawal of official subsidies and the rapid devaluation of the Mexican peso. At the same time, the total volume of credit destined to the agricultural and livestock sector by the national banking system declined 40 percent in real terms between 1980 and 1985 and approximately 60 percent between 1980 and 1986-1988 (de la Mora Gómez 1990, p. 947).

As a consequence, corn producers had to confront higher and higher costs with less and less crop credit; and they did so in a context of interest rates which increased constantly, not only in nominal terms but, as time went by, in real terms.[16] The acute inflationary process unleashed by the devaluation of the peso and concomitant increases in the interest rate wrecked havoc not only with programs of financial institutions servicing agriculture, but also with the balance sheets of agricultural enterprises themselves, hampering any medium-term planning and limiting the number of producers able to ask for credit or willing to utilize the total amount of credit for which they qualified, given their fear of the rising cost of money.[17]

These changes were particularly unfavorable to large and medium-scale farmers, long benefitting from governmental subsidies lowering the cost of electricity, irrigation water, fuel, and agricultural machinery. Adjustment measures were initially less unfavorable to peasant producers, since subsidies on chemical fertilizer, which was their principal purchased input, were for the moment maintained and even increased. Moreover, although short-term credit for annual crops provided through Banrural became increasingly insufficient in real terms, it was made available to a growing number of borrowers in an effort to ensure continued access to credit, fertilizer, and insurance on the part of clients of official programs. Such policy measures reflected the decision of the government to protect traditional corn producers during a period when benefits to the modern agriculture sector were being sharply cut.

---

targeting mechanisms. In addition, it is not clear that after targeting was introduced the subsidies really went to those who needed them most" (p. 1335).

16. Between 1982 and 1986, the level of subsidy on interest rates for agricultural credit was maintained and even increased slightly; but between 1986 and 1989 it dropped from 0.54 to only 0.09 percent of GNP. In 1987 Banrural interest rates approached those of the market (Gordillo 1990, p. 810).

17. For the case of long term credit, see Maydón Garza (1988).

It is nevertheless important to emphasize the extreme vulnerability of small and medium-scale commercial farmers, and especially of the relatively better off ejido-based producers, working irrigated or good rainfed land, in such a situation. Severely hurt by inflation and by the sudden reduction in the level of subsidies for inputs, ejido-based grain producers (as well as producers of certain other crops) began from late 1982 onward to engage in various forms of protest aimed at forcing the government to offset their losses through increasing the support price of corn.

Despite the relatively meager gains won by these protest movements, national statistics indicate that corn producers of all kinds continued cultivating their land with sufficient success to maintain prevailing levels of production until 1986. In fact, national corn production during the period from 1983 to 1985 was on average as high as in 1980 and 1981, the years just before the crisis. In addition to having benefitted from favorable weather conditions, it is clear that farmers were able to keep up their levels of corn production during the crisis in part because they took advantage of the immediate decrease in the relative cost of labor which was associated with the deepening recession. Between 1979-1982 and 1983-1986, the relation between the rural minimum wage and the nominal support price for corn decreased by one-third. To some extent, this counterbalanced the increasing cost of other inputs utilized by small, medium and large agricultural enterprises which expended resources on hired labor (see Ros and Rodríguez 1986, and Martín del Campo 1988, pp. 190-91).

For the majority of all corn producers, however, the reduction of rural wage levels was likely to do more harm than good: most peasant families counted on income from both urban and rural wage labor not only to meet consumption needs but also to defray a portion of their production expenses. In the context of declining income from off-farm sources, it would seem likely that part of the resilience of national corn production between 1983 and 1985 was attributable to the intensified use of family labor on smallholdings, as rural people attempted to offset difficulties in the labor market through bolstering subsistence strategies.

FROM ORTHODOX TO HETERODOX ADJUSTMENT MEASURES

If during the initial five years of recession and adjustment the government succeeded to some degree in protecting producers of basic grains from the full impact of the crisis, through raising support prices to keep pace with the evolution of the consumer index, increasing subsidies on fertilizers and trying (with decreasing success) to sustain subsidies on official agricultural credit, this protection began to be undermined in 1986. And by the end of 1987, the situation shifted abruptly, as macroeconomic policy was subject to fundamental modifications. From 1987 until the end of the decade, grain producers found themselves at an increasing disadvantage, as the level of support prices dropped sharply and the national grain market was increasingly opened to competition from foreign producers.

This shift in policy, involving sharply declining public support for producers and increasing dependence on the international market, was tied to implementation of a Pact for Stability and Economic Growth which signalled the end of five years of government reliance on an orthodox policy of macroeconomic adjustment. The orthodox adjustment strategy in effect from the outset of the crisis until 1987 was based on a systematic effort to leave the setting of key prices like exchange and interest rates as much as possible to the free play of market forces. The continuous devaluation of the peso was the centerpiece of this strategy, which was associated with a rate of inflation reaching the alarming level of 159 percent in 1987.

Threatened with the possibility of an uncontrollable inflationary spiral, the government abandoned its orthodox adjustment strategy toward the end of 1987 and adopted instead a heterodox program which set limits to the devaluation of the peso and established a mechanism for setting key prices within the national economy.

The peso would be defended by making use of the considerable fund of foreign currency accumulated after 1982 through sharp reductions in imports and a considerable increase in exports. Prices of most important goods and services were to be adjusted periodically through institutionalized consultation (or *concertación*) between the government and representatives of the principal sectors of Mexican society, including workers, peasants, and the leaders of industry and business.

Through a series of pacts which have been renewed on a regular basis since 1988 and are still in force today, both wages and prices have been allowed to vary only within certain specified limits. For its part, the government has assumed the responsibility to ensure stable prices for specified basic goods and services (including fuel, electricity, trains, telephones, and tortillas) -- a measure implying that programs to reduce or eliminate governmental subsidies must be slowed. Meanwhile industrialists, merchants and others within the business community have agreed to refer to negotiated guidelines when setting their prices. Labor representatives have accepted sharp restrictions on wage increases, in spite of the fact that the real income of the urban working class fell by 50 percent during the five years preceding the first pact. Finally, representatives of agricultural producers have collaborated, with great difficulty, in an effort to keep the prices of basic food staples low.

Between 1988 and 1991, this new strategy for dealing with economic crisis succeeded in sharply reducing inflation and allowed for modest economic growth in 1991. For the agricultural sector, however, both the pricing policy associated with the Pacts and the evolution of patterns of state investment proved highly unfavorable. From 1987 to 1989, the real support price for corn plummeted, advancing much more slowly than the consumer price index or the cost of agricultural inputs and contributing to a deepening recession in large areas of the Mexican countryside.

During the first year following the implementation of the heterodox adjustment strategy, the group of corn producers operating at a loss grew from 43 (1987) to 65 percent (1988) of the total; and the number who obtained profits of more than 40 percent above their costs dropped from 37 to 20 percent.[18] The worsening crisis among corn producers was reflected in national production levels, which had begun to fall (in response to inflationary pressures) during the year prior to the implementation of the Pact and remained very low throughout the period from 1987 to 1989.[19] In consequence, grain imports rose considerably.

To judge the overall impact of these developments on the livelihood of corn producers, and particularly on levels of living among small and medium-scale farmers, it is important to remember that the unprofitability of corn production was only one facet of a much wider crisis that affected the entire agricultural sector during the latter 1980s. There were few profitable alternatives to be found in the countryside at that time. According to official statistics, in the three years prior to 1989, the agriculture, livestock and forestry sector declined at an average annual rate of -0.8 percent. "Accompanying this tendency toward decreasing production was extreme instability in prices of products, cost of inputs, and income levels of producers" (SARH 1990, p. 988).

---

18. De la Mora Gómez (1990, p. 945), who employs data taken from the 1988 National Survey of Production Costs, Technical Coefficients and Yields, carried out by SARH.

19. The relative weight of these factors and of others related to the evolution of agricultural policy is analyzed in chapter 9 of this book.

RESTRUCTURING AND THE CORN PROVISIONING SYSTEM

It was in the midst of this generalized rural crisis and within the context of trade liberalization and a macroeconomic policy favorable to importing foreign goods,[20] that the Mexican government began to undertake a thoroughgoing reform of the structure of official support for the agriculture sector, including a reform of the institutional bases of the corn provisioning system. This effort, which began in 1989 and is still under way, forms part of a longer-term program to restructure the entire Mexican economy, in order to improve its ability to compete within the international market and to create a more "modern" institutional structure, less dependent upon paternalistic or clientelistic relations. In the agricultural sector, restructuring centered on institutional reform -- the elimination of various official agencies and programs and the reformulation of the mandate of several others, as part of a wider effort to redefine the role of the government throughout the economy.

This is an eminently political undertaking, involving debate among groups with contrasting -- and in some cases starkly opposing -- visions of the proper role of the public sector in the national economy. In fact, the group in power contains a faction which sees no viable future for the production of basic crops in Mexico and which would orient the process of restructuring toward sharply reducing official support to the countryside and leaving the provisioning of basic grains to the free play of forces within the international market.[21] It should be noted, however, that even among groups which would oppose such an extreme position and advocate varying degrees of governmental participation in the economy, there are good reasons for supporting a process of institutional reform within the agricultural sector. The cost of maintaining the old support structure was very high, resource utilization was often inefficient, and as already noted, governmental programs have all too frequently involved attempts at political control against which many peasant organizations have fought tenaciously.

In the last analysis, the current attempt to redefine the role of the Mexican government in the countryside implies, then, both an opportunity and a risk: the opportunity to create a support structure which is much more efficient and consonant with the interests of the majority of producers, and the danger that some of the public programs and initiatives which have constituted indispensible elements in supporting agricultural activities in the past will be eliminated. In the short run, of course, there are also the inevitable risks associated with any period of transition, when institutions are being dismantled, programs are being reoriented, and new rules concerning who will have access to services must be defined. Under such circumstances it is inevitable that both the continuity and quality of many services will be affected.

From 1989 onward, agricultural producers in Mexico have been affected by restructuring in a number of ways. In the first place, as a result of a progressive process of "disincorporation" or privatization of official enterprises, the normal channels through which small and medium-scale commercial farmers were accustomed to gain access to some goods and services have been modified or eliminated altogether. For example, the sudden closure of the National Agricultural and Livestock Insurance Company (ANAGSA), which had been poorly managed for many years, left all the clients of the official rural credit bank without a source of insurance. Reorganization of the government-owned manufacturer and distributor of chemical fertilizers (Fertimex) greatly increased the difficulty of obtaining that vital input in many rural areas. [22] Moreover, when

---

20. Protecting the peso against any serious devaluation from 1988 onward implied that exports, including agricultural exports, were in a relatively disadvantageous position within the framwork of the pacts, while imports became more and more attractive.

21. Raúl Salinas de Gortari (1990, p. 828) outlines different positions within the government. See also chapter 9 by Appendini in this book.

22. Fertilizer producing installations were offered to private industry and Fertimex was left with the secondary task of distribution.

a series of specialized commercial entities were put up for sale (such as the Mexican Coffee Institute --
Inmecafé, which provided production and marketing support for small-scale coffee producers), their clientele
ran the risk of losing access to basic inputs, technical assistance, and crop reception centers which in the past
had protected them to some extent from the vagaries of production for the international market.

Within the sphere of marketing of basic agricultural commodities, the state continued to provide corn
and bean producers with the option of selling their harvest to Conasupo, at the support price. The purchasing
role of Conasupo was, however, now strictly limited to reception of those two products; and since the agency
no longer regulated the market for other basic and semi-basic crops, most products faced increasing
competition from imports. In addition, although the national market for corn and beans continued to be
protected, industries which were important processors or buyers of grain exerted growing pressure for further
liberalization. Import licenses were thus progressively easier to obtain with every passing year.

The clientele of the official agricultural credit system was subject to great uncertainty and
experienced severe restrictions on access to productive resources at the turn of the 1990s, as that system
underwent far-reaching reorganization. Not only was there a reduction and reorganization of personnel within
official credit institutions, and a reform of operating procedures, but the basic mandates of credit institutions
were redefined and with this their future clientele. In 1989, faced with a vast portfolio of delinquent loans,
the Banrural stopped all lending to producers who were in default. Given the disastrous economic situation
prevailing in much of the countryside, a large proportion of all corn producers in Mexico had not been able
to pay their debts, and they therefore received no credit that year. Shortly afterwards, it was announced that
the official bank would only offer loans to the relatively better-off small and medium-scale producers with
clear productive potential. Such a policy left higher-risk producers to be attended within the framework of a
new initiative, known as the National Solidarity Program (Pronasol), which would respond to the needs of
groups with fewer resources.

At the heart of such restructuring was a clear intention to tailor official programs more closely to the
specific needs of various groups, providing "different treatment to producers, according to their income level
and their productive potential" (SARH 1990, p. 993). In fact, this was a demand long put forward by peasant
organizations themselves, as they criticized the extreme lack of direction or focus of subsidies awarded in the
agricultural sector. The effort could be judged sucessful to the extent that it had the effect of withdrawing
subsidies preferentially awarded to large-scale producers and channelling greater support instead toward
medium and small scale producers with productive potential. But as in the case of reform of the subsidy
directed toward consumers of basic food products, already discussed, a strict new effort to target programs of
official support toward a much-reduced group of producers was also demanded by those within the government
with a strong interest in sharply limiting the role of the state in the national economy. If the views of the latter
group prevail in the restructuring process, very few resources will be available to support small-scale producers
in the future.

Meanwhile, the effort to rationalize and reorient subsidies channeled toward agricultural production
confronts a series of difficulties which are to a certain extent inevitable. One of these has to do with deciding
who, within which group or region, will continue to receive preferential treatment from the state.[23] Another
arises from the need to define new forms of official support and to specify correct procedures for apportioning
it.

---

23. In the National Program for the Modernization of the Countryside, it was suggested that "a realistic census of producers, as
well as a system of reliable and up to date statistical information " be established, "... which would allow for precise identification
of producers in order gradually to individualize the commitments between them and the public sector" (SARH 1990, p. 1005).

Dialogue with peasant organizations obviously constitutes an indispensible element in any effort to define more efficient governmental support programs for the countryside. At the same time, an effort is being made to encourage private companies and consultants to provide a growing part of all goods and services formerly delivered to rural people by specialized agencies of the government. In the new arrangement, public funds earmarked for support of agricultural production will be preferentially channeled from the state to rural producers' organizations, so that the latter can utilize them to contract for services or purchase goods from the private sector as they deem appropriate.

How best to allocate public resources to these producers' organizations in the first place continues to be a problematic issue. At present, various kinds of organizations can receive funding for specific projects by reaching formal agreement (known as engaging in a process of *concertación*) with the Ministry of Agriculture (SARH), with the National Indigenous Institute (INI) and/or with Pronasol or, at the state level, by negotiating through state governments. Although this new procedure may reduce the role previously played by some official agencies and give greater opportunities both to organized producers and to the private sector, it is obvious that it does not eliminate the possibility that access to governmental resources will be conditioned by political negotiation.

It should also be noted that creating new opportunities for private initiative within the agricultural sector does not necessarily imply an immediate improvement in the conditions of production for farmers. In many areas of rural Mexico, there are no real incentives to invest in businesses which would replace state-run agencies; and in regions of greater economic potential, private interests tend as much toward collusion as toward competition. In a time of recession, the capacity of the majority of producers (and most particularly producers of basic grains) to organize in defense of their interests without governmental support is very limited.

THE IMPACT OF RECESSION AND RESTRUCTURING ON SMALL AND MEDIUM-SCALE PRODUCERS IN AREAS OF COMMERCIAL AGRICULTURE

In the principal regions of commercial agriculture in Mexico, where the use of modern technology allows for higher yields than the national average, small and medium-sized producers have not remained passive when confronted with problems stemming first from the debt crisis and later from the array of macroeconomic policy adjustments and attempts at institutional restructuring just discussed. Many commercial farming areas contain important ejido sectors which (contrary to the all-too-frequent stereotype of the ejido as universally poor and disorganized) carry political weight because of their significant contribution to national production and their high level of organization. To an increasing degree since the 1970s, these ejido-based producers have grouped together in associations and cooperatives in order to defend their interests and strengthen their negotiating position vis-a-vis both the government and the private sector.[24]

Throughout most of the 1980s, the demands of corn producers in commercial ejido areas centered on the possibility of raising support prices in order to minimize the overall effect of inflation, devaluation, and reduction of subsidies on agricultural profits. Since small farmers were likely to feel the extent of their loss most acutely at the time when they delivered their crops for sale, and since ejido-based producers in a number of regions were most likely to sell to Conasupo, demands for higher prices were often most forcefully presented around harvest time and in a number of cases took the form of occupying the warehouses of Conasupo in order

---

24. One of the principal actors in this process of ejido organization, Gustavo Gordillo, analyzes its development in his book (1988).

to prevent the shipment of grain from the region. At times strategic highways were also blockaded to assure that corn could not be moved.

Such protests were most frequent during 1982-1983 and 1985-1987; and as Luis Hernández explains in Chapter 2 of this book, the specific political context of each region or state had much to do with their success or failure. In general, producers' organizations obtained some concessions from the government in exchange for ending their take-over of Conasupo installations. But these tended to be short-term arrangements (involving one extra payment to producers from certain regions, a promised contribution to a particular regional development fund, and so forth), which did not significantly alter the fact that corn production was no longer a viable economic activity in many areas of small scale commercial agriculture in Mexico.

After the last series of producer protests in 1987, developments within the corn market itself began to reduce the strategic importance of Conasupo installations in the struggle for more favorable conditions of production, except insofar as the warehouses could be utilized by medium and small-scale producers to store grain which they planned to sell to private dealers. Because official support prices were kept very low, and private dealers offered to pay considerably higher prices in what was at the time a deficit market, fewer and fewer producers and small intermediaries could afford the luxury of delivering grain to Conasupo; and in consequence, state-run warehouses for the moment could no longer be considered the center of power within the regional supply system. The "enemy" of most corn producers was now not so much the government as the market, an infinitely more diffuse opponent and one on which it was much more difficult to apply political pressure.

Since few producers had the resources to construct their own storage facilities and since private control over such facilities tended to go hand in hand with monopoly pricing, it was imperative for medium and small-scale commercial grain farmers to ensure continued access to the existing public infrastructure for grain storage. Producers' organizations began to negotiate agreements with public institutions which would allow them temporary use of storehouses and silos until they could find private buyers for their grain. In some cases, Conasupo agreed to be the buyer of last resort, at the support price, if no better offer were forthcoming.

By the end of the 1980s, with the dissolution or reorientation of some of the major institutions formerly providing services to small-scale commercial corn farmers, the latter were confronted with the fact that they would have to create their own institutions to replace the infrastructure and services which had historically been provided by the government. There was an important precedent for such efforts. In fact, better organized ejido-based producers had already established a number of cooperative associations and regional unions during the late 1970s and early 1980s in order to facilitate the purchase of agricultural inputs at competitive prices, to process certain farm products, and to negotiate an advantageous sale price for particular crops. But this program had been carried out within a framework of access to basic governmental services; and although the struggle of the ejido-based producers in commercial areas long involved demanding a certain degree of independence in dealing with public institutions, as well as the improvement of governmental services, this was far different from coping with the total disappearance of some government agencies.

In parts of Chihuahua, Jalisco, Nayarit, and Chiapas, relatively strong organizations of medium and small-scale corn producers have recently begun to create credit cooperatives and insurance funds, and to build storage installations which their members must have if they are to continue to farm within the context of restructuring. They have also begun to establish programs which promote the substitution of other crops or non- agricultural activities for corn production. State funds, obtained through negotiations (concertación) of the kind just described, have been provided for these experiments. Nevertheless, as with producers' organizations throughout the country, they are working with members who have been deeply affected by years of unprofitable operations, overwhelmed by outstanding debts, and increasingly hemmed in by the need to be competitive in the international market. The general outlook is not encouraging.

Even in the case of several relatively strong agricultural associations, large investments made in better times have been imperilled by competition from imported products. For example, in the northern part of the state of Zacatecas, a processing plant for grapes which was profitably managed over many years had been idled by 1990 as both foreign grapes and wines made deep inroads into the national market. In the state of Jalisco, the efforts of some of the country's most productive small-scale corn farmers to form a marketing cooperative were at the same time being challenged by processing industries which turned as often as possible to foreign suppliers. In addition, better-off small farmers who have tried to avoid the corn crisis by raising poultry or pigs now find themselves operating in a depressed national market for animal products and in competition with imports from the United States (Cruz 1990).

The situation of small and medium-sized producers in areas of commercial agriculture is therefore far from promising. An increasing number of families in these regions respond by migrating to Mexican cities or to the United States, thus reinforcing the long-run tendency toward an oversupply of seasonal labor within U.S. agriculture and a consequent decline in the average agricultural wage in the United State (Runsten 1991). Such migration also contributes to seasonal scarcity of labor within some regions of commercial agriculture in Mexico, and is related as well to the fact that women are coming to form a larger and larger part of the agricultural labor force in these areas.

Some of the families remaining in the better-off agricultural regions of Mexico at the end of the 1980s produced less corn for the market and more for family consumption, and tried to return to the days when they had provided for most of their subsistence needs outside the market, through cultivating a variety of crops in family plots and backyard gardens. But withdrawing from the market has not been easy. Over several decades, many farm families systematically producing corn on a commercial scale have grown accustomed to purchasing the better part of their consumer goods and have lost some of the skills which formerly allowed them to maintain a greater degree of self-sufficiency.[25]

At the level of regional economies, recession and restructuring encouraged farmers in the most important commercial agricultural areas of Mexico to offer larger amounts of land for rent to those with the capital to diversify production and/or to produce for the export market. On small and medium holdings, the crisis was also reflected in a decreasing utilization of manufactured inputs and in descending yields. Levels of production in states and districts which had produced considerable corn surpluses over a long period of time began to diminish significantly during the late 1980s.[26] The tendency was reversed in 1990 when the support price for white corn increased 46 percent over the previous year, stimulating an immediate response by medium and small-scale commercial producers. Nevertheless the crisis is at present as much a question of institutions as of prices, and it is improbable that it can be resolved simply through raising the level of the latter.

---

25. Interview with Rolando Loubet and Milagros Camarena, Guadalajara, Jalisco, August 1990.

26. For a detailed analysis of changes in patterns of corn production and productivity, see Appendini (1992). The case of Jalisco is presented by Orozco Alvarado (1990).

CORN, CRISIS AND RESTRUCTURING IN AREAS OF SUBSISTENCE AGRICULTURE

The emigration of small-scale producers of corn from areas of commercial agriculture reflects a tendency throughout Mexican society as a whole to depend on increasingly complex survival strategies in the effort to cope with recession and restructuring. Nevertheless the overall context within which these strategies are developed varies markedly from one place to another; and for this reason it is important to distinguish the situation of small commercial farmers, analyzed above, from the pattern of change which predominates in what is usually called "subsistence agriculture".

In fact, the latter concept encompasses a very wide range of situations. All have in common the production of corn, as well as other agricultural crops and livestock, primarily for family consumption rather than for sale. But this goal is pursued within varied contexts implying different levels of participation in national markets of goods, capital, and labor, and therefore likely to be differentially affected by the national economic crisis.

At one extreme of the subsistence continuum is the pattern in which all basic needs of a rural household can be satisfactorily met through the efforts of unremunerated family labor, working on the family holding, communal lands or engaging in other forms of production within the community. This type of subsistence economy, in which there is only minimal participation in regional, national or international markets, can still be found in some parts of rural Mexico, like Plan de Hidalgo, Veracruz, which is analyzed in chapter 4. The people of Plan de Hidalgo have preserved a traditional system of diversified natural resource management based on hunting, gathering and fishing; and they practice slash and burn agriculture in a sustainable fashion within areas of extraordinary ecological complexity where the traditional Mexican corn field (or *milpa*) plays a central role.

For peasant families who can continue to make an adequate living in this way, recession and consequent restructuring of the national economy have been of relatively minor importance. This group represents, however, only a small minority of the rural population of Mexico. As a general rule, outside the principal commercial agricultural areas of the country, the cultivation of corn associated with beans, squash, or other crops has been carried out for decades within the context of a worsening livelihood crisis. Although corn production for family consumption continues to be the goal of the majority of families, the probability of satisfying their minimum needs with domestic production is becoming increasingly unlikely.

The deepening "corn crisis" in peasant areas, which preceded the general economic crisis of the 1980s and significantly conditioned its effects, is a phenomenon with multiple causes: population growth in rural communities where resources are relatively fixed; the low profitability of corn production in comparison with other agricultural and livestock options and, over long periods, even in comparison with the level of remuneration for labor; restrictions imposed on the availability of family labor by the seasonal and permanent migration of able-bodied members of the household; and the expansion of urban areas, livestock operations, and cultivation of forrage over large expanses which were previously dedicated to corn. In consequence, the cultivation of corn has been increasingly relegated to inhospitable areas and to a smaller proportion of the total available agricultural land.[27]

---

27. Under the direction of Carlos Montañez and Arturo Warman, two books (Warman and Montañez 1982, Montañez and Warman 1985) were prepared during the early 1980s which constitute basic references for anyone interested in understanding these processes. For an analysis of the development of sorghum cultivation in corn growing regions, see Barkin and Suárez (1985). A detailed study of the effect of all these modernization processes can be found in Tudela et al. (1989).

Even under difficult circumstances, however, peasant families continue their efforts to produce corn. As Appendini notes in chapter 9, slightly more than half of the total national output of corn is still cultivated on rainfed plots by farmers utilizing traditional methods. And of that amount, a further half is retained by producers for family consumption. Nevertheless corn production, even for subsistence, depends increasingly on the ability of households to generate off-farm income in order to finance indispensible purchased inputs. In many communties, for example, families must buy fertilizers because natural resources have been depleted and poorer agricultural lands are being cultivated. Emigration by some household members often leads to a scarcity of family labor, and then the need arises either to rely more heavily on labor-saving herbicides in the milpa or to contract day laborers, or both. At the same time, declining corn yields often oblige producers to purchase grain during several periods when their own supply of corn is not sufficient to meet family consumption requirements.

These expenditures, indispensible for the kind of "subsistence" agriculture which presently prevails in Mexico, are met with remittances from distant family members or with income generated through the sale of agricultural or non-agricultural (forestry, livestock, and handcraft) products; or they may be defrayed by diverting a portion of credit (in money or in kind) ostensibly requested to finance other crops. Among families with the potential to produce surplus corn when weather conditions are favorable, and who have been successful in gaining access to the official credit system, grain for family consumption can also be financed with loans from Banrural, and repaid with a portion of the harvest. Finally, the resources required to engage in subsistence corn production can be obtained from local moneylenders or merchants, to whom the borrower must deliver a prearranged amount of grain (usually at a prearranged price) even if production is not sufficient to satisfy minimum family consumption needs.

Such survival strategies closely integrate the low-income rural population into wider markets for labor, capital and goods, and make it extremely vulnerable to a whole range of negative changes related both to the economic recession and to recent efforts to restructure the Mexican economy. In the first place, of course, the periodic contraction of employment opportunities, especially within certain sectors of the economy consistently hiring peasant laborers, like the construction industry, has threatened the livelihood not only of low-income urban families but also of rural people who depend on remittances from family members who have migrated to the city. The relentless reduction in the level of real wages in urban and rural areas has obviously had the same effect.

In some cases, urban workers of peasant origin have reacted to the recession by abandoning the cities and returning to their communities to work in agriculture or to start a small business. Evidence of such strategies appears in chapter 4b (on the central region of Veracruz) and in chapter 5 (on the highlands of Chiapas). But under present conditions, it is difficult for many rural families to take advantage of the potential benefits which such an increase in the local labor force might imply. The situation is further complicated by the fact that in many communities the amount of available land is not sufficient to satisfy the minimum needs of the population, and there is no immediate possibility of increasing the size of agricultural holdings or providing new farm sites to landless families.

There is, then, an overall increase of emigration from areas of predominantly peasant agriculture, in spite of unfavorable conditions in the national labor market. This reduction of the labor force in the countryside appears to be related to two further phenomena. The first is a distinct increase in the "feminization" of the agricultural work force -- a process already under way in the 1970s. Thus at the present time, in Morelos,

Oaxaca, Guerrero, and the Tarascan plateau of Michoacan, it is increasingly likely that smallholdings will be cultivated by women, children and the elderly, often assisted by hired hands.[28]

At the same time, there is an increase in the frequency with which women accompany men who migrate in search of work as day laborers in commercial agricultural areas or in hopes of finding employment in the United States or Canada. In fact, a recent study commissioned by UNICEF concluded that "the phenomenon which has affected rural women most markedly during the 1980s is, without a doubt, their [growing] incorporation beside their husbands in salaried agricultural work". It is estimated that women now comprise about one-third of all the day laborers who work in the Mexican countryside (Arizpe, Salinas, and Velásquez 1989).

This increase in rural migration, especially when it involves the exodus of family members who have the greatest capacity to engage in hard physical labor, can also bring about a noticeable deterioration in the quality of farm practices on subsistence or semi-subsistence smallholdings. In fact, such a tendency is discussed in almost all the case studies in this book, whether with reference to historical experience or in the course of analyzing the impact of the present crisis.

The most extreme example of the kind of ecological disaster which can result from massive emigration of the rural population is presented in chapter 6 by Raúl García Barrios and Luis García Barrios, who present material on the Mixteco highlands of Oaxaca. Over the course of many years, continuing out-migration from the area encouraged the formation of an increasingly fragmented and "incomplete" local social structure, made up of small families with very few experienced workers. Under these conditions, it eventually became impossible to contribute the labor required to maintain the public works (including the local irrigation network) which are the backbone of productive agriculture in the region. Corn cultivation was gradually converted into an entirely monetized operation which depended on remittances from those who had emigrated. Essential agricultural practices were first reduced and then abandoned. Thus a vicious cicle of social disintegration and ecological deterioration set in. It is a scenario that is being repeated in many other communities throughout the Mexican countryside, although usually in a less dramatic and more potentially reversible fashion.

In addition to stimulating emigration and reducing earnings from wage labor, the recession of the 1980s has introduced other changes in the lives of millions of Mexicans who depend on corn production for family subsistence. For example, both the recession and the progressive elimination of barriers protecting the national market from foreign competition have reduced the income received by rural households from the sale of forest and animal products, as well as from handicrafts. Local economies are depressed, in part because products are being imported which compete with goods made by small rural industries, or by larger enterprises employing rural labor. Some of these products come from Bangladesh or China, where labor costs are lower than in Mexico, or from Japan and the United States where the level of technology is much higher.

TENDENCIES OF CHANGE IN RURAL GRAIN MARKETS

At the end of the 1980s, this set of factors influenced rural corn markets in a number of ways. In some microregions, the crisis in commercial agriculture stimulated subsistence corn production to such an extent that the amount of grain available on local markets increased considerably. This could be a highly positive adaptation to recession, which helped protect the level of living of the local population. Nevertheless it is important to remember that an increase in subsistence production can also mean a reduction in the amount of

---

28. Oswald (1990) and Zapata Martelo (1990). See also chapter 6 by R. García Barrios and L. García Barrios in this book.

grain available for sale, creating a relative scarcity of corn in certain rural areas and pushing up the prices paid for corn by deficit producers and landless families.

It appears that this was the situation in the Puebla Valley in 1988 and 1989. Smallholders who usually produced for family consumption but had previously been able to sell some surplus, reacted to the steep rise in production costs and low support prices by retreating into subsistence. This created a closed provisioning circuit, in which local farmers provided only for the extended family (including relatives living in urban areas) and sold little or no corn to deficit producers within the community. The valley experienced a considerable scarcity of grain, even though the deficit was lessened somewhat by the introduction of yellow corn imported from the United States.

In other agricultural areas of Mexico there were also clear indications that landless rural families and deficit producers were finding it increasingly difficult to meet their provisioning needs. For example, agricultural day laborers in certain regions of peasant agriculture began to request that they be paid not in pesos but in grain. [29] Moreover, as noted in chapter 5 (on Zinacantan, Chiapas), there were instances in which local people looking for work were willing to sell their labor to an employer before the agricultural season began, at a lower-than-market price and in return for prepayment in corn -- an arrangement which could only have developed in the context of severely limited access to grain.

These developments were of course attributable in part to the effects of inflation on rural livelihood and to restrictions which the recession itself placed on purchasing power. As the real income of many peasant families plummeted during the second half of the 1980s, their capacity to produce corn for subsistence and their ability to purchase grain were progressively reduced. In addition, the price structure which developed within some regional grain markets further worsened the situation of net buyers -- and for reasons not always related to a return to subsistence by local surplus producers.

During the last years of the 1980s, grain was scarce in many regions. As a consequence, its market price was sometimes as much as 50 percent above the prevailing support price. Therefore local farmers who did produce a surplus found it advantageous to sell to private intermediaries who in turn channeled the corn to urban areas. This tendency had severe effects on rural consumers, unless they had access to a Diconsa outlet. And high corn prices were often not even advantageous for the sellers of grain, many of whom sold only in order to meet a pressing need for income and might later have to buy at up to double the price they had originally obtained for their own corn, according to various studies included in this book.

Given this situation, rural people demanded a series of reforms in official provisioning policy. In the first place, they strongly advocated the extension of the network of Diconsa stores, since the crisis had significantly increased the number of net consumers in the countryside and the segmentation of the market had exacerbated their supply problems. The government responded positively to this request: the number of rural Diconsa stores doubled during the 1980s, even as other public services were being systematically reduced (Appendini 1992, p. 209).

At the same time, inhabitants of some regions insisted not only that the formal retail operations of Diconsa be expanded in rural areas, but also that the agency increase its support for community efforts to develop new forms of exchange among producers themselves. Chapter 4b, for example, describes an experiment in which peasant organizations within two different ecological zones of central Verzcruz have traded products with relative success, creating their own barter system within a general market context which

---

29. This fact was reported by several of the participants at the UNRISD Tepoztlan seminar in January 1990.

would otherwise have been unfavorable. And in chapter 8, other local provisioning experiments undertaken within the context of the Diconsa system are analyzed as well.

Organizations of small scale cultivators in the central and southern regions of the country (that is, outside the major areas of commercial agriculture in northern Mexico), have insistently advocated creation of a structure of credit and storage which can support local efforts to ensure that an adequate proportion of the corn harvest stays in the region where it is produced. The importance of these demands has been recognized in the recently published National Program for Modernization of the Countryside, which contains provisions to increase the number of regional centers for the purchase and storage of grain and to facilitate producers' access to these centers. In some cases, organized producers have even designed strategies which would allow them to withdraw almost all their production from the market. This attempt at self-sufficiency, financed with off-farm income, flows from the producers' conviction that they lose money both in their initial sale of grain and in their subsequent purchase of it; and that they would in consequence be better off if they concentrated on supplying their own needs outside the market.

Finally, the problems of both irregular supply and low quality of basic products in many rural stores have stimulated an attempt by some regional organizations to improve services to the consumer by taking over the management or ownership of local Diconsa stores and warehouses, which are usually run by the agency itself. Nevertheless, as Armando Bartra notes in his analysis of experiences in two regions of Guerrero, presented in chapter 8, this formal change in ownership alone cannot resolve the structural problems inherent in supplying low income familes who live in isolated and relatively small settlements. The task is a difficult one, especially when it means transporting grain over very long distances or bad roads; and unless high prices are charged, it is obvious that considerable subsidies are necessary.

CONCLUSIONS

By 1991, the future of Mexican agriculture and Mexican rural life depended fundamentally on pending decisions regarding integration into the North American Common Market. After a decade of recession, macroeconomic adjustment and institutional restructuring, what kind of basic provisioning structure in Mexico became the object of negotiation among parties to the proposed treaty? In the case of corn, which is the single most important element of that structure, one finds a system of production, marketing and consumption undergoing profound reorganization, beset by conflicts among groups with opposing interests and riven by the ideological differences that now permeate Mexican society as a whole.

For corn producers, and especially for those engaged primarily in commercial farming, international integration comes at a time of extreme vulnerability, when recession and restricted governmental investment in the countryside have seriously undermined the productive capacity of many agricultural areas, and when institutional reform creates additional uncertainty. A series of governmental programs providing goods and services which are indispensable for agricultural production have either been discontinued or are being reorganized. Until these processes lead to the creation of viable alternatives, Mexican producers operate within a context of disadvantage which is in sharp contrast to the situation prevailing in either Canada or the United States.

The farmers themselves, and especially the small and medium scale ejido-based producers who constitute the majority of the commercial sector, are being asked to play a leading role in restructuring the corn system -- to create the new institutions on which future grain production will depend. Such a call is in part a response to insistent demands that the rural population be granted a larger role in policy formulation and resource managment; and the countryside is now the scene of important experiments of this nature.

Nevertheless, it is unrealistic to expect producers to assume the primary responsibility for the development of the agricultural sector when strong and well organized support from the public sector is lacking.

At the present moment, commercial corn producers in Mexico require not only continued protection from international competition but also reconstitution of the basic infrastructure which provides essential support for modern agriculture, in Mexico as in any other part of the world. This is a torturous process, since it involves institutional reorganization and reform. It is, however, a task of vital importance and one which should not be relegated to a secondary plane under pressure from groups which stand to gain from indiscriminate opening of the national corn provisioning system to international trade.

Mexican commercial producers, like their northern counterparts, also have the right to conduct their business within a general framework of stability of the kind provided by a system of support prices. These prices must cover the average production costs of adequately-endowed small and medium-scale producers, making up the largest part of the commercial sector. Of course, a support price involves risks for any government. In years with good harvests, when market prices fall, payments made to sustain the official price may be considerably higher than the real market price; and this represents a drain on the federal budget. The problem is especially serious at the present time, when competition for scare public funds is fierce. The alternative, however, is a high level of insecurity for producers, which should be unacceptable in Mexico as it is in Canada, Japan, the United States and the European Economic Community.

Outside the commercial agricultural sector, in the majority of smallholdings where corn is cultivated primarily for family consumption, the support price cannot be the primary instrument which stimulates production, since it would not be rational from a national planning perspective to set that price high enough to cover the costs of very low productivity agriculture. Nevertheless, as several studies in this book emphasize, any serious rural development project in Mexico is more likely to be furthered by relatively more remunerative producer prices than by very low ones. On the whole, low corn prices are not advantageous for smallholders, even when the latter are net deficit producers. The private grain trade which predominates in many areas takes the prevailing level of support price into account when setting its own conditions for purchase. Therefore if the official price drops, deficit producers and their families lose when they sell small amounts in the market. Their loss is aggravated when they purchase corn at a later date, for the reasons analyzed earlier in this chapter.

As long as most rural communities in Mexico are marked by poverty, and as long as it is the poor who are most likely to obtain their grain through participation in oligopolistic private markets, it would be highly inadvisable to reduce or dismantle the programs which have been devised in the last two decades to challenge monopolistic practices in the grain trade. In fact, the experiences analyzed in this book emphasize the usefulness of the Conasupo/Diconsa program, as well as the importance of efforts made by organized producers and rural consumers to stabilize grain prices by creating greater regional storage capacity and establishing the necessary channels for obtaining grain from other regions when it is locally scarce.

It should be stressed that recourse to periodic importation of foreign grain has constituted in the past, and still constitutes, a central element in the continuing effort to make rural grain markets more competitive. As long as the basic interests of Mexico's commercial producers are protected, through establishing a just support price and maintaining strict governmental control over imports, purchases of corn abroad should of course continue to play an essential role in the regulatory process -- most particularly in moments like the present one, when urban poverty is increasing markedly. If the negotiation of a free trade agreement requires abandoning that protective capacity, however, the consequences for the rural economy of the country will be serious.

It is frequently asserted that an uncontrolled flow of cheap imported grain would improve the standard of living of the majority of rural people in Mexico, who are either subsistence producers, deficit grain producers, landless laborers, or entirely devoted to growing commercial crops other than corn. This assertion is false. It takes into account neither the complexity of rural subsistence strategies, in which locally-produced corn plays a major role, nor the complexity of local grain markets. Furthermore it assumes the existence of sufficient infrastructure to channel imported grain to widely scattered rural communities (something which often does not exist) and it fails to consider the high subsidies which such a program involves -- subsidies which could better be used to promote local production.

What is needed is not the destruction of the remaining productive capacity of subsistence or deficit producers, and the concomitant elimination of sources of work for landless households, but rather the improved regulation of local markets through the efforts of Conasupo/Diconsa and organized local people, and the creation of innovative rural development programs. It is here that Pronasol, in collaboration with a range of new producer and consumer organizations, has a key role to play. Despite all the problems which afflict the rural population, the variety of productive resources still available in many areas of the Mexican countryside -- the wealth of plant and animal life, forest resources and specialized knowledge which survives in spite of many decades of poverty and forced modernization -- is enormous; and the present challenge is how to ensure that resources are not further depleted and means of livelihood further undermined as a consequence of economic recession and restructuring.

Restructuring in a way which provides new opportunities for small farmers and rural communities, and some possibility of halting the advance of environmental degradation in the countryside, is expensive. But the price of the alternative option is, over the longer run, probably equally high. If inhabitants of the countryside are not supported as a farming population, they will have to be supported in other ways, and perhaps in other places, as the underprivileged, the unemployed, or simply the hungry.

Chapter 2

THE MOBILIZATION OF CORN PRODUCERS: FROM THE STRUGGLE FOR FAIR PRICES TO INTEGRATED RURAL DEVELOPMENT

Luis Hernández

Between 1985 and 1987, organizations of corn farmers in the widely separated Mexican states of Chihuahua, Nayarit, and Chiapas mobilized to demand increases in the support price of their principal crop. Although there was no formal coordination between these movements, the efforts overlapped and therefore eventually influenced each other.

The struggle of 1985 and 1987 grew out of an earlier wave of mobilizationsin 1983, based on the same demands. The later corn farmers' protest was also associated with a broad appeal for increased support prices by other small producers, including wheat farmers in the north, sorghum producers in the Bajio region (to the northwest of Mexico City), barley farmers in Tlaxcala and Hidalgo, and even coffee producers in Chiapas and Veracruz, although the latter could not count on official support prices. In fact, it is not too much to say that demands for higher prices constituted the central element in peasant mobilization throughout the country during the 1985-1987 period.

Although general demands and forms of protest on the part of corn growers were relatively similar in all cases, there were still important local differences among them -- differences in large measure attributable to the sociocultural heterogeneity of the Mexican peasantry. Corn producers throughout the nation suffered from such common problems as decapitalization and high interest rates, but some cultivated the infertile soils of overworked land, damaged by the intensive use of agrochemicals (as in Nayarit), while others made their living from the fertile, productive land of the Frailesca region of Chiapas and repeatedly won the national prize for corn production, known as the *Mazorca de Oro* ("the Golden Ear"). The farmers of Chihuahua made intensive use of agricultural machinery, while only a primitive hoe was used in Chiapas. Nevertheless, a common thread bound all regional struggles, despite their many differences.

THE ORIGINS OF THE MOVEMENT IN 1983 AND THE DEVELOPMENT OF A COLLABORATIVE NETWORK

Two regional organizations, the Union of Ejidos "Lazaro Cardenas" of Ahuacatlán, Nayarit (UELC) and what would later become the Union of Ejidos of Northwest Chihuahua (UENCH), provided the impetus for mobilization within the corn sector in 1983.[1] The first union had originally grown out of the promotional efforts of a rural development brigade in the 1970s. It gained ample experience distributing fertilizers, promoting rural marketing projects and overcoming interference from state officials attempting to impose an illegitimate leadership on the organization. The second union (the UENCH) was created at the beginning of 1983 as an outgrowth of protest by four ejidos of the municipality of Zaragoza over the rising cost of fuel. It

---

1. For a history of the UELC," see Hernández (1990a), Fox (1990), and Fox and Hernández (1989). For a history of the UENCH and its political organization, the Smallholders' Alliance of Northwestern Chihuahua, see "Entrevista al señor Paz Rojo, Secretario de Organización de la Alianza Campesina del Noroeste de Chihuahua," *El Día*, January 19, 1985.

was thus formed more to exert political pressure than to defend the broader interests of producers and was greatly influenced by the Unified Socialist Party of Mexico (PSUM).

The UELC launched its first offensive on December 12, 1982. A cost analysis had shown that, on average, corn producers were losing 6,014 pesos on every harvested hectare. Therefore, on that day, representatives from ten ejidos decided not to deliver their grain to the government marketing agency (Conasupo) and to speak to the governor about their decision. Shortly thereafter, the state government indicated that it would be possible to increase the support price only if the measure were extended to cover producers in the southern area of the state as well. This response, rather than discouraging the protesters, sounded the starting gun for efforts to organize other producers. A commission of ejido corn producers from Nayarit traveled to Mexico City to carry out further negotiations, and there they visited the same offices recently vacated by representatives of another strong smallholders' organization, the Coalition of Collective Ejidos of Sonora, who were seeking a higher price for wheat. Finally, after the movement received ample press coverage, producers from Nayarit returned to their communities with a promise of a favorable response from the national government. Some days later, they were informed of a victory: the support price of corn was increased from 8,850 pesos to 10,200 pesos per ton (Hernández 1990a).

The northerners, on the other hand, fought more intensely. On January 11, 1983 they marched en masse to the capital of the state of Chihuahua and occupied the main building of the state government. This initiative met with enormous popular support and revitalized a broader sociopolitical struggle in the state. Through their protest, members of the UENCH forced both a price increase (of the same magnitude just granted in Nayarit) and a reduction in the cost of state-provided tractor services (to 900 pesos per hectare instead of the previous 1,500); and they assured that the increase in the support price for corn would be granted even to those who had already sold their crop.

Months later, on September 3-4, September 30 and October 1, 1983, a congress of small producers was held in Mexico City to agree on a joint strategy for increasing support prices of grains and for seeking solutions to other common problems. These meetings had been preceded by others which promoted a new convergence among smallholders' organizations in various parts of the country, giving particular attention to issues of agricultural credit and marketing, but considering the problem of support prices only in passing.

In the First National Congress of Second Level Smallholders' Organizations,[2] the following conclusions were reached on support prices:

a) producers did not participate in fixing support prices;

b) although only one support price was authorized for the country as a whole, costs of production varied markedly in different regions of Mexico;

c) increases in support prices were not fixed prior to the delivery of the crop, but only in the period following the harvest. Therefore most producers lost money, since they received the previously quoted price;

d) calculation of the support price was based on the cost of the crop at the beginning of the agricultural cycle. This did not correspond to the actual investment in the crop or to the cost of living by harvest time (Costa 1989, pp. 83-84).

---

2. Second-level organizations group ejidos and ejido enterprises in Ejido Unions, ARICs, and other associational forms that operate in regions.

At the second meeting, twenty organizations from thirteen states within Mexico proposed to the ministerial-level coordinating committee for the farm sector, known as the national agricultural cabinet, that a movable scale of support prices be instituted which would compensate for increases in production costs. They demanded as well that representatives of producers participate in the price setting process and that regional agricultural committees be formed to measure the effects of inflation. Finally, during this session it was pointed out that at the time the government was paying 24,000 pesos per ton for imported corn, but only 16,500 pesos per ton to national producers. Smallholders' representatives demanded that the national support price for corn be increased to 35,000 pesos per ton.[3]

On November 17 and 18, during the Third Assembly of Smallholders'Representatives, held in the northern state of Sonora, it was decided to request an interview with the President, Miguel de la Madrid, in order to "present the demands of the assembly, expecially those related to support prices".[4] In preparation for this dialogue, the planning ministry (SPP) suggested that petitions of producers be previously ordered and systematized; and as they responded to this request, smallholders' organizations concluded that it was necessary to draft a proposal for a formal agreement between the federal government and the representatives of corn producers. Thus a struggle which had originally been focussed on short-term goals was reoriented toward strategic planning and the organizations involved moved from proposing immediate remedies to developing plans for influencing longer-term public policy.

EXPANSION OF THE MOVEMENT

Although the 1983 mobilization was basically spontaneous, the intense organizational activity of the following two years created a broad network of social support, opened new channels of an official and semi-official nature within some state development agencies, and provided new information about the rural world that converted the 1986-1987 movement into a much more organized effort than its predecessor had been.

Ironically, smallholders' mobilizations during late 1985 and 1986 in Chihuahua, Nayarit, and Chiapas, demanding an increase in support prices for corn, were spearheaded by the National Peasant Confederation (CNC) of the official party. Although it was the intention of the CNC only to exert pressure on the agricultural cabinet through press declarations and some other limited measures, producers themselves went beyond the plans of the leadership and shifted from words to action. In October 1985, the CNC-affiliated League of Agrarian Communities of the state of Chihuahua pointed out that the official price of 53,000 pesos per ton of corn was unjust since, according to its studies, the cost of production among its members was 70,000 tons per ton (Quintana 1988, Frente Democrático Campesino 1988).[5] On January 7, 1986, the League of Agrarian Communities of Nayarit took over the Conasupo storehouses where grain was received and demanded that the state agency liquidate the debts it had acquired when purchasing grain in the past. On January 8, 1986, members of the Agricultural Association of La Frailesca, Chiapas, occupied 54 Conasupo storehouses, as an outgrowth of a conflict which first emerged in October 1985 to protest the fact that payments to producers by Conasupo were two months in arrears.

---

3. *Unomásuno*, October 4, 1983.

4. As a result of these meetings, the National Union of Regional Autonomous Peasant Organizations (UNORCA) was formed. For further information see Fox and Gordillo (1989) and Gordillo (1988a).

5. See also Paz Chávez, "El movimiento campesino en el noroeste de Chihuahua", *El Día, Supplement on Rural Areas and Peasants,* June 13, 1986.

THREE HISTORIES, THREE CIRCUMSTANCES

Although these three movements were contemporary, each followed a different path and produced a different solution. It is important to understand the specific political context in each case.

In Chihuahua, the movement first developed during the 1983 elections, against the background of intense political strife, in which the opposition National Action Party (PAN) triumphed in seven major cities and demonstrated growing popularity throughout the state. The political situation was thus very favorable for the development of the corn producers' movement: its repression at the time would have been very costly for the government, since the official party needed the backing of small farmers to counteract middle class support for the PAN.

In Nayarit, the movement grew out of a CNC leader's initiative to strengthen the organization, which was internally divided and lacked the ability to mobilize its constituency. He confronted a political adversary, a populist governor and leader of the Confederation of Mexican Workers (CTM) in the state, who was accustomed to leading movements but not bargaining with them. The governor hoped to funnel all social demands through the corporatist channels of the official party, although he disposed of scarce economic resources with which to enforce his will.

In Chiapas, on the other hand, the movement confronted a governor who was overtly repressive, afraid of the peasant/teacher alliance which had been forged six years earlier in his state, and openly warring with important federal officials.[6] The governor saw the corn producers' movement as an attempt "sponsored by those in the political center" to destabilize his administration. Concomitantly, the leader of the smallholders, an ex-CNC representative, had won his popularity throughout the state precisely by using his power over the Frailescan corn producers to play upon contradictions between various state and federal bureaucracies.

In Chihuahua, mobilization in defense of higher support prices for corn began during an assembly of the Union for the Progress of the Smallholders of Lake Bustillos (UPCALA), held on November 18, 1985. The UPCALA had been formed in March 1985 by ten ejidos originally organized in bible circles and inspired by liberation theology. Initially, members demanded electricity for the towns on the shores of the lake,[7] but at the November meeting it was agreed to take over the Conasupo warehouse in Anahuac in protest against very low grain prices. Once the first storehouse was occupied on December 6th, the movement immediately spread to other regions, until a total of 62 grain reception centers had been taken. The protest widened, incorporating the Smallholders' Alliance of Northwestern Chihuahua, which at the time had a strong following in the municipality of Ignacio Zaragoza. The Alliance operated along the lines of a town council, carrying out a program of integrated rural development and a large project to help its members build and refurbish their own houses.[8] Together the two organizations formed what came to be called the Peasant Democratic Movement (MDC).[9]

---

6. For more details on this point see Neil Harvey (1990). In an interview conducted by Rogelio Vizcaíno with the corn producers' leaders (Tuxtla Gutierrez, Chiapas, 1986), the latter stated that in their interviews with officials of the SPP, they were told that since there was a surplus of 14 billion pesos in the state budget, the corn producers should try to resolve their problems through state government channels. For a complete chronology of the corn producers' movement, see Hernández Aguilar (1987).

7. Quintana, (1988) and Chávez, op. cit.

8. See "Ayuntamiento democrático y cabildo abierto: Plan Zaragoza (1983-1986)", in Costa (1989, pp. 181-83).

9. The movement drafted a petition with a list of demands:

   a) an immediate increase in the support price of corn; b) no increase in the cost of the state government program providing machinery used in plowing and threshing. Formation of committees, in which there should be smallholder participation, for planning and programming the use of the machinery; c) payment by the national

In this extremely politicized situation, different sectors of society began to take a stand on the conflict. Supporters of the corn producers ranged from the Archbishop of Chihuahua to the democratic teachers movement in the state. On January 6, 1986, representatives of the MDC and Conasupo agreed to an increase of the support price to 65,000 pesos per ton, plus a single compensatory payment of 5,000 pesos. However, the following day, during a meeting in which the PRI named its gubernatorial candidate, representatives of both the official CNC and the Independent Peasant Confederation (CCI) took credit for the support price victory. The MDC was angered by this subterfuge and resolved to go ahead with the mobilization. On January 15, amid outbreaks of violence, organized corn producers succeeded in obtaining an increase in the support price to 70,000 pesos per ton and 5,000 pesos for unspecified services. Thus the attempts of government officials to take control of the movement cost the federal government an extra 5,000 pesos per ton.

Meanwhile, in Nayarit, the independent union of ejidos (UELC) took up the original proposal of the state branch of the CNC and extended it throughout the region. A day after the the members of the union assembled, on January 8, they occupied the Tetitlan, Chapalilla, Jala, and Jomulco warehouses of Conasupo and demanded an increase in the support price for corn. At that time, the Union was in a strong position (it was carrying out a successful program of self-help housing among its members)[10] and had stable channels for negotiating with the state government. From the outset of the negotiations, the UELC assumed a flexible stance, suggesting compensatory payments when a general price rise seemed impossible. In addition to these direct payments, they demanded that the Mexican Institute of Social Security (IMSS) provide health care for rural families in their region and that financing be made available for a range of rural development projects. At the beginning of February, Union representatives had an interview with the deputy minister for regional development of the SPP, in which they presented alternative demands for a set of ejido projects totalling more than 204 million pesos. An attempt to lower production costs lay at the center of all these petitions, which were eventually approved by federal authorities.[11]

The Nayarit branch of the CNC did not make any optional proposals during this period and limited itself to taking credit for the 6,000 peso increase per ton which, in fact, the movement of independent organizations had won after a hard fight. In the end, however, many of these gains were to be negated. After the smallholders abandoned the Conasupo installations, the state governor refused to deliver resources approved by federal officials. Payments to corn producers were frozen; and the UELC took justice into its own hands, refusing to pay housing credits owed by the organization to the state government.

---

rural credit bank (Banrural) of agricultural credit to organized producers in one installment, one month prior to the beginning of the agricultural cycle; d) reduction of the bank interest rate for producers on rainfed land; e) reimbursement of 3 percent of the credit utilized by each smallholders' organization, so that the latter could use this money to contract for technical assistance; f) improvement of the administraton of machinery depots through smallholders' participation in planning and programming; g) continued subsidies for fertilizers, insecticides, and seeds utilized by authentic small producers; h) immediate resolution of pending agrarian problems in the ejidos of Northeast Chihuahua. (from "Movilización por el aumento a los precios de garantía del maíz" in Costa (1989, pp. 200-01).

10. This program supported housing improvements for 277 families and constructed 165 foundations for new houses, at the same time that it also strengthened the infrastructure and administrative capacity of the entire organization (Hernández 1990a).

11. These projects basically involved: a) refurbishing of abandoned infrastructure for pork production and dairy cattle; b) opening new areas to mining and forestry exploitation; c) promoting projects that could reduce production costs, such as organic fertilizers, certain kinds of agricultural machinery and inputs, and seeking ways to reduce interest rates; d) opening new areas to cultivation.

In Chiapas, the movement emerged in the context of support from the leader of the Agricultural Association of La Frailesca and the democratic teachers movement.[12] Word of the Chihuahua example had spread.[13] As dissatisfaction among local producers grew, they began to take over the warehouses of Villa Flores and Villa Corzo on January 8th, and shortly thereafter smallholders from Jiquipilas, Cintalapa and other areas emulated their example. This pressure brought about the initiation of negotiations with federal officials, but channels to the state government remained closed. By March, 110 storehouses in 21 municipalities had been occupied by the protesters, and by the beginning of April the number had risen to 300. The stubbornness of state authorities made the situation tenser. On the 28th, 29th, and 30th of April small corn producers took over the central square of the state capital, Tuxtla Gutierrez, and were then promised that they would have the opportunity to take their case before the economic cabinet of the national government. This promise, however, was only partially fulfilled. The commission sent by federal authorities arrived in Tuxtla with neither authority to negotiate nor proposals.

More than five months after the initial warehouse takeovers, corn producers resorted to a final action which had been undertaken by protesters in other states; they blocked the highways.[14] More than 10,000 people participated in the closing of the international highway which began on May 14. Repressive measures were taken by the state government that same day, and eventually seven of the leaders of the movement were jailed. In the midst of strong protests and to the great pleasure of the leader of the official smallholder organization (the League of Agrarian Communities of the CNC), the movement was disbanded.[15] It was time to begin planting the next year's crop.

AN EXPLANATION

The mass movements which developed at this time around the issue of increases in the support price of corn and other grains were a reflection of growing opposition between the better off, more commercially-oriented smallholders and the government. Behind immediate price demands one can find a broader questioning of governmental intervention in the agricultural sector, particularly in relation to the following points:

1) the fixing of support prices by the agricultural cabinet without consulting producers and without adequately considering the real costs of labor and the very large increases in input prices associated with inflation and the reduction of subsidies;

2) the importance of state control of the grain market in principal areas of commercial ejido agriculture. Although, as Appendini (1990) points out, Conasupo has traditionally played a limited role in the purchase of corn at the national level (handling between 10 and 20 percent of the total harvested volume in the country), its participation has been significant in regions like those just discussed. The role of the government was expanded when the Program of Support for Ejido Marketing (PACE) was

---

12. In 1979 primary and secondary school teachers from the state of Chiapas were in the forefront of a strong movement to democratize the National Union of Education Workers. When teachers gained control over their local section of the union, they oriented their program toward developing links with the peasantry. Hundreds of teachers became advisers to and organizers of regional peasant movements. For an analysis of this process, see Hernández (1990a) and Monsiváis (1987).

13. The leader of the Agricultural Association told Carlos Monsiváis: "We ... saw that our immediate future lay in working to increase support prices. We demanded the same level of payment as in Chihuahua, 16,700 pesos more than what we had at the moment, which would bring us up to 70,000 pesos per ton .... They set an example which we followed" (Monsiváis 1987, p. 186).

14. See Germán Jimenez, *El Día, Supplement on Rural Areas and Peasants*, June 18, 1986.

15. See the declarations of the CNC leader for Chiapas in *El Día, Supplement on Rural Areas and Peasants,* July 18, 1986.

inaugurated during the Lopez Portillo administration and increased further through implementation of the Program of Support for Rural Marketing (Fox 1991). Thus, in the eyes of many producers, the state agency was the first link of a marketing chain that had to be refashioned;

3) the ever-increasing cost of financing provided by the National Rural Credit Bank (Banrural), increases which were associated not only with the economic crisis as a whole but also with corruption;

4) the contraction of investment in rural areas for health, road construction, wells, and other productive infrastructure, as well as the drastic reduction in subsidies for agricultural inputs;

5) problems associated with the operation of governmental programs which rented agricultural equipment for clearing, plowing, and harvesting in some areas of commercial ejido agriculture, at times at subsidized rates.

In short, the explosion of peasant smallholders' discontent with the level of support prices reflected broad inconformity with governmental intervention in the fields of crop financing, marketing and certain phases of production, as well as in the fixing of the final price of grain. But these mobilizations were shaped by a series of factors related both to the structure of producers' organizations and to the nature of political opportunities. The protest movements would not have developed as they did without:

1) the existence of a large number of autonomous smallholders' organizations, operating outside the framework of the official peasant confederation. These had been created over roughly a decade of struggle, during the 1970s, and were oriented toward a strategy of strengthening the control of small farmers over key elements of production, marketing, and rural food supply;

2) the constitution of a network of these organizations, providing ideological and political support, and permitting regional groupings to have a national presence. The new, relatively more pragmatic leadership which developed within this network developed policy proposals that did not lead the movements down dead-end streets;

3) the deterioration of traditional, official peasant organizations, which no longer represented their consitutients adequately. These organizations tended to function more as transmitters of political and electoral information and as negotiators with the bureaucracy than as real defenders of producers' interests;

4) the precedent, during the SAM, of price increases for basic grains. This made the demand for increases in support prices during times of deep recession appear both just and eminently justifiable (Fox 1991);[16]

5) the fact that producers' movements were able to find allies within the government. This came about partially within the context of electoral and bureaucratic politics, but it also occurred because more progressive officals within the PRI saw the possibility of utilizing the mobilizations to challenge vitiated party institutions. Since producers' movements had to deal with both state and federal institutions, which did not necessarily have a common stance, the former had a margin for maneuver that could be useful both to the smallholders and to politicians and functionaries.

---

16. With regard to SAM, Alfredo Harvey (1989) stated: " The Mexican Food System (SAM) was, without any doubt, the best effort yet made in Mexico to mobilize agricultural resources, most particularly in the case of rainfed areas where the majority of the poorer and more marginal ejido producers and small private farmers live. It was conceived as a multi-sectorial effort to attain food self-sufficiency and improve nutritional levels. During the short life of the SAM, and in spite of resistance from the agrarian bureaucracy, it showed signs of success that over time seemed more likely to prosper. During the initial year of SAM the results were promising, since the production of basic grains and oilseeds increased 20 percent."

A NEW WAVE OF PROTEST

In July 1986, a part of the MDC of Chihuahua joined the Democratic Electoral Movement (MDE), an organization which had been formed to monitor the electoral process in upcoming state elections. It soon became clear that this initiative came more from the leadership than from the membership of the smallholders' organization, since popular protest against electoral fraud was limited in rural areas. However, the issue of agricultural support prices did play a role in the voting. In areas where the movement to increase producer prices had been strong, voters remembered the favorable resolution of their demands and supported the PRI, although there was a considerable increase of votes in favor of the PAN in the area of influence of the UPCALA (Quintana 1988). Both because previous mobilizations had strengthened producers' organizations and because the state governor was politically vulnerable, the MDC had no difficulty in negotiating an additional increase in the support price at this time. The governor proposed that 25,000 pesos per ton in cash and an equivalent of 25,000 additional pesos in construction of infrastructure be added to the support price of 93,000 pesos per ton which had been fixed by the agricultural cabinet. Producers did receive the cash, but they never saw the resources promised for infrastructure, which had either been programmed previously (and thus were already allocated) or simply never materialized (Quintana 1988).[17]

In Nayarit, on the other hand, corn producers were obliged to mobilize as never before in their history during the 1986-1987 agricultural cycle. To begin with, they had to confront a concerted effort on the part of the state government to strengthen its control over the agricultural sector through the creation from above of Regional Associations of Collective Interest in the north and the south central regions of the state. Although the UELC did not join this association and maintained its independence from the CNC, its room for manuever was reduced. Moreover, these developments coincided with two important electoral campaigns, one for governor of the state and one for the presidency of the republic.

According to estimates by the producers, production costs per hectare at this time were 314,000 pesos, while the support price was only 96,000 pesos.[18] It was necessary to protest; but this time instead of improvising the mobilization, the participants decided to plan it. To begin this process, they called a meeting of all producers in the region, including those working ejido land, small private landowners and holders of communal lands, and they founded the Alliance of Producers of Southern Nayarit (APSN). Then negotiations were initiated with the Minister of Agriculture. After waiting a month and receiving no response from the latter, producers seized the Conasupo storage facilities in five ejidos and blocked the Panamerican Highway. Although this initiative was close to failure several times, pressure did eventually bring results. The Minister of Planning and the Budget (SPP) invited leaders of the movement to negotiate.[19] This negotiation produced no immediate results, since the state governor reserved the right to have the final say. The producers continued to exert pressure: 3,000 marched on the governor's office in Tepic. Finally, the state governor informed the protesters of an increase of 8,000 pesos per ton of corn. The latter responded with boos and insults, but they demobilized.

---

17. See the paid notice placed in the newspaper *El Heraldo de Chihuahua* by the Smallholders' Alliance of Northwestern Chihuahua, February 13, 1987.

18. If we take into account that average production in the region was 2.5 tons per hectare, the producers lost, according to their own accounts, 72,000 pesos per hectare planted (Hernández 1990a).

19. Rolando Loubet, an advisor to the UELC, relates: "Time went by and the stalemate continued. The advisors sought interviews through friends and acquaintances. Finally, one of them talked to the Minister of Planning and the Budget on the telephone: "Mr. Salinas," he said, "you know what the problem is. We want it to be resolved." "Come on over here and negotiate," responded Salinas. "Stop blocking the highway" (quoted in Hernández 1990a).

The official League of Agrarian Communitiies was charged with administering disbursal of this increase. In fact, the League did not respect the rules agreed upon and distributed benefits primarily in areas where it controlled the movement. The leadership of the UELC was relegated to drawing up lists of producers eligible for the increase and verbally pressuring for compliance with what had been promised (Hernández 1990a).

In Chiapas, where the leaders of the movement were in jail, corn producers concentrated their efforts on freeing the former and reorganizing the movement. On July 12, 1986, representatives of 150 ejidos in 21 municipalities throughout the state celebrated the First Peasant Congress of the Union of Corn Producers of Chiapas. Out of this meeting and three further assemblies held between 1986 and 1988 came the stimulus for creation of an organization called Peasant-Teacher Solidarity (SOCAMA), and support for other efforts to promote community organization which were not directly related to the question of an increase in support prices.

CONSTRUCTING OTHER PATHS

After two years of continuous mobilizations, members of the organizations discussed above were aware of the enormous difficulties involved in continuing to press for increases in support prices. Confrontation with the government grew more and more acute, achievements were less and less significant, the danger of repression more palpable, and the strategies employed by official organizations to take credit for any successes increasingly sophisticated. In this context, the Peasant Alliance of Northwestern Chihuahua and the UELC of Nayarit began to consider other productive options, while the Chiapas association sought to reorganize. Only one sector of the MDC which had organized as the Peasant Democratic Front of Chihuahua (FDC) continued to fight with the same intensity for price increases.

The Alliance concentrated its efforts on the formation of a credit union and on forestry projects, as well as experimenting with the production and drying of apples. In fact, this was the first autonomous corn producers' organization which was able to develop a credit system that worked quite successfully. The experiment has involved setting up a series of credit cooperatives, denominated auxiliary credit institutions, which were later to play a key role in the programs of other autonomous organizations as well.

The UELC of Nayarit turned toward defending rural livelihood in its region through promoting a program based on the concept of a "war economy" (*economía de trincheras*). This project centered in part around a return to the small-scale production of food for family consumption (through the cultivation of vegetable gardens and raising of domestic animals), which was the responsibility of women's organizations. Members of the union also experimented with organic fertilizers.

In contrast, the FDC was inaugurated in a climate of tension: on December 6, 1987, a forum organized by the FDC called for direct action. Members then adopted a new demand, that corn prices be indexed to the cost of gasoline;[20] and shortly thereafter they reverted to a tactic they had previously used, seizing Conasupo grain storage installations on December 27. Finally, after taking over 67 storehouses, carrying out marches, hunger strikes and sit-ins in major cities throughout the state, gathering 76,000 signatures supporting the

---

20. As Quintana (1988) reported, it was stated in this forum that "the new price of 245,000 pesos per ton fixed by the government does not cover production costs reaching 283,000 pesos for rainfed areas and 330,00 in irrigated agriculture." At the time, a kilo of corn was worth 245 pesos and a liter of gasoline 267, so what was demanded initially was an increase of 22 pesos per kilo. The demand was ultimately modified because as the movement continued the price of gasoline shot up as high as 493 pesos per liter.

movement, and enlisting the strong backing of the Catholic Church, they won an increase of 60,000 pesos per ton for deliveries of up to 15 tons for all producers who sold less than 30 tons of corn to Conasupo.

A NEW PHASE

The efforts of the FDC in 1987-1988 marked the end of large scale mobilizations by corn producers during the decade of the eighties. From this time forward, first within the framework of the Economic Solidarity Pact and later of the Pact for Stability and Economic Growth (PECE), the large official peasant confederations, and especially the CNC, assumed responsibility for the struggle on a national level, emiting press declarations and pressuring bureaucrats in the hope of obtaining higher support prices for corn. Meanwhile regional organizations once again focused their attention on local negotiations.

In August 1988, immediately following the presidential election, the CNC announced that its continued support for the PECE would be conditioned on an increase in the support price to 435,169 pesos per ton.[21] A second group of independent and autonomous organizations, in the process of forming an alliance, demanded an official price of 773,000 pesos (This group included UNORCA, as well as the Independent Farmworkes and Peasants' Central (CIOAC) and the Popular General Union of Workers and Peasants (UGOCP). The echos of their demand reached the Chamber of Deputies, first through opposition parties and later as an initiative of legislators associated with the CNC. Finally, the Chamber requested that President De la Madrid himself reconsider the support price for corn.[22]

Additional pressure came through letters sent to the President. The leader of the Agricultural Association of La Frailesca, free after having spent twenty-two months in jail, proposed that 13 percent of a 3,500 million dollar loan recently granted to Mexico by the United States be utilized for paying a just price to small corn farmers. "What we are requesting is an insignificant [amount] if we take into account the social risk of not recognizing that the present price is very low" (Correa and Vera 1988).

Regionally, peasant organizations focused on signing agreements with the government which permitted access to rural development funds.[23] Even the FDC, an organization which was reluctant to become involved in that kind of political pact, eventually signed an accord on January 31, 1989, together with the Alliance, the CNC, and the CCI. As a result, they obtained agricultural inputs, reduced costs of machinery services and infrastructural works worth 6 billion pesos for rainfed corn producing areas. Nevertheless, six months after the agreements were signed, no resources had been delivered, and the FDC decided to reinitiate public protest. On November 11, 1989, taking advantage of a presidential visit to Chihuahua, the organization was able to wrest a new agreement from the federal government. This included financing to plow 11,000 hectares, which required an expenditure of approximately 800,000 pesos. As an incidental benefit, the Front also succeeded in extending its influence to more than 40 ejidos and settlements in eleven municipalities (Quintana 1991).

---

21. *La Jornada*, August 4, 1988.

22. *La Jornada*, October 11, 1988.

23. These agreements, called *convenios de concertación*, are accords signed by agencies of the federal government -- and at times even by the President of the Republic -- on the one hand, and various kinds of urban or rural organizations, on the other, for the purpose of providing federal financing for well-specified local development projects. The accords underline the fact that impetus for grassroots development should come not only or even primarily from state agencies, but must originate at the level of beneficiaries themselves. See Hernández (1990b).

Under the aegis of the UENCH, the Alliance, for its part, utilized the signing of a rural development accord with the government to obtain additional resources which could be used to strengthen its credit union, and to develop a factory to produce agricultural implements and a food dehydrating plant.[24]

In Nayarit, the leadership of the Union of Ejidos "Lázaro Cárdenas" (UELC) also shifted its position despite strong disagreement with official support price policy. The president of the organization stated to the press: "With its present policies, the government has forced us to tighten our belt to the limit. The support price for corn of 435,490 pesos does not cover the cost of our labor, and in spite of our proposals and demands in the price setting committees, no one has listened to us" (Hernández and Pérez 1989). Then the UELC joined those signing the rural development accords, basically in order to take advantage of financing for its projects to support production opportunities for women; and it began to place increasing emphasis on political activity.[25] In addition, the organization was required to confront the disastrous consequences of a sharp reduction in official credit within its area of influence: Banrural had closed its branch office in Ahuacatlán and in the end provided credit to only 27 percent of the 150 ejido producers of the community. The UELC responded by extending credits which involved no formal guarantee of repayment beyond the word of the borrower (*crédito a la palabra*). Members of the union confronted the crisis by declaring crop losses which were much greater than those actually suffered, in order to recuperate a part of their expenses from the federal insurance program (ANAGSA), by planting crops which promised to bring higher profits (vegetables, jicama, sugar cane, and peanuts), and by using as much corn as possible to fatten animals.[26]

In Chiapas, the alliance between the Agricultural Association of La Frailesca and the organization known as Peasant-Teacher Solidarity disintegrated shortly after their leaders were released from jail. In August 1989, the latter, which controlled seventeen municipal presidencies, organized the Fifth Meeting of Teachers and Peasants, at which more than 400 communities were represented. Participants opted to remain within the CNC and negotiated financing for farm credit through the National Solidarity Program (Pronasol), to be delivered to members in the form of crédito a la palabra (Martínez Vázquez 1990).[27] The grouping of peasants and teachers was also eventually able to obtain an additional 18,500 pesos per ton from Conasupo for grain delivered from the ejidos of Comitan, Trinitaria and Las Margaritas. This increase represented additional income of 635 million pesos for the producers involved.

A TRANSITORY SUMMING UP

By the end of 1990, the major producers' organizations involved in the fight to increase support prices for corn were shaken to the core by waves of crisis affecting the rural world. The progressive opening of the national economy to the international market, the reduction or elimination of subsidies, the reorganization of

---

24. See the letters of agreement between the Ministry of Agriculture and Hydraulic Resouces (SARH) and the National Institute of Rural Training (INCA-RURAL), January 6, 1989, p.21.

25. The president of the UELC joined forces with governor in a proposed effort to reform the CNC within the state. He was elected municipal president of Ahuacatlán on the PRI ticket, defeating a group of schoolteachers who had traditionally controlled the municipality. See López (1990b).

26. In Ahuacatlán, for example, women no longer use the family corn to prepare *masa* (dough) for making tortillas at home; instead most buy their tortillas at the tortillería. The few women who do prepare their own tortillas buy the masa. See López (1990a).

27. Crédito a la palabra, as it now operates, forms part of the program of Pronasol. This innovative credit arrangement was instituted after Banrural closed down its operations in high risk rainfed areas. Federal resources are used to form a fund, generally managed by local municipalities (although on occasion it can be managed by other organizations), which provides credit for up to two hectares per producer without the bureaucratic red tape which banks usually require. The idea is based on the experience of non-governmental organizations with community-based revolving credit funds.

many official institutions associated with the agricultural sector -- all these developments confronted small farmers with enormous challenges. At the same time, changes in the political strategy of the government, including the formation of the Permanent Agrarian Congress, the new importance given to the negotiation of rural development accords, and the creation of Pronasol have profoundly modified the circumstances in which the struggle for rural livelihood goes on.

As the institutional support structure which formed the basis for peasant-government relations is being dismantled, a new framework for co-operation must be designed. With few exceptions (such as that of the Peasant Alliance of Northwestern Chihuahua), attempts to implement alternative rural development projects are meeting with enormous difficulties. Nevertheless it is important to note that the political strength of the leadership of autonomous peasant organizations has grown significantly, to the point that negotiations with the government are being conducted under exceptionally advantageous conditions. In fact, leaders of key autonomous organizations are now privileged interlocutors of state development agencies. Several are municipal presidents, and others have been incorporated into official peasant unions. The stagnation of productive projects is not entirely unrelated to these political developments, although evidently it cannot be imputed solely to political factors.

The war over support prices continues to be a fundamental element of rural life. The recent neoliberal offensive, however, has changed the terms of combat, dramatically increasing the importance of capital and the market in calculations of advantage and disadvantage. Although the official discourse grants a privileged position to autonomous organizations of producers, the latter lack real authority when confronted with vastly more powerful economic players. As long as state policies do not take these inequalities into account, and as long as corporatist strategies are not completely eliminated, development of alternative regional projects elaborated by these organizations will be very difficult.

In the specific case of corn, producers must now confront problems arising from the disparity between the price of local grain and the price of corn on the international market. There is a large difference between the value consumers place on white corn, grown nationally, and yellow corn, which is imported and often produced for animal feed. Nevertheless the present inability of peasant organizations to establish "corn banks" in which to store production so that it can be utilized months after the harvest, does not allow them to capitalize on this advantage.

It is not clear whether organizations which previously played a fundamental role in the defense of the interests of small producers will be able to adapt successfully to the new rules of the game. In any event, the conflict continues, fueled by a stubborn refusali to abandon corn farming.

Chapter 3

THE IMPACT OF SUPPORT PRICES FOR CORN ON SMALL FARMERS IN THE PUEBLA VALLEY,1967-1989

Heliodoro Díaz Cisneros

While small corn farmers in some parts of Mexico were occupying government grain warehouses and blocking highways in an effort to win substantial increases in the support price, others dealt with the growing unstainability of grain production in a different way: they retreated into near-subsistence agriculture, progressively abandoning some of the farming practices which had permitted them higher levels of productivity and relying more insistently on off-farm income. It is particularly illustrative to look at developments of this kind in historical perspective, and from the point of view of small grain farmers in a region of central Mexico which has been the site of a highly successful technical assistance program for dryland agriculture.

From the latter 1960s onward, a world-famous agronomical experiment was conducted in the Puebla Valley. Known as the Puebla Project, it was based on a program of agricultural research and rural development aimed at increasing the corn yields of small farmers. Over time this "green revolution-like" initiative for rainfed areas significantly improved general levels of production and productivity among participating small farmers and converted the valley from a net deficit into a net surplus region, providing a growing volume of grain to the national market.

Toward the end of the 1980s, however, a series of changes associated with the economic crisis and with reorientation of national agricultural policy reversed this trend. As many small farmers found it impossible to continue to carry out the recommended practices of the Puebla Project, the region once more slid into deficit. Conasupo warehouses, which had previously bought and stored local corn, were by the end of the decade being utilized almost exclusively as channels for providing rural families with yellow corn imported by the Mexican government from the United States.

THE SITUATION IN THE PUEBLA VALLEY BEFORE THE PROJECT BEGAN

In 1967 the thirty-two municipalities of the Puebla Valley encompassed almost seventy rural communities containing from 300 to 15,000 inhabitants, as well as the capital of the state of Puebla with a population of 500,000. According to the baseline study for the Puebla Project, conducted in the winter of 1967-1968, average farm size, whether on ejido or private holdings, was about 2.5 hectares; and of an estimated 116,000 hectares of arable land available for cultivation, 80 percent was used to grow corn.

In 1967, according to the same study, the great majority of all farmers (nearly 70 percent) planted corn for the purpose of feeding their families. When farmers sold a part of their harvest (anywhere from 10 to 50 percent), they did so to cover urgent expenditures such as an illness, a loan repayment, or costs related to the children's education. Surplus corn was usually sold in the regional markets of San Martin Texmelucan, Huejotzingo, and Tepeaca to dealers who handled grain for local consumption. To a lesser extent, corn was also sold to larger private merchants, who had wider contacts, or to Conasupo. In 1967 the price paid per ton of corn ranged from 850 to 940 pesos. Although Conasupo offered higher prices, most local farmers felt at the time that it was advantageous to sell to private dealers, since the latter paid immediately and did not discount for humidity or impurities as the government agency was then required to do.

A majority of the small farmers in the region had already incorporated some elements of modern technology, such as chemical fertilizers, into their production strategy. However, tillage practices and prevailing plant density per hectare had not changed over many years; and in fact, some of the elements of corn farming in the Puebla Valley could be traced back to pre-Columbian Choloteca culture. Average yields per hectare did not surpass 1,500 kilograms, partly because knowledge about the correct amount of fertilizer to be applied was limited (in most cases the dosage was too low) and in part because the fertilizers purchased, which were the only ones available on the local market, were often inappropriate for local needs. Although a majority of all farmers were familiar with hybrid seeds and more than 50 percent had tested them in their plots, less than 1 percent of those surveyed used them regularly. Most farmers indicated a preference for planting local varieties which over time had proven to meet their nutritional needs and which were also well adapted to the soil and climate of the region.

In 1967, the average dosage of fertilizer applied per hectare by the 250 producers interviewed during the baseline study was 25 kilograms of elemental nitrogen, 14 kilograms of phosphorus, and about 8 kilograms of potassium. Average seed density for that year was about 31,000 plants per hectare -- a situation congruent with the low fertility of the soil in the region and the inadequacy of fertilizers applied during the growing cycle. In the opinion of researchers, practices related to conservation of humidity, weed control, and soil management seemed adequate and required little change.

During the survey year, the great majority of farmers in the Puebla Valley financed their own production without receiving loans from any source. Official credit services benefited only 6.8 percent of the producers (the Ejido Bank accounted for 6.4 percent and the Agricultural Bank 0.4), and local moneylenders extended agricultural credit to a further 4.4 percent of the farmers of the area. While interest on official loans was 9 percent per year, private loans (granted for periods ranging from one to three months) carried an interest rate of up to 10 percent per month. The latter did not, however, appear to be linked to the kind of arrangement common in states like Veracruz, Guerrero and Oaxaca, in which borrowers secured their loans by pledging to sell their corn crop to local moneylenders at a much reduced price (see CIMMYT 1974).

Only those farmers working with the official banks had access to agricultural insurance, which was an integral part of official credit arrangements. At the same time it could be said that, for all practical purposes, technical assistance was nonexistent: in 1967 there were only five extensionists for the entire state of Puebla.

THE PROJECT STRATEGY FOR INCREASING THE PRODUCTIVITY OF SMALL FARMERS

In the spring of 1967, the first steps were taken within the Puebla Project to design an effective strategy for supporting small producers in rainfed areas who planted basic grains for family consumption. The effort was undertaken by a group of researchers from the Graduate College (CP) of the National Agricultural University and from the International Center for the Improvement of Maize and Wheat (CIMMYT), all of whom believed that small farmers, working ejido and private land, should have access to modern production technology and to the range of services available through governmental institutions (including agricultural credit and insurance, as well as purchase of grain at guaranteed minimum prices). Their concern for small grain producers grew out of a detailed analysis of the 1960 Agricultural Census, as well as a series of studies based on field research in different regions of Mexico, which dramatically documented the growing crisis in the agricultural sector.[1]

From this analysis it was clear that those who benefitted most from technological innovation in the Mexican countryside, and from the development of official programs of support to agriculture, including credit, crop insurance and technical assistance services, were medium and large-scale commercial farmers. The great majority of all small farmers, usually tilling rainfed plots, did not benefit. They continued to utilize the traditional technology which had been handed down from one generation to the next, adapting it without benefit of support from agricultural science or access to an institutional support structure.

The team that conceived and implemented the Puebla Project strategy was convinced that small producers could adopt and benefit from modern agricultural technology. This belief was in sharp contrast to the view held by most agronomists and decisionmakers in the 1960s, who attributed small producers' backwardness to their lack of interest in change (or "need for achievement"); commercial farmers, however, were supposed to be motivated by this value to adopt modern technology (Rogers 1969, pp. 1-41). The project team rejected this view and maintained that if small producers had access to a technology appropriate to their ecological and socioeconomic conditions and if the relation between the sale price of their crop and cost of inputs was favorable, they would adopt the new technology with as much or more rationality than had larger commercial farmers. From the outset of the project, researchers insisted that the recommended technology should complement the farmer's traditional knowledge, not discard it.

ELEMENTS OF THE STRATEGY IN OPERATION

The Puebla Project was based upon making the following elements available to small farmers:

1. high-yielding varieties of corn, developed through research within the region;
2. information on efficient farming practices;
3. effective dissemination of information derived from continuing research in the area;
4. an adequate supply of agricultural inputs, easily accessible to farmers;
5. agricultural credit at reasonable rates of interest;
6. access to agricultural insurance, to protect the investment of farmers adopting the technology recommended by the project;
7. a favorable ratio of costs to benefits of the recommended technology;
8. access to rural markets where surplus production could be sold at a relatively stable price;
9. orientation and assistance to producers, so that they could form associations facilitating access to credit and inputs and promoting the development of rural infrastructure.

The implementation of this project was the responsibility of an interdisciplinary team of ten professionals in the agricultural and social sciences who were based in the region. In addition to conducting research of an agronomical, economic, and social nature, they were involved in dissemination and technical assistance, as well as in fostering the participation of official agencies in the experiment. From the outset of the project, the team established evaluation and monitoring procedures and conducted periodic surveys of participating and non-participating farmers. It is precisely the information gathered through these studies that now makes it possible to document the evolution of the experiment over the past few decades in such unusual detail.

---

1. For an analysis of unfavorable trends in the agricultural sector from 1945-1965 see Reyes Osorio et al. (1974, pp.1-174).

GENERATION OF TECHNICAL RECOMMENDATIONS AND THEIR GRADUAL ADOPTION BY SMALL PRODUCERS

The first stage

The pilot phase of the Puebla Project began at corn planting time in the spring of 1967, when experiments were established at sites considered to be representative of the major soil types of the region. Twenty-seven soil fertility experiments were conducted to study the dosage and application of fertilizers, plant density per hectare and planting dates. Applying the same criteria of representativity, thirty experiments concerned with the genetic improvement of corn were also inaugurated. Tests were conducted to compare the performance of local varieties of corn with that of available hybrids, produced in experimental stations under ecological conditions considered similar to those of the Puebla Valley.

At the end of the first year of experimentation, researchers concluded that soils in the region could yield 3,700 kilograms per hectare when 130 kilograms of nitrogen and 40 kilograms of phosphorus were applied. No positive response to the application of potassium was noted. Optimum plant density per hectare under conditions prevailing in 1967 was 50,000. This recommendation was codified as 130-40-50,000. As previously mentioned, the dosis of fertilizer and plant density generally prevailing at the time (25-14-31,000) yielded 1,300 kilograms per hectare.

Improved varieties (principally hybrids) obtained by geneticists from experimental stations located in high altitude valleys did not demonstrate a greater capacity for yield than the local varieties already used by small producers.[2] Given those test results, and taking into account the fact that with recommended practices it seemed possible at least to double corn production, the project team decided to promote the recommendation on a community-wide basis. A few weeks before planting was scheduled to start in 1968, they issued an invitation to corn growers through municipal and community authorities. More than 500 producers responded positively to the initiative; however, since participation required that farmers acquire the inputs themselves, either through obtaining credit or through investing their own money, only 103 producers, with plots ranging in size from 0.25 to 1.0 hectares, joined the program in 1968. A total of 76 hectares were planted by these first volunteers.

After assisting the volunteers to acquire the necessary inputs (using credit or personal resources), the dissemination unit organized local demonstrations to explain the correct use of the recommendation. Participants themselves applied the new dosis of fertilizer to their plots and planted seeds according to instructions provided by project personnel, so that the correct density of plants per hectare could be assured. Thus, if the yields at harvest time were convincing, participants could continue to apply the recommendation in their own plots in succeeding years.

Weather conditions, which were excellent during the 1968 agricultural year, contributed to the success of the experiment. The first participants in the Puebla Project obtained an average yield of 3,985 kilograms per hectare in contrast to a regional average of just over 2,000. The dissemination unit took advantage of this

---

2. Beginning in 1969, project plant breeders, with assistance from the CP and CIMMYT, initiated a corn improvement program which tested genetic material gathered both within the region and outside it. This program was formally terminated in 1973, when economic support from the Rockefeller Foundation, as well as collaboration with CIMMYT, came to an end. Nevertheless, research continued under the direction of a field assistant within the project research program (and with counsel from the CP), utilizing strains of local corn which had been demonstrated to be superior to hybrids. After eight years of breeding, researchers delivered an improved variety called Blanco Tlaltenango, which could be profitably utilized on 12,000 of the 80,000 hectares planted with corn in the region. In the rest of the Puebla Valley, producers continued to use other local varieties with good results.

At the same time, from 1975 to 1981 participating producers, whether they acquired the recommended fertilizers through the credit program or by utilizing their own resources, developed and consolidated organizations that facilitated the acquisition, transport, storage, and distribution of inputs. Moreover, they gradually developed a rural infrastructure through construction of community grain storage facilities, roads and bridges, and deep wells. The latter allowed some producers to change over from rainfed agriculture to irrigation.

As a result of the advances described above, average yields for the region as a whole reached nearly 3,000 kilograms per hectare between 1975 and 1981. During that same period, pressure from regional smallholders' organizations brought about changes in the grain acquisition procedures of Conasupo, thus ensuring that an increasing proportion of all regional corn production would be sold to that agency. To simplify regulations governing the receipt and payment of corn, Conasupo abandoned its former policy of reducing the price offered for colored corn; and it also began to purchase grain just as it came from the fields, with the usual level of humidity of 14 percent, although it had previously penalized producers who delivered grain with a level of humidity of more than 12 percent. In addition, Conasupo accepted delivery of quantities of grain ranging from 10 kilograms to ten tons instead of restricting purchases to a minimum of 500 kilograms per vendor, as it had done before.

Participation in the Puebla Project, whether of a direct or indirect nature, reached its highest point in 1981 when, under the auspices of the SAM, special benefits were provided to producers of basic grains. A discount of 30 percent on the cost of fertilizer was offered both to farmers receiving official credit and to producers who organized to acquire inputs with their own resources. In addition, the fact that the National Program to Support Rainfed Agriculture (PLANAT), funded by the World Bank, had since 1979 made resources available for the development of rural storage infrastructure (some ten storage facilities had been constructed in coordination with smallholders' organizations) permitted the timely delivery of the inputs subsidized by SAM. In various regional forums it was noted that for first time since the agrarian reform there was persuasive evidence of strong official support for small farmers.

Participation from 1982 to 1989

As Table 1 illustrates clearly, there was a noteworthy decline in regional yields from 1982 onward. In part this can be attributed to unfavorable climatic conditions and in part to the economic crisis and the evolution of national agricultural policy. To judge the relative importance of these factors in affecting corn yields, the evaluation and research units of the Puebla Project gathered experimental data, as well as consulting accumulated survey information, in order to carry out a retrospective evaluation of the twenty-one year period from 1969-1989. The results of that analysis are presented in Table 2.[3]

For comparative purposes, a year with favorable weather conditions (1968) was chosen as the standard. It can be seen in the table that during the period under consideration, there were twelve years characterized by a less favorable climate for corn production, three years with similar conditions (1978, 1981 and 1989), and another six years (1976, 1977, 1980, 1984, 1985, and 1987) which had better climatic conditions than the base year.

---

3. For further details on this study see Esquivel (1986).

Table 2

Estimated Effects of Technology on Yields for All Producers (YGRAL), and Estimated Climatic Effects Based on Change with Respect to 1968 Experimental Yields (YTTR)[a]

Year	YGRAL kg/ha (A)	YTTR kg/ha (B)	Climatic effect (% change from 1968) (C)	Estimated yield (kg/ha) with constant technology (D)	(A - D)	Change due to technology (E)
1967	1,310	2,303				
1968	2,090	2,394	Base	2,090	0	0.00
1969	1,662	1,963	-18.00	1,714	-52	-3.03
1970	1,917	2,035	-14.99	1,777	140	7.88
1971	1,883	1,892	-20.97	1,656	227	13.71
1972	2,442	2,250	-6.02	1,964	478	24.34
1973	2,552	2,250	-6.02	1,964	588	29.94
1974	1,714	1,649	-31.12	1,440	274	19.03
1975	2,099	2,044	-14.62	1,784	314	17.63
1976	3,356	2,599	8.56	2,269	1,087	47.91
1977	2,953	2,708	13.12	2,364	591	25.00
1978	3,011	2,396	0.08	2,107	904	42.90
1979	2,803	2,255	-5.81	1,969	834	42.36
1980	3,096	2,863	19.59	2,499	597	23.87
1981	3,095	2,341	-2.21	2,095	1,000	47.73
1982	1,300	1,794	-25.06	1,566	-266	-16.98
1983	980	1,582	-33.92	1,381	-401	-29.04
1984	2,281	2,558	6.85	2,233	48	2.15
1985	2,664	2,985	24.68	2,606	58	2.23
1986	2,008	2,233	-6.73	2,076	-68	-3.27
1987	2,172	2,648	10.61	2,311	-139	-6.01
1988	1,523	1,695	-29.20	1,480	43	2.71
1989	2,414	2,426	1.34	2,092	12	-0.57
Average	2,229	2,255	-6.18	1,974	284	14.38

[a] Average yield obtained in agronomic experimentes using the traditional technology of 1968, codified as 50-25-30 000.

During that twenty-one year interval, years classified as disastrous were 1974 (marked by serious frosts), 1982 and 1983 (devastated by severe drought). In these three cases, the effect of the climate (and diminished yields, as compared to 1968, by -31.12%, -25.06%, and -33.92% respectively. In spite of the frosts, however, use of the project technology improved yields in 1974 by +19.03%. The recommended technology corresponding agricultural practices) had a negative effect on yields in 1982 and 1983. Since the crop lacked humidity in virtually all phases of the growth cycle after the second tillage was completed, the high dosage of fertilizers in fact damaged the plants.

On the whole, the recommended technology was used to favorable effect from 1970 to 1981, with a low positive impact on yields of 7.88% in 1970 and maximum benefits of +47.91% and +47.73% in 1976 and 1981, respectively. The average favorable effect of the recommended technology over the twelve year period was 28.53%.

The sharp drop in yields in 1982 and 1983 was attributable to the climate. Nevertheless, from 1984 to 1989 the weather was favorable in four of the six years analyzed. Consequently, the considerable drop in regional yields (2,177 kilograms per hectare over those six years) must be imputed not to the climate but rather to changes in agricultural practices. As is shown in Table 2, the average effect of technology on yields was -0.46% during the period under scrutiny. That figure reflects a gradual abandonment of some elements of the technological package developed by the Puebla Project and utilized by small corn farmers up to 1981. To fully comprehend this process of change, it is necessary to discuss the evolution of support prices for corn and their relation to corn production.

SUPPORT PRICES AND THEIR RELATION TO THE COSTS OF PRODUCTION

Table 3 provides a list of the nominal support prices for corn in effect from 1968 through 1989, as well as real prices in pesos of 1978. In real terms, the maximum level of support prices was reached in 1976 and 1981, when farmers were offered the equivalent of 3,508 pesos per ton. In descending order, the next best years were 1983, with a real support price of 3,504 pesos, 1984 (3,491 pesos), 1985 (3,480 pesos) and 1986 (3,376 pesos). The lowest prices during this period were in 1987 (2,662 pesos per ton), 1989 (2,236 pesos until October 31st, and 2,634 pesos after the first of November), and above all, 1988 (1,778 pesos per ton, which was the lowest point reached in twenty-two years). It is therefore not surprising that beginning in 1988 the gap between the level of official prices and those paid by private grain dealers began to widen significantly, even though the market had previously tended to be unified around the level of prevailing support prices. (This is not to suggest, of course, that there were not always some differences in sale conditions in individual cases.)

Studies of the changing cost structures associated with different kinds of corn production, conducted periodically within the Puebla Project from 1967 onward, make it possible to analyze the impact of producer price fluctuation on the level of profitability of grain farming at various times over the past two decades. For example, looking first at 1968, when the support price was 940 pesos per ton or 0.94 pesos per kilogram and the costs of nitrogen and phosphorus were 4 and 2.81 pesos per kilogram respectively, one sees that applying the recommended dosis of fertilizer, coded as 130-40-00, cost the producer the equivalent of 671 kilograms of corn.[4] Nevertheless, given the fact that yields rose to 3,985 kilograms per hectare, the use of the recommendation was an attractive alternative for the majority of the peasants beginning in 1969.

A comparison of production costs borne by users and non-users of the recommended technology during the 1968 agricultural cycle (including both the real cost of hired labor and the imputed cost of family labor) shows that small corn farmers adopting the recommended technological package had to spend almost double the amount spent by those continuing to cultivate their grain in the traditional way. (The corresponding figures were 2,197 vs. 1,144 pesos per hectare.) Since yields were much higher in the former case, however,

---

4. The cost of inputs, stated in kilograms of corn, which would be required to comply with the recommendation coded as 130-40-00 was calculated on the basis of information gathered during project evaluation surveys conducted in the region from 1967 through 1988.

Table 3

Prices Paid by Conasupo per Ton of Corn, 1968-1989

Year	Nominal Price[a]	Deflated Price[b] (Constant 1978 pesos)
1968	940	3165
1969	940	3082
1970	940	2928
1971	940	2798
1972	940	2685
1973	1200	2963
1974	1500	2852
1975	1900	3209
1976	2340	3508
1977	2900	3376
1978	2900	2900
1979	3480	2939
1980	4450	3007
1981	6550	3508
1982	8850	3087
1983	19200	3504
1984	33450	3491
1985	53300	3480
1986	96000	3376
1987	175000	2662
1988	245000	1778
1989 to 10/31	370000	2236
1989 from 11/1	435000	2624

[a] Prices provided by the Boruconsa office for the eastern region of Mexico, with headquarters in Puebla.

[b] Consumer price index for food and beverages (see below). From Banco de México, *Indicadores Económicos*, (diciembre de 1989).

Deflator:

1968 = 29.7	1976 = 66.7	1983 = 547.9
1969 = 30.5	1977 = 85.9	1984 = 958.3
1970 = 32.1	1978 = 100.0	1985 = 1,531.5
1971 = 33.6	1979 = 118.4	1986 = 2,843.5
1972 = 35.0	1980 = 148.9	1987 = 6,572.5
1973 = 40.5	1981 = 186.7	1988 = 13,771.8
1974 = 52.6	1982 = 286.7	1989 = 16,578.9
1975 = 59.2		

farmers participating in the Puebla Project had a net profit of 1,309 pesos per hectare, compared to only 737 pesos for non-participants.[5]

The tendency for average yields per hectare to increase throughout the 1970s, combined with a relatively moderate increment in the prices of agricultural inputs, reinforced the profitability of corn production throughout the decade. In 1981, the substantial decrease in the price of chemical fertilizers brought about within the framework of the SAM further reduced the cost of adopting the technological package coded as 130-40-00: in that year producers in the Puebla Valley needed to destine only 364 kilograms of corn per hectare to pay the cost of the recommended fertilizers -- in other words, only 54 percent of the cost in 1967.

From this low point in 1981, costs began to rise. The following year, 397 kilograms of corn per hectare were required to pay for the recommended fertilizers; and by 1989, the figure stood at 474 kilograms per hectare -- a level not as high as the original cost of the recommendation in 1968, but still much above the amount which had to be spent at the beginning of the decade.

Let us look in greater detail at how production costs were structured during the 1982, 1984 and 1989 agricultural years. Table 4 analyzes the situation during 1982 and 1984, the first marked by disastrous weather conditions and the second by recuperation. These calculations include not only the level of direct expenditures on inputs and services, but also the cost attributed to the use of family labor and the imputed value of land rent. Table 5 registers the total value of corn production (including both grain and stubble) at average rural prices in 1982 and 1984, as well as the net gain or loss during each year, calculated within three different analytical contexts: 1) considering production costs to include the value imputed to family labor and land; 2) considering only the imputed value of family labor to constitute a cost; and 3) including neither of the above in production cost.

It can be seen from Table 5 that for the 1982 cycle, when production costs are defined as in option one, a loss of 6,486 pesos per hectare is sustained on a holding with an average size of 4.38 hectares (in other words, a total loss of 28,422 pesos per holding). The second option, in which the imputed rental value of the land is no longer considered a cost, suggests that there would still be a net loss 9,709 pesos (2,216 pesos per hectare). Under the third option, when neither labor nor rental value of the land is taken into account, there is a small profit of 8,378 pesos for the 4.38 hectares, or 1,912 pesos per hectare.

In 1984, with a better support price and greater productivity, when the costs of production according to option one are subtracted from the value of production 3.93 hectares of corn per family, there is a net profit of 22,286 pesos (or 5,657 pesos per hectare, in pesos of 1982). Obviously the profit margin increases when production costs do not include the imputed rental value of the land. In that case, there is a total profit of 36,328 pesos (or 9,220 pesos per hectare). When neither labor nor rental value of the land is considered, the overall profit rises to 48,618 pesos, or 12,340 (1982) pesos per hectare.

The favorable situation for farmers of the Puebla Valley in 1984, and the even better one in 1985, became gradually more unfavorable. By 1988, when the support price was at its lowest level in the 21 years under analysis and climatic conditions were once again disastrous for corn production, farmers suffered serious losses and total production was not even sufficient to satisfy regional consumption needs.

---

5. For further information on the 1967 analysis of production costs both among producers who followed the recommendation and among those who did not, see Myren (1969).

Table 4

**Production Costs for Corn Planted Alone or in Association
with Beans during the 1982 and 1984 Crop Seasons
(in constant 1982 pesos)**

Component	1982 Survey		1984 Survey	
	Amount	Percentage	Amount	Percentage
INPUTS		14.46		16.80
Chemical fertilizers	8,096.88	61.85	9,049.48	68.63
Organic fertilizer	2,750.43	21.00	973.27	7.38
Seeds	1,158.95	8.85	1,356.53	10.29
Insecticides	83.01	0.63	152.86	1.16
Herbicides	497.98	3.80	579.64	4.40
Fuel and lubricants	103.84	0.93	87.54	0.66
Packing and boxes	176.00	1.34	776.32	5.89
Irrigation water	80.25	0.61	55.91	0.42
Other	144.01	1.10	155.30	1.18
Subtotal	13,091.95	100.00	13,186.85	100.00
SERVICES		35.67		38.66
Machinery costs	10,103.95	31.27	7,749.28	24.55
Draft Animals	15,404.54	47.68	10,851.36	34.86
Land rental	308.82	0.65	315.58	1.04
Sharecropping payment	538.11	1.67	3009.27	9.92
Transport	3,995.50	12.37	4908.90	16.17
Interest paid to private parties	123.35	0.38	0.00	0.00
Bank interest payments	489.63	1.52	2,072.12	6.83
Agricultural Insurance	89.94	0.28	897.26	2.96
Other	1,355.72	4.47	1,115.64	3.67
Subtotal	32,309.55	100.00	30,249.41	100.00
LABOR		29.21		26.65
Hired labor	8,367.81	31.63	8,628.86	41.25
Family Labor	18,086.67	68.37	12,290.46	58.75
Subtotal	26,454.48	100.00	20,959.32	100.00
LAND RENTAL		20.66		17.89
Irrigated field rent	2,246.88	12.00	2,639.42	18.80
Dryland field rent	16,360.02	87.42	11,347.99	80.82
Good dryland field rent	106.51	0.58	53.65	0.38
Subtotal	18,713.45	100.00	13,903.70	100.00
TOTAL corn production costs	*90,569.39*	*100.00*	*78,496.65*	*100.00*

Table 5

**Profit (or Loss) Obtained by Small Farmers in the Plan Puebla Area
in the 1982 and 1984 Crop Seasons[a]
(in constant 1982 pesos)**

Item	1982 Survey		1984 Survey	
	Amount	Percentage	Amount	Percentage
(A) Total value of corn produced	62,147.03	100.00	100,783.14	100.00
1. Value of the grain	34,180.87	55.00	78,641.08	23.08
2. Value of the forage (storage)	27,966.16	45.00	22,142.06	26.97
(B) Total cost of production	90,569.39	100.00	78,496.55	100.00
1. Value of family labor	18,086.67	19.97	12,290.46	15.66
2. Rental value of the land	18,713.91	20.66	14,041.07	17.88
3. Other cash expenses	53,769.31	59.36	52,165.12	66.46
(C) Net profit (or loss) = A - B	-28,422.36		22,286.49	
(D) Net profit (or loss) taking into account the value of family labor = A + B1 - B2 - B3	-9,708.95		36,327.56	
(E) Net profit (or loss) taking into account the value of family labor and the land = A + B1 +B2 - B3	8,377.72		48,618.02	

[a] 1982 n = 352, 1984 n = 320

By 1989, the majority of all families in the region were so disillusioned by low prices and high costs that they no longer invested in all elements of the technology they had employed in 1984-1985. Reacting to the increasing cost of fertilizers, small scale producers significantly decreased the dosage of fertilizer per hectare. Nevertheless good weather conditions permitted average yields in that year to reach 2,400 kilograms per hectare.

To gain a better picture of producer profits and losses in the Puebla Valley in 1989, it is useful to look at data obtained from twenty families cultivating different kinds of land, considered to be representative of the most important soil types in the region. The data come from a survey, carried out as part of a research project funded by the National Council for Science and Technology (Conacyt), which sought to understand why traditional farming practices essential for ensuring the conservation of humidity in the soil were being discontinued by producers.[6]

In the twenty cases studied (including ten families who continued to carry out the traditional practices and ten who did not), average yields were just 1,797 kilograms per hectare. Producers estimated that they received an average rural price of 451,650 pesos per ton for their grain, when the support price was 435,000, so that the total value of production per hectare was 811,890 pesos. In addition, the corn stubble was valued at 217,700 pesos per hectare. When the imputed value of family labor and land were taken into consideration in calculating costs of production per hectare, the latter reached 1,542,370 pesos.

If we subtract the costs of production (1,542,370 pesos per hectare) from its value (811,890 pesos per hectare), there is a net loss of 512,7000 pesos. Even if we eliminate the imputed costs of family labor and rental value of the land, there would be a profit of only 224,087 pesos per hectare (or approximately 80 US dollars). If family labor is given a monetary value when calculating production costs, however, there is a net loss of 136,508 pesos per hectare.

CHANGES IN LIVELIHOOD STRATEGIES AS A RESULT OF THE CRISIS

Even when confronted with such a noteworthy decline in the profitability of farming, producers in the Puebla Valley have not engaged in protest movements of the kind frequently found in other regions of Mexico. Instead, producers have chosen to respond in a more individualistic manner, abandoning sales to Conasupo and searching out regional dealers who pay more than the support price for grain in a deficit market, or, alternatively, dropping out of the corn market altogether. In such a case, the entire crop is consumed by the extended family and by farm animals. In addition, the labor resources of farm families, which have always been flexibly utilized, have been reallocated to meet the current economic challenge.

To understand this last element in the response of small corn growers to the crisis, one should remember that there has been a significant process of industrialization in the Puebla Valley during the last few decades; and this coupled with the proximity of the region to Mexico City has allowed family members to earn off-farm income on a permanent basis or to seek temporary urban employment when bad weather decimates corn production. Thus even in 1967, when the initial Puebla Project survey was conducted, 41 percent of the income of farm families was derived from non-agricultural activities. (The proportion of total income attributable to agricultural activities was 30 percent and that from livestock, 28 percent.) Net family income during that year was 8,335 pesos.

In 1970, thanks to improved corn yields and attractive profit margins for the sale of surplus corn, small farmers devoted more effort to agriculture, generating 36 percent of their income from these activities and 30 percent from their livestock. Off-farm activities declined to 28 percent, the lowest percentage throughout the period under analysis (1967-1989). Total household income rose to 10,320 pesos.

The tendency for rural families in the Puebla Valley to give increasing importance to agricultural production continued unabated through 1981. Conditions during the 1970s allowed the majority of these households to generate most of their income on the farm. At the end of 1981, total household income among

---

6. The conservation of residual humidity allows farmers to plant in the month of April, before the rainy season commences. An outstanding example of the potential of such practices has been provided by the Zapopan system in the state of Jalisco, which has been studied by agronomists from many parts of the world. Careful conservation of humidity allows dryland farmers to obtain yields of about 4,000 kilograms per hectare and in unusual cases up to 8,000 kilograms per hectare.

the corn producers surveyed by Puebla Project personnel reached a maximum figure of 27,811 pesos, 234 percent higher than the level registered in 1967 (in constant pesos of the latter year).

The situation changed radically in 1982. Climatic conditions were disastrous, farmers suffered significant net losses, and off-farm activities generated 50 percent of the net family income. Although agriculture recuperated during 1984 and only 38 percent of family income was derived from off-farm activities (average family income was 25,544 pesos, still in pesos of 1967), the low return on investment in recent years has reinforced the tendency to abandon modern technology, revert to subsistence farming and to withdraw from the marketplace. In 1989 the average income of the families surveyed was 5,942,390 pesos (or 10,645 1967 pesos); only 18 percent of this total was derived from agricultural activities.

In order to make ends meet, rural people in the Puebla Valley are counting more and more on the support they can receive from family members working in urban areas. In fact, over the course of the last two decades, the children of many smallholding families have found permanent jobs in the urban labor force. With more years of schooling than the previous generation, some are employed in the factories of the Puebla-San Martin Texmelucan industrial corridor. Others have invested in small businesses in their communities, where they run stores, make bricks or transport urban passengers or agricultural products. Concomitantly, the importance of temporary off-farm employment (particularly as agricultural day laborers) has decreased in relative terms.

In order to satisfy the consumption needs of the extended family, children who work in urban industry or in the service sector often continue to live within rural communities, even after they are married. They contribute cash to the extended family, which in turn provides them with corn and beans. By the latter 1980s, the low return on investment in the corn crop had created a closed supply system which meant that less and less grain was available outside these family networks.

The development of such strategies has begun to modify grain provisioning structures in ways which are particularly harmful for smallholding households without sufficient members to contribute off-farm income, for families who do not produce enough to satisfy their consumption needs and for households which have no access to land.

According to information provided by Conasupo, the Boruconsa grain storehouses located in the Puebla Valley have been almost empty for the last three years, although those same installations held nearly 80,000 tons of corn in 1981-1982 and 40,000 tons in 1985-1986. At the present time, when producers do sell some of their grain, they deal with private merchants who, given the prevailing deficit in the market, pay up to 50 percent above the support price; they do not sell to Conasupo or to neighbors who are looking for grain to buy. In fact, Conasupo's only role in the region since 1986 has been to sell imported corn from the United States to rural landless families or to families whose harvest was insufficient to satisfy their consumption needs. The latter, who previously purchased local corn from neighboring families, are reduced to buying imported yellow corn sold by Conasupo, since the price of the latter is lower than that of the small quantities of local corn presently available in the region.

Table 6 illustrates this trend toward the increasing sale of imported corn in the Puebla Valley in recent years. The potentially dramatic impact of this development on local supply networks, as well as its effect on the living standard of poor families, are best understood by reviewing the evolution of producer and consumer prices in rural markets. Given the scarcity of white corn, the average price paid to producers in the Puebla Valley in November 1989 fluctuated between 550,000 and 600,000 pesos per ton; the reference price fixed by the government on the first of November was 435,000 pesos. Regional dealers from San Martin Texmelucan, who paid the higher producer price, then retailed the corn at 650 to 800 pesos per kilogram. Thus

Table 6

Sales of Corn to Rural Consumers in the Puebla Valley by Various Conasupo (Boruconsa) Rural Storage Centers, 1984 - 1989

(in tons)

Center	1984	1985	1986	1987	1988	1989[a]	Total
La Magdalena Tetela	0	0	0	438	876	337	1,615
San Jerónimo Ocotitlán	46	1	43	370	698	203	1,361
San Agustín Tlaxco	18	0	71	383	695	603	1,770
Santa Ana Coatepec	27	0	0	0	0	0	27
Malacatepec	2	0	0	0	0	0	2
Benito Juárez	0	0	0	0	0	0	0
San Felipe Teotlalzingo	0	0	0	0	0	0	0
San Juan Tlautla	213	0	65	352	640	516	1,786
El Salvador El Verde	104	5	0	0	0	0	109
Santa Ana Acozautla	0	0	0	0	0	0	0
Tepeaca	52	0	171	338	506	604	1,671
San Andrés Cholula	0	0	0	0	0	0	0
Emiliano Zapata	18	14	0	0	0	99	131
Guadalup Zaragoza	108	6	0	0	0	0	114
Santiago Coltzingo	12	10	0	0	0	0	22
Total	600	36	350	1,881	3,415	2,362	8,664

Source: Boruconsa (*Oficina Regional Oriente*)

[a] Data for 1989 is from January to November (inclusive).

rural consumers who were not able to buy from a Conasupo warehouse or rural store were left with no alternative but to pay very high prices to ensure access to the most basic element of their diet.

The problem may well be more serious still. A Conasupo warehouse visited in November 1989 had sold 470 tons of corn at the official price to families in the region between May and September (of the 470 tons, 110 were from the region and the remaining 360 were imported); at that time the warehouse was open to the public two days a week. As of September, in spite of continuing demand for grain, none was reported to have been sold, since the warehouses were empty. Peasants in neighbouring communities who had corn to sell approached Conasupo to ascertain the new support price. However, when they were informed that it remained unchanged, they opted to sell their surplus to private dealers.

If policies which decrease corn production (including the setting of extremely low support prices and gradual disintegration of official programs supporting the rural population) are sustained, the present scarcity of basic grains on the regional market will be exacerbated. The majority of the peasant families in the valley will respond to the crisis by intensifying their strategies to diversify off-farm income. More and more family members will join the urban labor force, leaving the farm with fewer qualified laborers and making it impossible for the farm to produce optimally -- and very difficult for it to function at even an acceptable level.

In a 1989 study of five families which still employed traditional methods for conserving the humidity in the soil during the winter months, for example, the average age of the heads of household was more than seventy years. The latter were responsible for supervising work on their ejido land. Carrying out the Puebla Project recommendations, they harvested over three tons per hectare even during average years. In three of the five cases, corn production was destined strictly for the consumption of an extended family containing between 10 and 12 members.

In every case, the heads of household received cash contributions from children working in the cities, money which was in turn paid to laborers working on the family farm. Without these cash contributions, it would have been impossible to keep the farm running, since there were not sufficient family members available for the task. In fact, there is a relative scarcity of labor in the agricultural sector of the Puebla Valley, and this has raised salaries for agricultural workers to a level about 30 percent above that of the prevailing minimum wage.

In the cases studied, it should be noted, an income diversification strategy without declining yields was made possible by the fact that the head of household remained on the farm. At the same time, children engaged in off-farm activities were assured access to the basic foodstuffs produced on the family holding, and this supplemented their often meager earnings and provided a certain security. In other cases, however, the situation is quite different. In families whose circumstances require that the head of household himself leave the community to seek employment, farming must be neglected to a greater or lesser extent and yields can fall as much as 2,000 kilograms per hectare.

It is important to add before closing that although strategies to diversify family income through off-farm activities predominate among small grain producers of the Puebla Valley, these are not the only options available. During recent decades, about 20 percent of all ejido households have adopted the alternative strategy of diversifying on-farm sources of income. This minority has attempted to increase value added to its corn by developing livestock and dairy operations and selling milk, meat, and eggs. In such cases family livelihood becomes dependent upon the market value of these products. Unfortunately, up to 1989, developments in these markets were not favorable.

In summary, the experience of the Puebla Project from 1967 through 1989 proves that the majority of all smallholding families responded positively to production stimuli offering significant profits. They also responded rationally when agricultural activity generated systematic losses. At present, it is the latter situation which predominates in the Puebla Valley; and in consequence, an important agricultural region is producing at deficit levels and the adequate utilization of both traditional and modern technology is being undermined.

Chapter 4

THE NEVER-ENDING BATTLE OVER CORN: FACETS OF LOCAL PROVISIONING IN THREE AREAS OF VERACRUZ

Luisa Paré, coordinator

During the past two decades, the production of corn in the state of Veracruz, on the Gulf coast of Mexico, has fallen considerably. As livestock and citrus production increased, the area dedicated to corn cultivation shrank from 859,000 hectares in 1970 to slightly more than 435,000 in 1987, and that dedicated to beans from 161,000 to just 31,000 during those same years. This process of crop substitution, coupled with the rapid advance of cattle raising, occurred within a context of accelerated development of the petroleum industry, which had important implications for rural livelihood within a number of areas of the state.

Since Veracruz is marked by extraordinary cultural and ecological diversity, it is impossible to generalize about how rural society has been affected by this process or how the place of corn in the survivial strategies of rural families has changed. Not only has the course of modernization varied considerably from one region to another, but significant differences have developed in patterns of social stratification among producers themselves. To talk in general terms about categories like "producers" or "peasants," or even "rural consumers" is therefore not particularly useful.

In the following pages, the complexity of corn provisioning issues will be explored in three areas of Veracruz. Each of the latter forms part of a region where the production of commercial crops and/or livestock competes strongly with the cultivation of basic grains, and in the first two cases, where grass-roots organizations are searching for ways to deal with growing difficulties in ensuring adequate access to corn for local consumption. All may be thought of as recent episodes in what many rural people describe, in almost milennarian terms, as a never-ending battle over corn.

1. The first region, made up of thirty-four municipalities in the southern part of the state, has traditionally been one of the most important corn producing areas in Veracruz. Its strikingly varied landscape stretches from the crests of the Santa Marta mountains (the home of Zoque-Popoluca and Nahua indigenous peoples) to the plains of Acayucan and Jaltipan, where a mestizo population engages in commercial agriculture and livestock production. The regional economy has been strongly affected both by the development of the petroleum industry and by its subsequent stagnation; and as a consequence of a series of events, including the general economic crisis of the past decade, this area has evolved over the 1980s from a corn surplus to a corn deficit status.

2. The second study, carried out in the central zone of Veracruz, also examines a situation of growing regional deficit created in part by the encroachment of commercial agricultural interests on lands formerly planted in corn. This is occuring within a less favorable ecological context than that characteristic of the first case, and in the midst of strong natural and technological restrictions which threaten the self-sufficiency of individual households.

The region in question surrounds a volcano known as the Cofre de Perote and contains two clearly distinguishable ecological settings, descending from the highlands (Perote is located at 2,465 meters above sea level) to the coastal plain, where Tlapacoyan is only 650 meters above sea level. Although this region was historically populated by the Totonaco people, it is today almost entirely mestizo. The case study focuses on efforts made by rural people, organized in cooperatives, to exploit the advantages of ecological complementarity, through engaging in barter, and to pressure the government for reform of its grain provisioning policies.

3. In neither of the preceding two cases do most rural households engage in subsistence agriculture, strictly defined. Although most families produce grain and other goods for their own consumption, they are also partially integrated into the market. Some of them raise cash crops, and most sell a part of their grain at harvest in order to repay production or consumption loans. Many depend upon remittances or other off-farm earnings for an important part of household income. In sum, they might best be characterized as semi-subsistence, or semi-proletarian, farmers.

There are, however, some areas of Veracruz in which rural communities continue to grow maize within the context of an extremely complex and sophisticated subsistence economy. Such a situation is described in part three of this chapter: in a region of northern Veracruz which has been transformed over the past few decades into a sea of pastureland for cattle, one Totonac community, called Plan de Hidalgo, located within the municipality of Papantla, has managed to preserve an island of subsistence agriculture which still provides an adequate livelihood for the entire population. The final study thus demonstrates how the conservation of a strategy of diversified natural resource use can in some cases assure self-sufficiency not only in basic food staples but also in a variety of other consumption goods.

CASE-STUDY A -- Descendents of Homshuk: From Corn Self-Sufficiency to Scarcity in Southern Veracruz

José Luis Blanco and Florentino Cruz

The first Mesoamerican societies to produce a surplus of corn were located in an area, rich in water resources, between the Papaloapan basin and the Tonalá river in Veracruz. This cradle of Olmec civilization, where Homshuk, the god of corn, has been worshiped for many centuries,[1] underwent fundamental transformations during the mid-twentieth century. Commercial cultivation of coffee and development of pastureland for cattle increasingly encroached upon the fields where corn was traditionally produced. Nevertheless, until the beginning of the 1970s, this area continued to be the leading producer of corn in the state.

It was in the latter decade that the most modern petrochemical installations in Latin America were established in southern Veracruz; and in conjunction with the inexorable expansion of cattle ranching over ever larger areas of land, this industrial development soon altered the economic and social life of rural areas. Many communities withdrew before the advancing herds of cattle, and many peasants stopped farming their land in order to earn wages in the expanding construction or oil industries.

Entire villages, which had previously been surrounded by cornfields, were converted into bedroom communities. This was particularly the case for villages like Zaragoza and Oteapan, which were near the burgeoning oil center of Minatitlán. Although others were affected to a lesser extent, it is true that under the impact of agricultural and industrial change, many communities in the southern area of Veracruz stopped producing a suffecent quantity of corn for their daily diet. At the same time, the fact that the population was attracted to off-farm activities created a new and constantly increasing consumer demand for corn. Under these circumstances, and given the relative stagnation of productivity and overall production of corn, the region moved from the early 1980s onward from a surplus to a deficit position. Moreover, with the exception of the brief period from 1981-1982 when the program associated with the Mexican Food System (SAM) was carried out in Veracruz (under the name "Plan Granero"), this deficit continued to increase as the years went by. (For a summary of these tendencies, see Tables A.1 and A.2).

Implicit in this process are a series of fundamental changes in the corn market of the region during the last three or four decades. With many communities moving from self-sufficiency to participation in the consumer market, new actors have appeared in the chain of local and regional provisioning and new social relations have developed. Although many rural households still produce corn for their own use, the number of small retail stores operated by Diconsa/Conasupo has grown, and there are more and more tortillerías where rural people can buy corn already processed into dough (*masa*) or finished tortillas.

In the village of Soteapan, these changes are reflected in the narrative of Doña Estefana Lanche, who inaugurated a new era in the history of corn provisioning in her village around 1970.

Nineteen years ago we set up the first tortillería. In the beginning, it was not very successful. Around 1970, people didn't buy tortillas; everyone had his or her own corn. At that time, two

---

1. Homshuk, sculpture #00322, Museum of Anthropology, Xalapa, Veracruz. Olmec Room II. Made of basalt, this carving of a human face was found on the island of Tenaspi, in Lake Catemaco.

hundred kilos of tortilla dough lasted us about three days. Even so, though, we did make enough to pay for our investment.

About five years ago, we started buying Maseca-brand corn flour because there wasn't enough grain to meet our needs during the entire year. From June to August, when there was a scarcity, we had to use Maseca, even though people don't like tortillas made of corn flour (produced on an industrial scale from imported yellow corn) and would far prefer to buy tortillas made with white corn kernels. Now we have to buy Maseca all year long, even when the local supply of grain is sufficient, because if we stop buying it for a few months, the company won't supply us when we need it.[2]

The level of sales at our tortillería depends on the time of year. After the harvest, from October to February, when there is an abundant supply of corn, sales are low. In March, not everyone plants the second corn crop (knownas"tapachole") and corn begins to be scarce. Then tortilla sales increase. In May, sales continue to rise. The most notable period of scarcity comes between June and August. Then we prepare 25 sacks-worth of tortillas during the week and 40 on Sundays, when people from coffee-growing communities, like San Fernando, come to buy. Sales fall again in September, as corn starts to be harvested. Each year this cycle is repeated. When corn is harvested, tortilla sales are low.

It is important to note that Soteapan is a community which even today produces more corn than it needs to satisfy the basic needs of the local inhabitants. Thus the cycle of deficit and surplus that is characteristic of the corn market in this village is related less to the drop in production, although that has been considerable, than to the creation of a regional and national market which channels corn out of the area after the harvest, only to return it later at a higher price.

In an earlier period, the corn market in the village operated through traditional, personalized networks controlled by local or regional political bosses and grain merchants. The village drygoods store, wheresmall farmers could sell small quantities of their grain and buy a few indispensible manufactured products, and where credit was available, generally stood at the center of these networks. As time passed, however, both the balance of power between the local shopkeeper and his clients and the manner in which middlemen operate at higher levels of the marketing chain have undergone some modification. At present, the influence of those who purchase corn in southern Veracruz is usually not limited to one village or to a credit relationship. Grain traders operate over large areas which extend beyond the region and even the state. The clients to whom they sell corn, who are generally shopkeepers, may also have operations in different villages and cities. These shopkeepers, if they need to, can resort to buying grain at Conasupo warehouses.[3]

There are also a number of reasons why rural households are now less dependent on relationships with shopkeepers in their communities, or with one particular shopkeeper, than they were in the past. In the first place, because growing corn is an increasingly unprofitable business, many people are producing less for the market and prefer to keep what they produce for family consumption. Second, many families receive incomefrom other agricultural or non-agricultural activities, and this reduces their dependence on local traders for credit. Finally, the influence of private storekeepers has diminished in the region owing to competition

---

2. At the beginning of the 1970s when the region was the largest corn producer in the state, two large processors of corn flour, Maseca and MINSA, set up plants in Jaltipan and Chinameca. Now Maseca processes imported corn (100,000 tons per year) and the 3,000 tons which supply MINSA come from Soteapan, Acayucan, and Minatitlán, Veracruz.

3. At the end of the 1980s, 40 percent of the total volume of corn production in the southern part of Veracruz was marketed. Of that 40 percent, 10 percent was handled by Conasupo.

Table A.1
Corn Production and Consumption in Southern Veracruz[a]
1970-1990 (in tons)

Year	Minimum Regional Corn Requirement	Regional Production	Deficit or Surplus
1970	149,771	476,097	326,326
1971	155,392	n.d.	n.d.
1972	161,221	480,040	318,819
1973	167,269	449,968	282,699
1974	173,539	200,725	27,186
1975	180,042	355,900	175,858
1976	188,081	378,680	190,599
1977	194,501	292,076	97,575
1978	202,541	n.d.	
1979	210,899	n.d.	
1980	218,745	216,308	-2,347
1981	227,750	256,110	28,360
1982	237,156	295,557	58,401
1983	246,958	227,698	-19,260
1984	257,149	214,493	-42,656
1985	267,770	241,741	-25,989
1986	278,829	217,664	-61,165
1987	290,281	230,386	-59,895
1988	302,335	261,573	-40,762
1989	313,595	238,050	- 75,545
1990	327,681	n.d.	

[a] The region is comprised of the 34 municipalities that make up the SARH Rural Development Districts of Las Choapas, Jaltipan, and Los Tuxtlas.

from Conasupo and to the increase in the number of small village stores brought about as families turn to commerce as one way to make ends meet during a time of economic crisis. Under such circumstances, the capacity to manipulate purchase and sale margins on the local market is somewhat reduced.

With ever greater frequency, corn which is sold in the regional grain market does not come from small farmers, who are producing for their own domestic needs, but rather from medium- scale producers who can absorb the high production costs and low sale price of the grain. During the 1970s, and especially during the last years of the Echeverria administration (1970-1976), a series of programs were implemented, including the opening of a road to the mountains, which facilitated the participation of small-scale producers in regional markets. But soil depletion, increases in fertilizer prices, and the damage caused by pests ultimately undermined the ability of small farmers to compete with producers from the more technified and easily

Table A.2

Corn in Southern Veracruz,[a] 1970-1988

	Area (hectares)			Production	Yield
Year	Planted	Damaged	Harvested	(tons)	(tons/ha)
1970	287,320	***	287,320	476,097	1.66
1971	n.d.	n.d.	n.d.	n.d.	n.d.
1972	261,360	***	261,320	480,040	1.84
1973	242,785	***	242,785	449,968	1.85
1974	267,965	160,779	107,185	200,725	1.87
1975	284,904	14,245	270,659	355,900	1.31
1976	238,904	***	238,908	374,680	1.57
1977	215,246	***	215,649	292,076	1.35
1978	n.d.	n.d.	n.d.	n.d.	n.d.
1979	n.d.	n.d.	n.d.	n.d.	n.d.
1980	208,601	30,157	178,444	216,308	1.21
1981	185,245	18,744	166,501	256,110	1.53
1982	209,464	26,206	183,258	295,557	1.61
1983	176,908	21,059	155,849	227,698	1.46
1984	205,171	53,198	151,973	214,493	1.41
1985	171,814	15,889	155,925	241,781	1.55
1986	156,027	12,997	143,030	217,664	1.52
1987	165,011	7,627	157,384	230,386	1.46
1988	209,228	17,341	191,887	261,573	1.36

[a] The data correspond to the same municipalities indicated in Table A.1
***The data for these years do not record damage, although it may have occurred.
n.d. - No data is available.

Source: SARH, Delegation for State of Veracruz, from district-level documents.

accessible plains area. Nicéforo Pachejo Santiago, a grain trader in Oteapan, explains how surplus producers in the Nahua-Popoluca region have been redefined:

> In 1983, production in the more mountainous areas began to decrease. From that time onward, grain supplies flowed more readily from Acayucan and Los Tuxtlas, Juan Rodríguez Clara and San Juan Evangelista. There, producers farm ten or more hectares, receive credit from Banrural, utilize tractors, and have higher yields. Now no one purchases from the older sources of supply, where those with land produce only for family consumption. It isn't profitable for small farmers to plant corn anymore, because the price is just too low for them.

In addition, production costs are high, and especially the cost of money:

> The bank has lent us 260,000 pesos, but we don't want to take any more because the interest rate is somewhere around 46 per cent. It's just too much for us. They could give us

up to 500,000 pesos, but then we would be up to our necks in debt. So we don't ask for all the credit they would give us, just the bare minimum. . . (Modesto Arizmendi Cruz, Morelos, Soteapan, September 25, 1989).

Given such circumstances, there are many deficit producers in the region and there are even more consumers who cannot produce corn. As the reader will recall, according to Table A.1 the corn deficit in the state grew from 40,000 to 60,000 tons between 1986 and 1988. With the rise in unemployment in oil producing areas, associated with economic recession, and the relentless increase in the cost of living, there are indications that many rural families have attempted to return to corn cultivation. This tendency has been reinforced by a deep economic crisis in coffee growing regions during recent years.

As they attempt to return to subsistence production, however, small cultivators in many areas of Veracruz are faced with the tight limits on available land imposed by the progressive expansion of cattle ranches. In the 1940s, cattle operations occupied only 8 percent of the southern area of Veracruz (Los Tuxtlas, Jaltipan, and Las Choapas Rural Development Districts) (De la Peña 1946). By 1986, they had spread over 50 percent of the area. With the aid of credits from the World Bank and the Interamerican Development Bank, managed by the Mexican government agencies FIRA and Banrural, cattle ranchers had far better opportunities to progress than grain producers. Even in ejidos with common lands, small groups of peasants responded to these incentives by converting their farms and those of their friends into pasture land.

Recently, thanks to exceptionally low-cost loans granted for cattle production, that activity has expanded still further into the mountainous regions inhabited by the Popoluca people, the land of Homshuk. Thus while there were some 3,721 head of cattle in Soteapan in 1970, there were 18,880 in 1988. This growth is greater than that of the population, with the result that now there are more cattle than people, and this blocks any attempt to increase the number of hectares planted in corn.

We are surrounded by pastures, and my family (which has 20 members) can use only three hectares to plant corn and about a half hectare for beans.Although we would like to plant more corn and beans, we don't have any more land now that the cattle anchers have their pastures (Domitilio Santiago,Soteapan, Veracruz).

While it takes more than a hectare to maintain a cow, within the system of extensive grazing which prevails in the region, the area available for corn cultivation is now much less than one hectare per person. In Soteapan, the ratio was 0.30 hectares per person in 1980. There was still sufficient grain in the local market when this study was carried out, but the progressive approximation of production to local consumption forewarns of a deficit. It should also be noted that the advance of cattle ranching has reduced areas available for hunting, and thus affects a significant source of food for many rural people. The only options left are to raise chickens and turkeys using corn as feed.

Given the vulnerability of the peasant economy, agricultural authorities have promoted the production of corn on ranches with better quality land and the capacity to engage in mechanized agriculture. Cattlemen were asked to dedicate 10 percent of their land to producing basic crops; but they have responded without enthusiasm and placed conditions upon their compliance. In particular, they demand guarantees that their holdings will not be subject to expropriation for exceeding the limits set by agrarian legislation on the size of private farms.

Meanwhile, in many of the communities in the southern area of Veracruz, such as Zaragoza, where the peasants have become laborers or urban workers and corn production is no longer possible for the majority of the population, there is a growing supply problem. This is the central issue of the following study.

CASE-STUDY B -- *The Stepchildren of Conasupo: An Independent Regional Marketing System in Central Veracruz*

María Eugenia Munguía

Since the end of the 1980s, a cooperative operating in the central part of Veracruz has attempted to develop an alternative regional marketing system, administered by representatives of the rural communities. One of the purposes of the program is to take advantage of the complementarity of different agroecological zones within the region, facilitating trade between subtropical and highland areas. Another is to influence official policies related to the purchase and distribution of basic grains in central Veracruz, pressuring Conasupo to develop a provisioning system which will give priority to satisfying the basic needs of the local population.

In order to understand the work of the cooperative, it is first necessary to look briefly at the context of rural livelihood in the two distinct ecological areas where the members of the organization live: the subhumid tropics of Tlapacoyan and Atzalan, with an average temperature of 22.8 degrees centigrade, and the cold highland zone including Perote, Villa Aldama, Acajete, and the higher areas of Ixhuacán de los Reyes, where the average temperature is 15 degrees centigrade and frosts are a constant threat.

THE HUMID SUBTROPICS: COFFEE, CITRUS, AND CORN

In Tlapacoyan and Atzalan, which are located within the Rural Development District with headquarters in Martínez de la Torre, Veracruz, the cultivation of corn has slowly given way over the last thirty years to coffee and citrus crops, as the latter have been promoted by various official programs and corn has not. By 1989, although corn was planted on 20,406 hectares, this amounted to only 6 percent of all the agricultural land in the district. Table B.1, which presents data for Tlapacoyan and Martínez de la Torre, where corn is now hardly produced at all, will illustrate how this process of substitution advanced between 1980 and 1989.

The proximity of urban areas is another factor which has contributed to the displacement or cessation of corn farming. Even so, a great many families continue to produce corn on a small scale, especially in the most remote communities. The majority of the smallholders participating in the cooperative work an average of 2.5 hectares, of which one-half to one hectare is dedicated to corn. The rest is planted with coffee or citrus trees, used as pasture or given out to be sharecropped by landless families.

In fact, there is strong pressure on the land in this region: a great many landless families who eek out a wretched existence picking coffee, oranges or pepper are anxious to supplement their income by sharecropping corn on uncultivated ejido plots. For members of the ejido who hold land but lack the resources to work a part of it, sharecropping is a useful arrangement, since if they were to leave the land untilled it could be reapportioned by ejido authorities. Half the harvest is delivered to them by sharecroppers, who thus invest a disproportionate amount of labor for the benefit obtained. Nevertheless sharecroppers assure corn for family subsistence and supplement the meager salaries earned while working as agricultural day laborers on large commercial farms or for other smallholders.

Table B.1
Land in Production, Tlapacoyan and Martínez de la Torre

		Area (in hectares)		
Municipality	Year	Orange	Coffee	Corn
Tlapacoyan	1980	886	1,264	596
	1987-88	1,504	2,834	110
	1989			14
Martínez de la Torre	1980	9,470		1,093
	1987-88	13,645		486
	1989			643

The cultivation of corn is difficult for a number of reasons. The technology employed depends on utilization of the digging stick, machete, and hoe. Moreover, the scarcity of available land makes it impossible for land to lie fallow; most land is in fact planted twice a year. Erosion is exacerbated by the unevenness of most corn fields and by the effect of subtropical rain. Finally, there is the risk of occasional droughts and strong winds which damage the crop.

In part, the fact that ejido members themselves do not cultivate more corn on their own parcels can be explained as a response to relative prices: for many years other crops, such as coffee and citrus, have been more profitable than corn. Their farming decisions are also affected by the degree of compatability between activities related to corn cultivation and those related to alternative crops. And finally, storage problems are an important consideration.

Looking at the first factor, we see that even when price fluctuations in the coffee and citrus markets are taken into account, these products are more profitable than corn, and that corn cultivation may in fact result in losses. At the beginning of 1989, when the official price of corn was 370 pesos per kilogram and the real price on the local market was as high as 450 pesos per kilo, the production cost for a farmer harvesting an average of 1.5 tons per hectare was 513 pesos per kilo.

This situation is closely related to a second factor, the way labor requirements for alternative crops condition the effort which can be dedicated to corn. Work in the cornfields of the region is almost always carried out by unremunerated family members. The Totonac tradition of exchanging labor without charge (the *mano vuelta*) has been lost in this region, along with most other characteristics of the indigenous culture. Under these conditions, farmers can only cultivate corn when they are assured of other simultaneous options for remunerated agricultural work in the community. In other words, they cannot work full-time in an activity that offers almost no hope of profit or income, but they can manage to do so on a part-time basis.

This means that there is a limited amount of labor available for corn cultivation, just as there is a scarcity of all other productive resources. Without access to technical assistance, credit and other inputs for corn production, the majority of all corn farmers (who also produce coffee) find ways to divert resources from other crop programs to corn production.

In a certain sense, coffee has been subsidizing corn for a long time in this region, since fertilizers alloted for coffee production tend to be apportioned between coffee and corn. Such a strategy has permitted local people to maintain an average yield of 1.5 tons of corn per hectare, even though soils are eroded. Coffee production, of course, has been hurt by this procedure: transferrence of fertilizers creates large differentials in productivity between small-scale coffee producers (usually harvesting less than three hectares), who have average yields of 3 tons per hectare, and larger producers who harvest an average of 10 tons of coffee per hectare, and sometimes as much as 20 tons.

A glance at Table B.2 will highlight certain aspects of the symbiosis of coffee and corn in the region. The fact that planting corn can be combined with work in the coffee groves, and that it also overlaps with the citrus harvest, permits families to redirect part of the money they receive for the latter to corn production. Financing from the Mexican Coffee Institute (Inmecafé, now liquidated) could be utilized to hire workers to cultivate corn and/or to subsidize family consumption during the planting stage. In like manner, income from the sale of citrus fruit is what sustains producers during the corn harvest.

Despite such strategies, many heads of families who have very small parcels of land, or who do not have the income sources described above, must leave their communities in search of work during the months of March, April and May, when there is little to do in agriculture.

A third factor which limits the amount of land planted in corn is the climate, which makes it difficult for stored grain to remain in good condition between harvests. Although local people practice some forms of conservation, such as drying the corn before storage or leaving the husks on the cob, or even applying lime or insecticide, they are unaware of other methods which could extend the period of storage. Thus three or four months after each harvest, producers must sell their grain before it rots, even though they know they will have to buy corn shortly thereafter at a higher price.

It is evident, then, that the corn which is marketed in this region does not represent what producers would consider to be surplus production: the local harvest does not even cover family consumption needs, and yet it is precisely the corn needed for family consumption which is sold. What remains of the June-July harvest has to be marketed in September or October, and the November-December harvest must be marketed between March and May. The situation is exacerbated during the latter period by the lack of employment in the region at that time of year, which forces families to sell grain at village stores in order to buy staples such as beans, cooking oil and rice. Later the storekeepers will resell the grain to those from whom it was purchased, but at a higher price.

HIGHLAND AREA

While problems of local corn supply and distribution in the lowland region are aggravated by an inability to store grain over a sufficient period of time in a tropical climate, the factor which works against self-sufficiency in the colder region is the high probability of weather-related damage to the crop. In the foothills of the volcano known as Cofre de Perote, and the surrounding highlands, corn can be stored in good condition for more than a year; but frosts destroy two out of every three corn crops. For example, of the 47,635 hectares planted with corn in the spring-summer season of 1989, 23,358 were destroyed by frosts. For this same reason, very few producers receive credit for corn, which can be planted only once a year.

As in other places, the area planted with corn has decreased over time and most of the arable land is utilized for more profitable crops or for those which are more resistant to cold, such as broad beans, potatoes and dried peas. Peasant families also plant plum, apple and avocado trees and utilize part of their land for pasture. In 1989, they were able to make profits of about 900,000 pesos for each hectare of potatoes harvested,

Table B.2

Calendar of Productive Activities for the Communities in the Region

Activity	Jan	Feb	Mar	Apr	May	Jun	Jul	Aug	Sep	Oct	Nov	Dec
Corn planting (tonalmil)	X	X										
Cultivating tasks		X	X	X	X							
Tonalmil corn harvest							X	X				
Maize planting (rainfed)							X	X				
Cultivating tasks						X	X	X	X			
Rainfed corn harvest											X	X
Cultivation of coffee		X				X	X	X	X	X		
Cultivation of citrus	X	X				X	X	X				
Citrus harvest	X	X								X	X	X
Pepper harvest								X	X	X		
Coffee harvest	X	X	X								X	X
General day-labor			X	X	X	X						

and showed a deficit of 32,000 pesos for each hectare of corn (if the cost of family labor is taken into account). Nevertheless, those interviewed in 1989 indicated that approximately one-third of the family holding had been planted with corn.

When the crop is not destroyed, average yields of corn are about 1.4 tons per hectare. Animal traction or tractors are utilized on level ground and the digging stick, machete, or hoe on hillsides. Since the land is never left fallow, chemical fertilizers are a necessity. There are, however, no improved seeds for these climatic conditions; local seed varieties produce better results.

Even though many official programs have been implemented to respond to the marginality and poverty of the local people, which is especially critical in Villa Aldama and Acajete and serious in Altolonga, Ixhuacán, and Perote, these efforts have not proved very effective. Many rural families are landless and have little possibility of acquiring land; and for the majority, who do have land, the average size of holding is only six hectares, according to our study. Thus, within a situation characterized by poor climatic conditions and low yields, in addition to low sale prices of the harvest, many smallholders in the Perote region have to supplement their income with employment outside their communities.

Some people seek employment in Puebla and Mexico City, three to four hours by bus from their homes. In these cases, they rent their land to members of the community with sufficient resources to work it. Other members of local families engage in shorter-term migration, picking coffee in the Cosautlán and Teocelo areas; and those from San Miguel Tlalpoala go down to the area around Martínez de la Torre between August and April to harvest the citrus crop. In the highlands (Los Molinos), the ANDSA grain warehouses of El Rubín and Totalco offer jobs as carriers and handlers. In many cases, if it were not for remittances from migrants, it would be impossible for peasant families to continue cultivating their land.

Clandestine woodcutting in the sparse forest areas around the Cofre volcano provides another source of income, especially at times when wages paid for harvesting coffee and citrus are insufficient. At present, extremely low prices for coffee have created a situation in which laborers are unwilling to harvest the crop. Thus, if income-generating projects are not implemented or employment opportunities increased in the area, the forest will be overexploited. In response to this problem, some have suggested the possibility of transforming the Naolinco-Xalapa-Coatepec region into a center for assembly plants (*maquiladoras*), which could utilize the labor of the unemployed in the region. It might be argued, however, that equal attention should be given to promoting self-management options in these regions in order to take advantage of available resources.

PROBLEMS OF PROVISIONING AND CONSUMPTION IN BOTH REGIONS

The Quicempaccayotl Cooperative has launched a program of the latter type, in an attempt to protect the income of its members through a series of interventions in the market for agricultural products and staple consumers goods. The cooperative was officially formed on April 25, 1989, by some 400 people, the majority of whom were smallholders, although a few landless workers also joined the organization in hopes of obtaining additional income. The roots of the effort go back to 1985, when the majority of the communities now active in the cooperative participated in the rural distribution system promoted by Diconsa. The center of this regional supply system was the Conasupo warehouse located in González Ortega, Puebla, and the mechanism which linked Diconsa with the rural population was the Community Provisioning Council, made up of a delegate from each participating community.[4]

The Council took advantage of the Diconsa marketing program to launch its own initiative, managed outside the official system. Broad beans, potatoes and dried peas from the highlands were bartered for coffee, citrus products and corn from the subtropics, utilizing the warehouses and vehicles of Diconsa, as well as some start-up capital provided by the agency. Producer prices were fixed above private market levels and consumer prices were set below those prevailing in the market. After repaying the loan from Diconsa, there was money left over, which was managed by the Community Provisioning Council of the González Ortega warehouse.

Attempts were also made to deal with problems of corn distribution in the region. As previously noted, there was considerable dissatisfaction with the way the local grain market functioned. The margin between producer and consumer prices was high in the subtropical area;[5] and the quality of grain sold to rural families by private merchants or Conasupo was, and still is, of worse quality than that delivered by the small farmers at harvest time. Members of the Council wanted to establish mechanisms which would allow them to influence the provisioning policies of Conasupo and to facilitate the exchange of corn among members of the organization.

In the area where the Council was founded, a network of small grain reception centers already existed. Operated by Boruconsa, they purchased and stored local corn. The effectiveness of this system was, however,

4. Each community has a store affiliated with the Diconsa program of rural provisioning. The highest authority in the community, its general assembly, designates a rural supply committee to oversee the operations of the local store, as well as a person who will represent the community within the regional Community Provisioning Council.

5. In the highland region, both the nearness of major highways and the presence of the large ANDSA warehouse complex create a relatively competitive market in which large numbers of traders sell corn at prices which can be below those of Conasupo. In contrast, the grain market in the subtropical zone is characterized by very large margins between producer and consumer prices. Thus in 1989 private merchants bought corn from producers for 400 pesos per kilo and resold it to community stores at 600 pesos. The latter then offered corn to the public at 800 pesos per kilo.

seriously limited by a series of operational problems. Producers delivering their grain to the rural storehouses complained that payments were slow and furthermore were not in cash, and that many discounts were applied. Moreover, the corn purchased by Boruconsa was shipped out to ANDSA warehouses; and from there it was later distributed by Conasupo to millers, to Diconsa, or to private local dealers or traders from outside the region. The operational regulations of Conasupo prohibitted the sale of corn stored in its small rural storehouses to local consumers.

For a time, the Council was successful in changing this policy. Corn deposited in the local grain reception centers of Boruconsa would no longer be sent to other parts of Mexico; it was to be delivered to the regional warehouse serving the Diconsa rural stores, where it could be sold to those living in the participating communities. In addition, producers could take their grain directly to the Diconsa warehouse, where they could sell it at the support price; and this local grain could then be channelled immediately to rural consumers at the official price. Thus the Council began to demonstrate its ability to supplant Diconsa as manager of the regional corn supply.

Within this context, the Quicempaccayotl Cooperative was founded in 1989, when some of the members of the Community Provisioning Council operating in the highlands merged with a part of the Association of Pepper, Banana, Citrus and Coffee Producers from the subtropical area. The latter organization had also been formed in 1989 to facilitate marketing of its products at both national and international levels; and since it was a legally constituted entity, the Association could negotiate credit. By forming the Cooperative, its members hoped to reinforce their institutional capacity to promote the exchange of products between complementary agricultural regions.

The Cooperative also tried to insist upon the rights of the rural population to be informed about operations within regional grain markets and to have a say in the formulation of policy. In the final analysis, however, the brief experiment with local control over the provisioning system could not be sustained. Diconsa rejected the participation of the Cooperative in the purchase and storage process and opted to continue channeling white corn out to other buyers and selling yellow corn through rural stores in peasant areas. This was not only advantageous for Conasupo but, in a certain sense, also for peasant consumers, since the price of imported yellow corn was cheaper than regional prices for locally produced white corn.

The Cooperative nevertheless continues to defend the interests of rural consumers, building upon the previous experience of the Community Provisioning Council. After continuous mobilizations and protests during 1987, the latter organization had won the right to have access to the national grain storehouses of ANDSA in El Rubín and Totalco, in order to verify inventories and check on the quality of corn that would subsequently be sent to the Diconsa warehouse at Villa Aldama, and from there would be supplied to rural retail stores. Since many of these stores were later associated with the Cooperative, this program of inspection has continued to be carried out through coordination with the Community Provisioning Council.

Even though the large ANDSA warehouses are generally well-stocked, the Council hears constant complaints from its local rural stores, related not only to shortages but also to the low quality of the corn and beans which they receive -- in such bad condition, one often hears, that "even the animals don't want to eat it". People are unhappy that good corn is channeled preferentially to private dealers, or to provisioning programs in cities where elections are about to be held, while rural stores receive imported corn of the worst quality. Delays in supplying grain to local stores have also been traced on occasion to disruption of services at the large ANDSA warehouses, when workers affiliated with the official National Workers Confederation (CTM) are being transported to increase the size of the crowd at election rallies.

The present crisis in the coffee market, as well as the recent demise of Inmecafé, create new challenges for the Cooperative. Both developments imply a marked reduction in the income of rural people, whether coffee producers or wage laborers. Many will try to return to subsistence corn production, or increase current output, in order to make up for the decline in coffee prices and to find a reliable solution to basic provisioning problems.

The Quicempaccayotl Cooperative is therefore complementing its efforts to improve the grain distribution system with a new program of support for corn production. It is necessary to search for new ways to prolong storage of corn in tropical areas, as well as to negotiate credits and obtain technical assistance which can promote an increase in yields. Nevertheless, given the prevailing level of producer prices for corn and the relatively low productivity on most holdings in the region, corn cultivation does not generate sufficient income to offset the sharp fall in levels of living experienced by coffee producers. It would thus seem more important than ever before to strengthen the system of exchange among rural producers and consumers, and among rural regions, so that provisioning options are not totally dependent on often unfavorable trends within the national market.

CASE-STUDY C -- Exceptional Abundance: Traditional Resource Management in the Totonac Community of Plan De Hidalgo, Veracruz

Narciso Barrera Bassols, Sergio Medellín and Benjamín Ortiz Espejel

In the forty-one municipalities of northern Veracruz inhabited by the Totonac people (and known as the Totonacapan), the destruction of cornfields and forests to make way for pasture land and new commercial crops is far advanced. Trees now cover only 9 percent of the area of the region, which once was a zone of dense tropical forest. Figure C.1 illustrates the way corn and bean production began to lose ground about 1970 and how they have continued to decline precipitously during the last two decades. At the same time, pasture land increased from 3 percent of the total area of the region in 1930 to 72 percent in 1980.

The inexorable advance of cattleraising has largely destroyed the ecological setting within which local people previously practiced a highly complex and diversified subsistence agriculture. By the mid-1970s, the region was no longer self-sufficient in basic grains and had become an area of chronic deficits.

Even so, some areas of vegetation which are capable of supporting traditional systems of resource management can still be found within the Totonac region. One of these islands in the sea of pasturelands is a block of land belonging to the ejido of Plan de Hidalgo, in the municipality of Papantla. Just an hour by bus from the county seat (the city of Papantla), some 165 families work 1,591 hectares of ejidal land, drawing upon a fund of sophisiticated traditional knowledge of the environment which permits them to hunt, gather and cultivate a great variety of products, to assure ample satisfaction of their own subsistence requirements and to produce some additional income as well.

A special factor explains in part the resistence of this community to outside pressure for change. In spite of the fact that the territory won after a hard-fought agrarian struggle in 1933 was designated as ejido land, the older indigenous form of communal control over the entire area was preserved; and furthermore, local people took up and defended Article 164, sections I and II of the Agrarian Reform Law, which sets forth the obligation of ejidos to preserve, restore and conserve their forest lands (Medellín 1988, pp. 55-57; and Rodríguez 1987).

In the following pages, the complex susbistence strategies developed by the people of Plan de Hidalgo will be analyzed in detail, as will some of the problems which they confront as they attempt to continue to satisfy their basic needs by traditional methods.

PLAN DE HIDALGO: THE DEFENSE OF DIVERSITY

The land of Plan de Hidalgo is located on the coastal plain of the Gulf of Mexico, within the subhumid tropics and at an altitude that varies from 100 to 250 meters above sea level. There is abundant rainfall in summer and part of the fall, with early morning frosts in winter.

FIGURE C.1
Soil Use in the Totonaca Region, 1950 - 1980

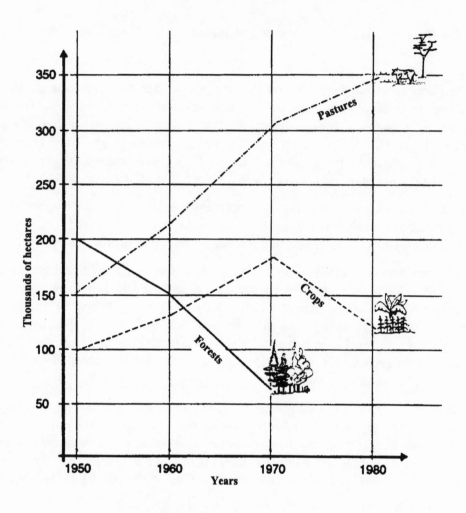

Sources: 1950, 1960, and 1970 Agricultural Censuses. Annual Statistical
Bulletins for the States of Veracruz and Puebla, 1984.

The population is entirely Totonac: 29 percent of the inhabitants of the ejido can speak only Totonac and the remaining 71 percent are bilingual (Totonac/Spanish). In 1989, there were only three monolingual Spanish speakers living in the ejido. The most remarkable characteristic of the structure of economic activity in the community is its homogeneity: 85 percent of all males aged thirteen years or more work in agriculture, another 10 percent in livestock husbandry, and the remaining 3 percent in commercial activities or as artisans.

Subsistence agriculture is the central activity in the life of all local families (Medellín 1988, p. 73). Although there is no precise information on the land area dedicated to various productive pursuits, both a 1989 household survey and aerial photographs of the ejido (Ortiz 1988) suggest that 30 percent of the ejido is utilized for crops and 10 percent for pasture, while 60 percent is in woodlands (see Map C.1). By community agreement, the land has never been divided into parcels held in perpetuity by village households, but rather is periodically redistributed as individual needs dictate.

The pressure of population on natural resources is beginning to be reflected, although in a moderate fashion, through the migration of about 4 percent of the population, principally within the group of 18 to 34 years of age, as well as in a certain incipient social stratification within the community. In addition, a tacit agreement among all ejido members prohibits new settlers from establishing themselves in the ejido.

At the same time, the need to search for new alternatives has recently led to acceptance of new productive options such as the introduction of cattle, the purchase of fertilizers with loans from the National Indigenous Institute (INI) and the use of herbicides. Three cooperatives have been formed, two for livestock and one for citrus. The latter, also financed with INI loans, has planted a ten hectare orange grove on the plot of land set aside for the use of the local school. Finally, the community has agreed to allow two cattle ranchers, with a total of 100 head of cattle, to usufruct twenty hectares of land each on the outskirts of the ejido. This agreement was apparently reached in order to avoid later forceful occupation of the land.

To carry out these productive projects, the ejido utilizes a traditional labor arrangement called _mano vuelta_ or _diamakapuchoko_ ("today you help me, tomorrow I'll help you in return"), which is rapidly disappearing or has already disappeared in most other parts of the Mexican countryside. The importance of this collective use of non-remunerated labor will become obvious in the economic analysis of subsistence agriculture to be presented in the following sections.

PRODUCTION STRATEGIES

Within the ejido it is possible to distinguish 14 different practices through which the community benefits from its natural resources. In the first place, local people gather and extract various kinds of plant and animal products, both from woodlands and from their _milpas_ and the grounds around their houses. These are used as part of the family diet, as medicines, as sources of energy (in the case of firewood), and for construction (in the case of lumber, vines, palm fronds, and reeds).

Second, they plant vegetable gardens in their yards and consume the harvest themselves. They also grow fruit trees, especially citrus trees and banana palms, primarily to ensure family consumption. Any surplus fruit is sold locally or in the region. The flowers which are cultivated in Plan de Hidalgo are utilized in magical-religious ceremonies and, to a lesser extent, are sold within the region.

Corn may be grown either by itself, as a single crop, or as a polyculture, in conjunction with other crops in the milpa. Sugar cane, chiles, sesame, and beans, among others, are produced by many households and the surplus sold within the community or in Papantla. In addition, the inhabitants of Plan de Hidalgo produce edible mushrooms for family consumption and for sale. Cultivation of the vanilla plant has traditionally been an important activity with high market value; now, however, it is of less consequence because of demographic pressure on the land, continual theft of the plants, and a depressed national market for that product.

Two forms of livestock production are practiced: 1) raising small species such as poultry (chickens, turkeys, geese, and ducks), and to a lesser extent pigs, in areas around the house; and 2) producing beef cattle for marketing outside the community. Other complementary activities include hunting birds and small mammals, fishing in local streams for fresh water shrimp, and beekeeping of three local species.

MAP C.1
Photoidentification of Soil Use in Ejido Plan de Hidalgo

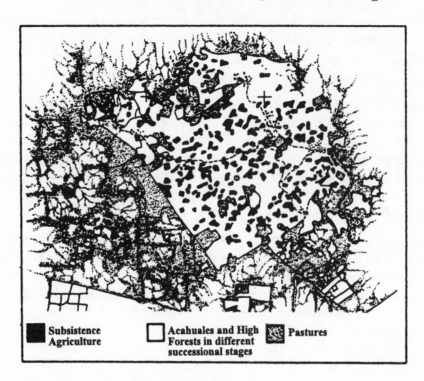

Source: B. Ortiz (1988).

In addition to engaging in such primary activities, some ejido members also dedicate a part of their time to processing (Rodríguez 1987, and Medellín 1988). Families who produce and market chilies, for example, seed and cure their product in order to earn a higher price in the regional market. Grinding sugar cane and making brown sugar and alcoholic drinks is a labor intensive activity which involves entire families and provides some income. Baking bread for family consumption and for sale is another important household task, so important in fact that an oven is to be found in the patio of every home. Carpentry and the repair of wooden utensils are specialized but not well-remunerated activities which are carried out by a few members of the community. A small number of men and women produce arts and crafts, although this is not an important economic activity in Plan de Hidalgo. Finally, pottery is produced for community needs, some people are wood carvers, and others dedicate themselves to making traditional Totonac costumes.

Primary productive activities have transformed the natural environment of the community in a variety of ways. In fact, it is possible to distinguish eight distinct local environments, which have been grouped into three sets, defined through consideration of whether the original ecosystem has been maintained or altered (Toledo and Barrera 1984) as well as through reference to the degree of intentionality with which the environmental units and their resources are managed (see Figure C.2).

The concept of the natural, unmanaged environment (MAN) can be applied to an area in which the logic of reproduction has not been affected by human intervention. Such conditions are found in high tropical forests, which in this region are more than eighty years old and have trees up to sixty meters high. We have designated areas with these characteristics as unmanaged high woodlands.

The concept of managed environments (MAM) applies to ecological areas where there is human intervention. In these environments, there has been a deliberate selection of certain plants and trees, the tolerance of others, and the introduction of new species; and this semi-intensive management allows for natural reproduction of the ecological unit and its principal species. Within this kind of environment in Plan de Hidalgo, three different agroforest areas can be distinguished. (1) The managed high woodlands maintain a structure similar to unmanaged high woodlands; nevertheless, their forests, with 100 year-old trees more than seventy meters high, contain useful species introduced and promoted by the people of the community. (2) The managed *acahual* represents an emergent, successional phase of cut high woodland, in process of regeneration, but within which certain species are deliberately introduced and certain others are tolerated. In areas like these, vanilla might be grown and wood extracted for household use. (3) The unmanaged acahual represents a secondary phase of natural regeneration in tropical forests of medium height,in which, among other things, diverse species are extracted and firewood is collected.

Finally, the transformed environment (MAT) refers to those agroecological areas whose structure and reproduction are dependent on human intervention and which are thus developed as a kind of ecological artifice. Such environments within Plan de Hidalgo include the milpa, the yards surrounding individual houses, and plots of land where crops are cultivated alone or in combination with others. The yards around houses contain small family gardens where local people are continually experimenting with fruit trees, annual crops (including certain varieties of corn), perennial foodcrops, and medicinal and ornamental plants. Here they also tend domestic animals and keep beehives. The other two elements of the transformed environment (the milpa and cropland dedicated to mono- or polycultivation) will be analyzed more fully below.

The fact that this Totonac community makes diversified use of the natural resources at its disposition, exploiting some 345 different biological organisms in a way favoring their long-term availability (Medellín 1988), has permitted its members to maintain an adequate and varied diet, as well as to satisfy other basic requirements for an acceptable livelihood. As in the case of most rural people, the production of corn has constituted a central element in the economy of this community; but corn in Plan de Hidalgo occupies a much less vulnerable place in the overall strategy of subsistence and production than it does in many other parts of rural Mexico. Given their circumstances, the people of Plan de Hidalgo have had less need for money than most of their counterparts in the Mexican countryside, and in consequence they have suffered less from the current economic crisis.

THE CULTIVATION OF CORN IN THE MILPA

Although corn can be cultivated in Plan de Hidalgo in small family gardens, this is of much less economic importance than slash and burn agriculture, or *katukuxtu*, on areas of ejido land dedicated to the milpa. As in other Totonac communities on the coastal plain, the grain is planted twice a year, in a December to June cycle called *tonalmil* and a summer cycle beginning in July and ending in November. The latter is the more productive one.

At an annual meeting attended by the 165 members of the ejido, called by the community council, ejido plots are distributed to producers. The average size of a plot is 8.22 hectares, which may be dedicated to a variety of uses according to the strategy adopted by each household. A survey of 10 percent of the population suggests that each producer utilizes an average of about 2.75 hectares for corn (which works out to 453 hectares of milpa among the 1,519 hectares available in the ejido or 30 percent of the total).

FIGURE C.2

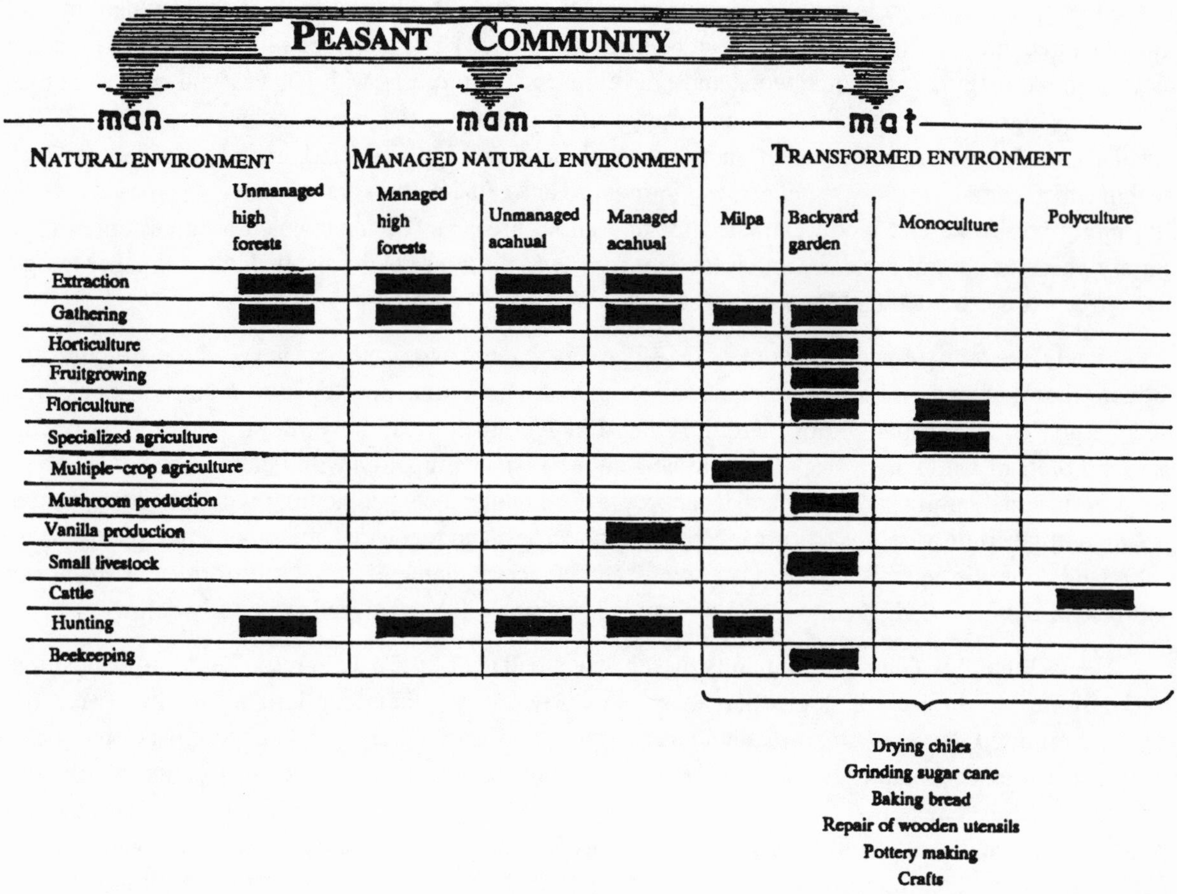

PEASANT COMMUNITY

— man —   — mam —   — mat —

	NATURAL ENVIRONMENT	MANAGED NATURAL ENVIRONMENT			TRANSFORMED ENVIRONMENT			
	Unmanaged high forests	Managed high forests	Unmanaged acahual	Managed acahual	Milpa	Backyard garden	Monoculture	Polyculture
Extraction	■	■	■	■				
Gathering	■	■	■	■	■	■		
Horticulture						■		
Fruitgrowing						■		
Floriculture						■	■	
Specialized agriculture							■	
Multiple–crop agriculture					■			
Mushroom production						■		
Vanilla production				■				
Small livestock						■		
Cattle								■
Hunting	■	■	■	■	■			
Beekeeping						■		

Drying chiles
Grinding sugar cane
Baking bread
Repair of wooden utensils
Pottery making
Crafts

It is important to understand that the milpa is a unit of land in which not only corn, but a wide variety of other species are either cultivated or tolerated. This polyculture, of Mesoamerican origin, involves as many as 31 different species and varieties of plants utilized for food (47 percent) and for medicinal purposes (49 percent), not including plants which are tolerated and also collected as part of the productive process (Medellín 1988, pp. 181-93).

The milpa of Plan de Hidalgo can contain up to five different agroecological micro-areas. Some are oriented toward polyculture, in which corn predominates, and others toward monoculture (principally, sugar cane, blue corn, sesame, and a tuber called taro), toward cultivation of varieties of squash and sweet potatoes, or toward the production of edible mushrooms (Medellín 1988, 149-50; see also Map C.2). There are also areas of boundary growth between plots (the acahual) which act as a reserve of germplasm and protect the milpa from fire at times when underbrush is being burned in nearby fields.

MAP C.2

Spatial Distribution of 31 Useful Species within a Totonac Milpa of Plan de Hidalgo

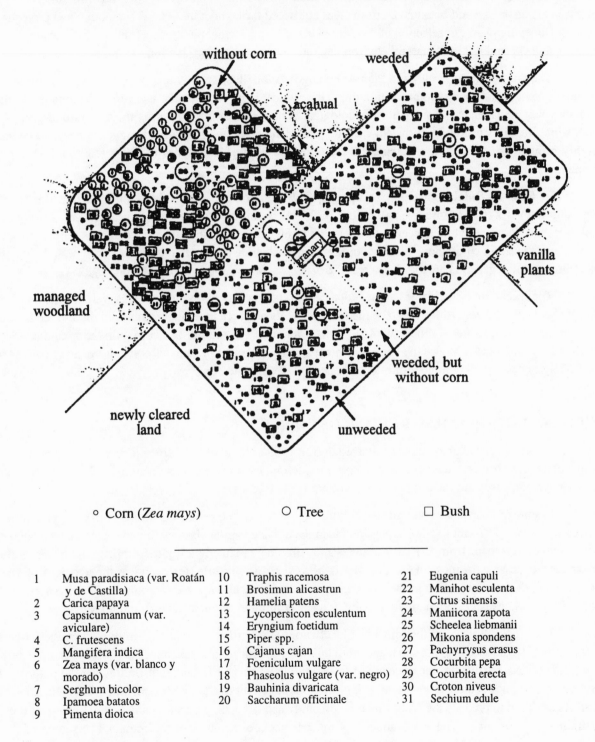

∘ Corn (*Zea mays*)   ○ Tree   □ Bush

1	Musa paradisiaca (var. Roatán y de Castilla)	10	Traphis racemosa	21	Eugenia capuli
2	Carica papaya	11	Brosimun alicastrun	22	Manihot esculenta
3	Capsicumannum (var. aviculare)	12	Hamelia patens	23	Citrus sinensis
4	C. frutescens	13	Lycopersicon esculentum	24	Maniicora zapota
5	Mangifera indica	14	Eryngium foetidum	25	Scheelea liebmanii
6	Zea mays (var. blanco y morado)	15	Piper spp.	26	Mikonia spondens
7	Serghum bicolor	16	Cajanus cajan	27	Pachyrrysus erasus
8	Ipamoea batatos	17	Foeniculum vulgare	28	Cocurbita pepa
9	Pimenta dioica	18	Phaseolus vulgare (var. negro)	29	Cocurbita erecta
		19	Bauhinia divaricata	30	Croton niveus
		20	Saccharum officinale	31	Sechium edule

Source: Medellín (1987).

Within these five micro-areas of the milpa, the most important one is that utilized for polyculture, which requires careful management. Principal practices include a) selective clearing of the land, b) protection of useful species, c) protection against fires, d) selection of tree trunks appropriate for cultivating mushrooms, e) interspersing annual and biannual crops in areas cultivated throughout the year, f) promotion and protection of useful creeping plants, g) selection of the germplasm of some annual plants, especially corn, h) manual pest control, and i) promotion of a natural environment auspicious for the production of vanilla.

The complexity of a milpa in Plan de Hidalgo can be illustrated by mapping the spatial distribution of the different useful species found within one fairly typical unit (see Map C.2). Figure C.3 summarizes the way in which management of such an agroecological system is coordinated during the agricultural year -- a task which requires profound knowledge of the plants and soils involved -- and suggests the intricate and highly refined play of spatial and temporal relationships within which corn is cultivated in this Totonac community.

In Plan de Hidalgo, the part of the milpa utilized for polyculture is planted during four to six agricultural cycles (two to three years), before lying fallow during three to twelve years more. During the fallow period, forest growth reappears, and is cleared through use of slash and burn techniques before the land is once more used for cultivation. Students of Mexican agriculture recognize this kind of agricultural strategy as falling within a general category known as *barbecho medio* (Warman and Montañez 1982).

The recent use of herbicides in the milpa, and of insecticides for storing corn, as well as the imminent use of chemical fertilizers which are to be made available through credit arrangements with the INI, constitute the only technological innovations adopted by the community in the field of corn cultivation and storage. Herbicides could quickly reduce the variety of plant species tolerated in areas of polyculture, and their use is also likely to decrease the number of man-days needed to cultivate corn.

THE PRODUCTION AND MARKETING OF CORN

As already noted, the families surveyed during 1989 cultivated an average parcel of 8.22 hectares of which about 2.75 hectares were devoted to corn production. The maximum area cultivated with corn was 4 hectares (in one case) and the minimum one hectare (in two cases).

In spite of their socioeconomic and cultural homogeniety, the producers utilized different production strategies. In two cases, for example, they continued to cultivate vanilla plants within the acahual, while others who had received loans from INI grew oranges and still others planted part of their milpa with beans, chile, sugar cane, or sesame. Almost all those surveyed, however, owned cattle (ten head was the average), as well as some smaller animals raised in their yards. In addition, they all engaged in poultry raising. There were around 17 chickens per ejido member, as well as a lesser number of ducks, geese, and turkeys.

The corn cultivated in the milpa is a local variety (boletillo, *Zea mays l.*), improved by the farmers themselves. Hybrid seeds are not sown and, until this year, chemical fertilizers have not been applied. Manure is widely utilized. No one has received credit from a public or private financial institution for the purpose of producing corn, nor is there any system of informal private credit available for corn cultivation. No salaried workers are hired to produce the crop, which is still cultivated using digging sticks and hoes. In spite of these restrictions, community yields are about one ton per hectare, better than the municipal average of 800 kilograms per hectare, and in the middle range of yields within the Totonac region.

FIGURE C.3

The Five Agroecological Units of a Totonac Milpa in Plan de Hidalgo

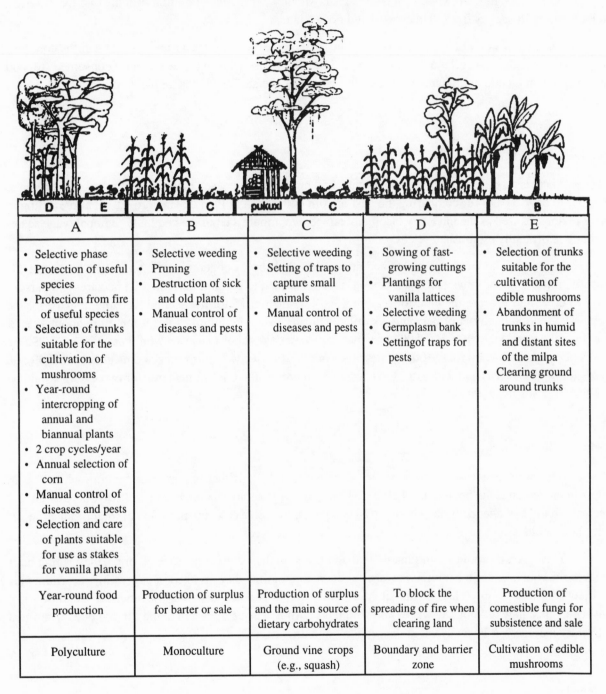

A	B	C	D	E
• Selective phase • Protection of useful species • Protection from fire of useful species • Selection of trunks suitable for the cultivation of mushrooms • Year-round intercropping of annual and biannual plants • 2 crop cycles/year • Annual selection of corn • Manual control of diseases and pests • Selection and care of plants suitable for use as stakes for vanilla plants	• Selective weeding • Pruning • Destruction of sick and old plants • Manual control of diseases and pests	• Selective weeding • Setting of traps to capture small animals • Manual control of diseases and pests	• Sowing of fast-growing cuttings • Plantings for vanilla lattices • Selective weeding • Germplasm bank • Setting of traps for pests	• Selection of trunks suitable for the cultivation of edible mushrooms • Abandonment of trunks in humid and distant sites of the milpa • Clearing ground around trunks
Year-round food production	Production of surplus for barter or sale	Production of surplus and the main source of dietary carbohydrates	To block the spreading of fire when clearing land	Production of comestible fungi for subsistence and sale
Polyculture	Monoculture	Ground vine crops (e.g., squash)	Boundary and barrier zone	Cultivation of edible mushrooms

It is important to note that corn production in the community under study exceeds local requirements by about 60 percent; in other words, production from the two plantings is almost twice the amount consumed. In consequence, a significant volume of corn is sold, whether within the community (in the two local stores), in Papantla or to dealers from Plan del Rio and Poza Rica.

The majority of all families interviewed in 1989 (some 60 percent) consumed about half the corn they produced during the two cycles and sold the rest. The other households in the community consumed from 60 to 75 percent of their total production. These differences can be attributed in large part to the size of the family itself.

Production Costs

There is no wage labor in the community, and producers do not sell at the official price. Nevertheless, in order to have a basis for comparing the cost of corn cultivation in Plan de Hidalgo with that prevailing in other regions, as well as the monetary income obtained, we impute a labor cost equal to regional wage scales and utilize officially established prices.

We begin with information obtained during the 1989 survey concerning the amount of time invested in corn production. Sixty-two and a half person-days are needed to produce corn on 2.75 hectares (30 person-days to clear and prepare the land for planting, 7.5 for sowing, 15 for the second weeding, and 10 for the harvest). The total number of person-days utilized during two agricultural cycles is therefore about 125. If the prevailing regional wage of 7,500 pesos per day were paid, labor expenses would amount to 1,289,062 pesos per year. If we add to this 60,000 pesos for purchasing needed tools (hoes and machetes) and 49,500 pesos for inputs such as herbicides, the total cost of corn production on 2.75 hectares for two cycles would be 1,389,563 pesos in 1989.

Value of the Harvest

Supposing an average yield of one ton per hectare and taking the support price for corn which was in effect in the region at the beginning of 1989 (310,000 pesos per ton), the gross value of two harvests on 2.7 hectares would hypothetically have been 1,674,000 pesos. In such a case, the net value of total production per farm household would have reached some 275,437 pesos per year.

Thus even if producers in Plan de Hidalgo had sold their corn at the official price, they would have received the equivalent of the minimum wage for the period of time they invested in cultivating the grain, plus a small additional sum. Their actual situation, however, was better than the hypothetical condition just outlined, since they did not pay wages and sold their corn at a price higher than the official one. Their real monetary income will be analyzed in the section on marketing.

Storage

Both in the case of corn used for family consumption and in that of corn which is destined for sale, grain is removed from the cob by family labor. Until recently, lime was applied to protect the stored harvest; but now an insecticide called Aldrin or Defasa (banned in many countries because of its high level of toxicity) is applied. This permits grain to be kept for up to six months without spoiling. With two crops, a six month storage period insures there will be no long periods of corn scarcity in the community.

Consumption

Considering that the majority of homes utilize half of the corn they produce, we estimate average family consumption at 2.75 tons per year. If we subtract the 610 kilograms of corn which are consumed by domestic animals, then 2.14 tons per year are left for human consumption. For a family of 8.4 members, this impliies an annual average consumption per individual in Plan de Hidalgo of 254.7 kilograms, or 697 grams of corn per day. We should point out that in 1982 COPLAMAR estimated an adequate minimum level of consumption at 353 grams of corn per individual per day. Thus, according to our estimates, residents of Plan de Hidalgo consume almost double the amount of corn required to sustain adequate nutritional levels. (Medellín 1988, pp. 61-64).

Marketing

Until recently there was a Conasupo store in the community which, in addition to buying local corn, sold basic staples. However, the store was closed because its level of profits were below the minimum required for operation. This lack of economic viability can be related both to the large surplus of corn generated in the community and to the relatively lower prices paid for the grain by Conasupo, when compared with other dealers who paid amounts above the official price.

The majority of all producers in Plan de Hidalgo sell their surplus corn in Papantla to dealers whose storehouses are located near the central market. It is customary for an ejidatario who travels to that city to take with him around three sacks of grain which, in 1989, fetched 600 pesos per kilo -- double the support price at that time. Thus a producer who sold 50 percent of his crop received 1,650,000 pesos per year, if he sold only in Papantla. The single expense involved was the cost of transport from Plan de Hidalgo to Papantla.

The second marketing option available to local producers was sale to middlemen who came to Plan de Hidalgo once a week from Papantla or Boca del Rio, and who offered around 400 pesos per kilogram in 1989. The price fluctuated somewhat according to the time of year, and was highest when grain was scarce during September and October. If a producer selling 50 percent of his crop decided to sell to these middlemen, he received an average of 1.1 million pesos per year.

The third option is to patronize one or more of the three privately-run stores within the community, where producers tend in fact to sell only small quantities of grain. The price they receive fluctuates between 470 and 500 pesos per kilo, and the price paid by consumers is more or less fixed at 470 pesos per kilo. The storekeepers in turn sell grain to dealers from Papantla. The fact that they buy and sell corn at about the same price must be attributed to the abundance of the product. Such a situation clearly sets Plan de Hidalgo apart from the majority of rural communities in the state of Veracruz.

Local producers do not, of course, sell through one single channel. Depending on circumstances and household requirements, they sell at times to buyers in Papantla and at times to intermediaries. When they deal with local storekeepers, the transaction seems to involve an exchange of commodities more often than monetary payment. Thus storekeepers gain access to corn with no cash outlay, and later sell it outside the community.

FINAL REMARKS

Although Plan de Hidalgo is an atypical community, its strategy of diversified resource use, taking advantage of ecological complementarities, is characteristic of the economic and ecological rationality of many indigenous communities in Mexico, most of which are in process of dissolution. Traditional systems of production are based on a profound understanding of nature and a refined handling of ecological microregions, through which indigenous groups seek to assure the economic and sociocultural reproduction of all families within the community.

This form of production is maintained in Plan de Hidalgo as part of a valued cultural heritage and as an element of ethnic resistance to wider changes in the region. Even in the midst of regional and national agricultural crisis, such a strategy has allowed the families of the community to satisfy their basic needs, to maintain self-sufficiency in corn and to enjoy a wide variety of other benefits from fields and forests.

The ejido nevertheless stands on the threshold of change. It confronts population growth within a framework of limited resources and is thus constrained by a type of production which is traditionally oriented less toward increasing agricultural yields than toward conservation of naturally established patterns of output. Increasing emigration and social differentiation are signs of an imminent rupture of the precarious equilibrium which sustains the community.

The passage toward agricultural modernization, recently undertaken in the community through acceptance of credit from INI for the purchase of chemical fertilizers and herbicides and for the initiation of citrus production, is not of a kind well suited to the local natural environment or congruent with the idiosyncracies of the local society. In coming years, this process of modernization may well generate a worrisome degree of ecological and socioeconomic disequilibrium. It is therefore imperative to search for more creative approaches to rural development, in which the community can participate in determining a viable future for itself.

Chapter 5

SEEKING FOOD AND SEEKING MONEY: CHANGING RELATIONS OF PRODUCTION IN ZINACANTÁN, CHIAPAS[1]

George A. Collier

The processes of change which have led first to the reinforcement, and then ultimately to the loss of provisioning capacity on the part of large numbers of people in rural Mexico are well illustrated in the case of Zinacantán, Chiapas. Chiapas is one of the most important corn-producing states in Mexico, and relations between its highland Indian communities and lowland plantation owners and cattlemen are among the most conflictive. Indigenous people, like those in the Tzotzil-speaking district of Zinacantán discussed below, have maintained a separate identity, based not only on language but also on a distinctive social structure in which rank and authority within the community have traditionally depended upon age and careful fulfilment of ceremonial obligations.

Despite this cultural singularity, the agricultural economy of such communities has been increasingly integrated into regional and national markets. In the case of Zinacantán, corn farmers in the highlands have during certain periods migrated to lowland cattle areas, where they have cleared rented fields for corn cultivation, and the Tzotzil have also periodically been absorbed into and expelled from the wage labor force of lowland farms and cities.

During the oil boom of the late 1970s, new opportunities for making money in off-farm occupations wrought fundamental changes in the economy and society of Zinacantán. Many men became construction workers or went into commerce, leaving fewer behind to farm. Corn cultivation was in consequence transformed from a labor-intensive to a relatively capital-intensive venture, increasingly dependent upon purchased fertilizers and herbicides.

When the collapse of the oil boom and the subsequent economic crisis curtailed possibilities to earn a living outside agriculture, and outside Zinacantán, the cultivation of corn gained renewed importance in the livelihood strategies of local people. But within the context of the late 1980s, a growing number of families could no longer afford to farm: to cultivate corn in the mass of contiguous plots already conditioned to the use of herbicides and fertilizer required a monetary investment beyond their means.

A relative abundance of laborers, and a very low level of rural wages, permit those with capital to make a profit from corn farming. Returns to capital have in fact not been low in Zinacantán during the latter 1980s. But returns to labor have been so low that they serve as a profound disincentive to small cultivators who invest their own time in production. For the latter to earn a return on their labor equal to the prevailing minimum wage, corn prices would have to have risen much above their level at the end of the eighties.

---

1. The research upon which this paper is based was supported by the Center for Latin American Studies, Stanford University, and by a research grant from the National Science Foundation, BNS-88-04607. Writing was facilitated by support from the same NSF grant and from the Stanford Humanities Center. I am grateful for comments and advice from Frank Cancian, Jane F. Collier, Akhil Gupta, Cynthia Hewitt de Alcántara, Victor Ortiz, Richard S. Price, Sally Price, Renato Rosaldo, Jan Rus, Orin Starn, Arturo Warman, and others. I am also grateful to Daniel C. Mountjoy for permission to use milpa budget data he collected in Apas during 1988 with support from the Inter-American Foundation and from Stanford's Center for Latin American Studies.

Over the past decades there has thus been a marked polarization of life chances within Zinacanteco society. Not only has population growth created new groups of landless villagers, but socioeconomic and technological change has encouraged formation of a large semi-proletariat composed of people with nominal access to land but insufficient capital to work it. And at the same time, wealth has been increasingly concentrated in the hands of a new class of indigenous merchants, truckers and moneylenders who were able to accumulate capital during the boom years. For reasons to be examined below, the process of change has also favored the young over the old, men over women, and has altered the meaning of working together within extended families.

The structure of social relations within Zinacantán traditionally provided an opportunity for relatively more disadvantaged groups, who could not engage in "seeking money," to "seek food" for their subsistence. But clearly this situation is eroding.Let us look at this process of change in some detail, taking up the analysis at the point, at the end of the Cardenas presidency in 1940, when land reform made it possible for virtually all Zinacanteco families to specialize in the labor-intensive farming of *milpa*.

ZINACANTECOS IN A CHANGING REGIONAL ECONOMY

During the early decades of this century, access to land among the Tzotzil was very unequally distributed. In the hamlet of Apas, for example, only a handful of wealthy families held tracts of communal land before 1940, and other Zinacantecos had to work for them. But in 1940 almost all married men in Apas received ejidal land, substantially ameliorating differences among them based on property (see Figure 1).[2] And for the first time every Apas household farmed milpa, although some poorer men continued to work for others as well.

At the outset Zinacantecos concentrated on farming in the highlands in labor-intensive swidden, or slash-and-burn, cultivation. But the ejido could not sustain intensive cultivation on the part of a growing population, among whom the landless began to grow in numbers. Zinacantecos began to rent marginal farmlands in the Grijalva river valley below them from ranchers who were eager to convert scrub forest to grazing land. As roadways opened up the Grijalva valley during the 1960s, Zinacantecos followed them (see Map 1). They rented little-used marginal ranch land, they reaped the higher yields obtainable from fallow lands, and they moved on. Zinacantecos farmed to the limits of their household labor and beyond, employing workers from neighboring Chamula. They produced for profit as well as subsistence, selling much of their crop directly into the federal corn warehouse system established by ANDSA in the early 1960s. Some began to experiment with hybrid seed and chemical weed sprays.[3]

Not all Zinacantecos benefited equally from the mid-century expansion of corn farming in the lowlands. Labor-intensive milpa production gave greatest advantage to elder Zinacantecos who could combine two strategies for accumulating rights in others' labor. One was to subordinate youth of their own households by indebting them through a marriage system based on bridewealth. During the 1950s and 1960s, Zinacantecos elaborated costly and time consuming courtships that left young couples financially obligated to continue working for their parents rather than independently. The second strategy was not simply to employ

---

2. Land ownership was surveyed in 1967 on the basis of detailed aerial photographs, which were used to reconstruct the history of land ownership and use of all Apas land back to the 1930s (see Collier 1975). The land parcel database was updated in 1989.

3. Cancian's studies (1965, 1972) provide the most complete information on these developments in Zinacanteco milpa farming through the 1960s. My own study of Apas (1975) devotes greater attention to milpa farming in the highlands in relation to lowland rental farming.

FIGURE 1

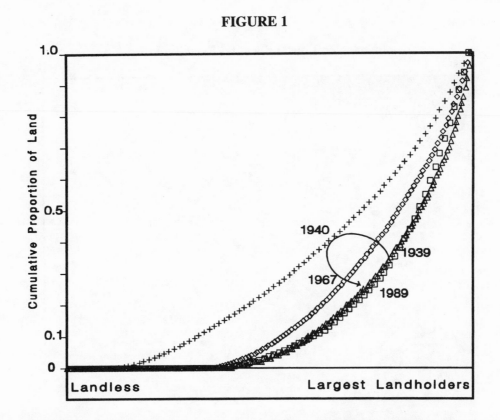

The Changing Distribution of Property in Apas, Zinacantán. The cumulative distributions of land held by married men in Apas are shown for 1939, just before the distribution of land in the ejido; for 1940, just after the distribution; for 1967, at the time Apas farming was first studied by the author; and for 1989. In the graphs, individuals are ranked from left to right in terms of the amount of land they owned, and the curves show the total proportion of all property owned by a given individual and by all those with less land. Equal ownership in a given year would have resulted in a plot along the diagonal of the graph of cumulative distribution for that year. Disparities in property ownership in 1939 were evened out through distribution of ejido land in 1940 to most, but not all, married men. By 1967, many maturing younger men lacked land, and disparities had begun to reappear. In 1989, although minifundia prevail, the disparities are as great as they were in 1939.

poorer Zinacantecos in farming, but to coopt them into political followings elaborated in the system of ritual office-holding or *cargos*. In the heyday of lowland corn farming in the 1960s, Zinacantecos were neither egalitarian, as peasants in a closed-corporate community facing outward into a capitalist agrarian economy are often thought to be, nor differentiated by capitalist class relations. Rather, rank was the dominant idiom for differentiating followers from leaders, juniors from seniors, low status cargo holders from more prestigious ones, and poorer peasant households from those who engaged in successful entrepreneurial farming (see Figure 2).

The 1970s, and in particular the oil-led boom of the Lopez Portillo presidency (1976-82), transformed the economy of the region and Zinacanteco participation in it. In the highlands, demographic growth had almost negated the benefits of land reform, swelling the ranks of landless Zinacantecos (Figure 1). In the lowlands, Zinacanteco and other sharecroppers (*aparceros*) found it difficult to find land to rent as landowners

MAP 1

Zinacanteco Lowland Rental Farming in 1967

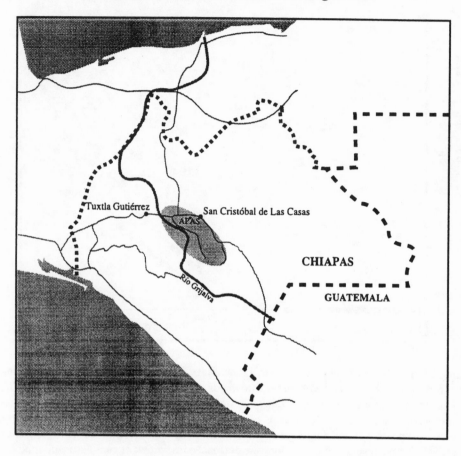

Apas is at the top of an escarpment dropping down to the Río Grijalva. Zinacantecos from Apas and other hamlets primarily farmed parcels rented in the lowland area shaded on the map. (For a detailed analysis of Zinacanteco lowland rental farming in the 1960s, see Cancian 1972.)

turned property over to increasingly profitable cattle raising.[4] At the same time hydroelectric projects at Malpaso, Angostura, and Chicoasen, and the construction of housing spurred by oil development in and around Villahermosa drew all but the most advantaged Zinacantecos into wagework. Relatively wealthier inhabitants of the hamlet of Apas experimented in commerce, buying fruits, flowers and vegetables wholesale to sell retail in urban markets. By 1981, Zinacantecos had virtually abandoned lowland rental agriculture, although better-off, older men still farmed marginally in the highlands to provision their households (Collier 1989). To a substantial degree, Zinacantecos had been drawn into regional relations of class, and the primary differentiation

---

4. Jan Rus (personal communication) argues that shortly after 1977, the guaranteed price of corn (indexed for inflation) fell to its lowest levels over the previous decade in Chiapas, driving both landowners and sharecroppers out of milpa. In the meantime, after 1975, landowners turned over property to cattle ranching, converting Chiapas into the second largest beef producing state in Mexico by 1985. Rus thus emphasizes the factors pushing peasants out of agriculture during this period at the same time that hydroelectric dam and oil-related housing construction began to draw former peasants into construction jobs.

FIGURE 2

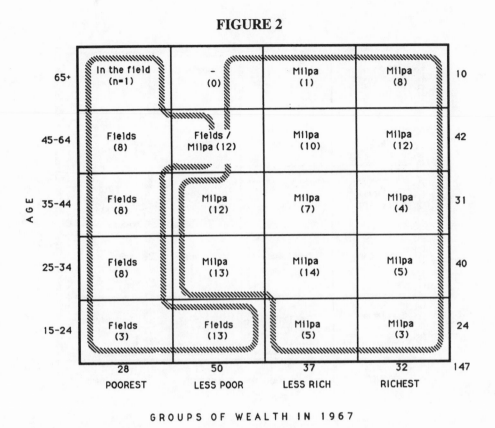

The Productive Activities of Apas Men in 1967. For each group of married men of a given age and wealth, the corresponding cell shows the predominant occupation. Most men farmed milpa, but a small underclass of poor Zinacantecos made their living primarily by working in the fields of other Zinacantecos as fieldhands.

among them had come to be between those who worked for others, and those who undertook commercial ventures for themselves (see Figure 3 and Map 2).

When construction slackened after the 1982 economic crisis, many Zinacantecos returned to corn farming, usually in combination with wagework or commercial enterprise (Collier 1989, Collier and Mountjoy 1988; see Figure 4). But their milpa cultivation differs now from that of the 1950s and 1960s in three interrelated ways: 1) it is technically altered; 2) it requires new and more extensive capital inputs but less labor; and 3) it rests on relations of production in which women's roles are changing and in which newly-rich youth are wresting power from established elders.

TECHNICAL CHANGE IN MILPA AGRICULTURE: A BALANCE SHEET

Bearing in mind that farming milpa is only one of the ways in which the people of Zinacantán make a living, we can learn much about the constraints and opportunities in local agriculture by examining costs and returns to farming in the recent 1987-88 agricultural cycle. Table 1 summarizes data collected by my colleague, Daniel C. Mountjoy, who collected retrospective budgets from 22 Apas farmers, selected as a sample stratified by age and wealth across the categories of Figure 4. These men farmed a total of 57 parcels

FIGURE 3

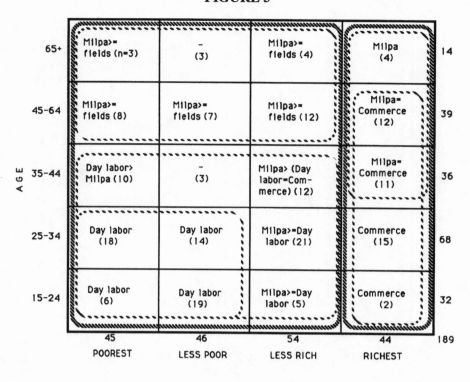

Productive Activities of Apas Men in 1981. The oil-led boom semiproletarianized all but the wealthiest Zinacantecos. Most men in Apas reduced milpa farming to a minimum, shifting into wagework in the regional economy as unskilled construction workers or as field hands for farmers outside their community. A minority of wealthier Zinacantecos went into regional commerce.

in the highlands near Apas and in the Grijalva river valley. One can see from the budget data why Zinacantecos now choose to farm close to home on relatively less productive highland properties rather than in the more distant, albeit more fertile lowlands.

Various technical changes -- all deriving from broader economic transformations -- have made Zinacanteco agriculture more local, more concentrated, and much less labor intensive. Changes in transportation have favored Zinacanteco cultivation in the highlands, for example. Cuts in fuel subsidies after the 1982 economic crisis made long-distance transport much more costly. At the same time, new roadways have made the nearby highland ejidal and communal lands accessible to motor transport. The Apas farmlands are on an escarpment dropping precipitously from 2400 meters in altitude behind Apas to 1600 meters just above the Grijalva valley. The farmlands are relatively unfertile at higher elevations close to Apas but more productive at lower elevations (see Table 1) that used to be accessible only by foot or horse. But Apas' first trucker and leaders of the Zinacantán ejido recently convinced local people to allow loggers -- who are active throughout the state -- to build dry-season roads to pine forests far down the escarpment, in part because these roads facilitated truck transport through farmlands. The change in transport, in costs and access, was one factor bringing Zinacanteco cultivation closer to home when farming revived after 1982.

MAP 2

Zinacanteco Livelihood Strategies in the 1970s and 1980s

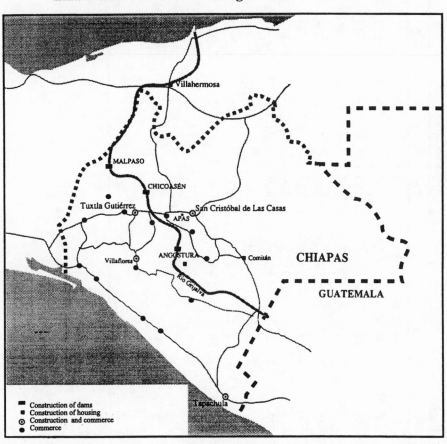

Dam construction drew many Zinacantecos into wagework, as did the oil-led boom in housing, as far from Apas as Villahermosa, Tabasco. Zinacantecos also entered commerce as wholesale-retail fruit, vegetable, and flower vendors throughout western Chiapas. The map shows places where men from Apas have worked and do business.

Chemical inputs[5] -- heavily promoted by agricultural extension agents and manufacturers -- also allowed for concentrating Apas farming closer to home, increasing the acreage that Zinacantecos can keep in cultivation by eliminating the need to fallow milpas to recuperate their fertility. Highland fields were once fallowed for eight to fifteen years after being cultivated for two or three seasons at most. Over time, the required fallowing grew because as Zinacantecos put it, "the land tired," and highland yields -- 44 units of harvest to each unit of seed in 1967 -- began to drop. Farmers in the community had experimented with fertilizer as early as 1967 but came to use it regularly only after subsidized fertilizer became available locally in the early 1980s. They used it first in the lowlands and then in the highlands. Now, they say, highland fieldsmust be fertilized to be worth farming, even though fertilizer subsidies have been cut. With fertilizer, Zinacantecos get yields averaging 53 units of harvest for each unit sown. They farm fields almost continuously

---

5. No attempt is made here to analyse the long-term ecological and health consequences of the use of fertilizers and herbicides, although this deserves serious study. Herbicides pose serious health risks when misapplied; and Zinacantecos routinely apply herbicides in ways that do not even begin to meet the precautions recommended by manufacturers.

Table 1

Milpa Expenditure Budget for the 1987–88 Agricultural Year

| | Highlands, Apas | | | | Lowlands, sharecropping | | | | |
| | Altitude | | | Total / | Almudes sown | | | | Total / |
	2,400m	2,000m	1,600m	Avg.	1 – 1.9	2–2.9	3–3.9	4–5	Avg.
Number of surveys	17	8	15	40	4	3	4	2	17
Proportion of crop	0.22	0.10	0.20	0.52	0.08	0.10	0.18	0.12	0.48
Familiar labor, days	30.2	36.5	33.7	32.8	46.7	50.2	20.1	18.2	35.0
Hired labor, days	6.8	5.9	7.8	7.0	6.6	5.0	16.3	26.9	12.4
Transport costs[a]	3,473	4,606	8,365	5,534	35,824	8,001	12,789	15,228	19,147
of fertilizer & herbicides[a]	19,482	15,371	17,335	17,855	27,442	15,528	28,136	28,208	25,024
of hired labor[a]	12,850	12,397	15,872	13,893	16,619	10,279	40,793	63,157	29,754
Total costs[a]	35,805	32,375	41,572	37,282	79,886	33,809	81,718	106,593	73,925
Harvest, almudes	36.21	56.65	71.49	53.53	91.29	75.00	99.08	99.35	91.17
Share rental, almudes	4	0	3	3	12	6	14	12	11
Net harvest value[a]	38,506	59,781	76,831	57,156	84,982	94,040	95,235	105,478	93,380
Net profit[a]	2,755	27,406	35,259	19,874	5,096	60,231	13,517	-1,115	19,455
Return to family labor[a]	91	751	1,046	606	109	1,200	672	-61	556
Return to capital[b]	0.08	0.85	0.85	0.53	0.06	1.78	0.17	-0.01	0.83

[a] In March 1987 pesos (US$1.00 = 1,018 pesos)
[b] After recovering costs, in March 1987 pesos

Table 1, continued

Costs and returns to rain-fed milpa farming, based on averages per *almud* (.75 liter) of corn seeded. Data are for the 1987-88 agricultural year and show average per-almud inputs and returns on parcels cultivated by a sample of 22 Apas farmers in the highlands and the lowlands. The almud is a standard unit of measure for corn and corresponds roughly to the amount seeded per *tablon* or hectare of land. Highland parcels, all of approximately 1 hectare in size, are grouped by altitude zone because yields vary considerably by altitude. Lowland parcels, which vary minimally in altitude (they are all at approximately 500 m.), were generally rented plots and are grouped by size to show variations in returns to scale.

All values are per-almud values for a given group of surveyed parcels, shown as averages. Because parcels in a group vary in size, values in a column, showing average values per almud, do not add up precisely. Costs are deflated to March 1987 peso equivalents. Family labor, in days, includes unsalaried work in the field and management. Fertilizer and herbicide costs are cash outlays for the purchase of these chemical inputs. Rental costs are in almud withdrawn from harvest to deliver to land owner. Almost all lowland parcels were rented; almost all highland parcels were not.

The value of the net harvest per almud (after rent), which includes the value of fresh corn (*elotes*) harvested early, is based on the price received by Zinacantecos who sold corn at harvest time (February 1988). Zinacantecos received about 258,500 pesos per ton, as compared to the 310,000 peso guaranteed price. Many farmers waited until later in 1988 to sell at a higher price. Net returns are figures obtained after deducting costs, but not the value of family labor. Returns to family labor are shown in pesos per day (deflated to March 1987 values) and compare unfavorably to then-prevailing daily wages for fieldhands (1500 pesos with food, 2000 pesos without), and for unskilled and skilled construction workers (2500 pesos and 5000 pesos, respectively). Returns (after costs and rent) to capital are shown as a ratio (after indexing) of net returns to total cash outlays. Harvest yields are shown as the number of almud harvested per almud of corn seeded.

Daniel C. Mountjoy compiled these budgets in Apas in March, 1988.

FIGURE 4

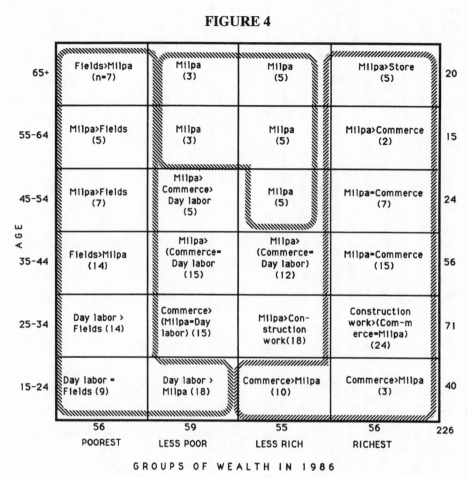

Productive Activities of Apas Men in 1986. The economic crisis of 1982 returned Zinacantecos to farming in the highlands, although many younger men continued to work for wages in the regional economy as field hands, construction workers, or skilled masons. Wealthier Zinacantecos combined milpa farming with commerce.

through regular application of fertilizer and by using chemical weed sprays to control the runner grasses that used to strangle the milpa after a year or two of use. Once a scrub forest punctuated by scattered milpas, the Apas ejidal and communal lands are today a virtual sea of milpa.

Although during the 1960s, the people of Apas undertook only about 20 percent of their farming in the highlands and the rest on rented lowland fields, by 1987 highland acreage accounted for 52 percent. Among the 22 farmers that Mountjoy studied, 12 farmed solely in the highlands. Only 10 also farmed in the lowlands, where farming proved profitable only at a very modest scale with a minimum of hired labor. Several of the 10 in fact suffered losses in the lowlands, and no one farmed exclusively there.

Zinacanteco farming now requires substantial capital (see Table 1). Simple tools and equipment (machete, hoe, billhook, bags) and a reserve of corn sufficient to feed one's household and field workers are no longer enough to enable a household to farm. Fertilizer and weed sprays must be purchased. Workers, if they are hired, no longer wait for payment in kind after the harvest; they expect payment at the time of their work. Local truckers must be paid to haul the harvest home. At the same time, those who have capital can expect reasonable returns to expenditures in farming as long as they keep hired labor costs down. Zinacantecos who farmed in the highlands during the 1987-88 season consistently earned returns to working capital of about 85 percent, after inflation, except at the highest altitudes.

Returns to capital invested in lowland farming were poorer, except for parcels of modest size farmed with a minimum of hired labor. One can see that returns to lowland farming drop when Zinacantecos farm there on a large scale. If more than 2 almud of milpa are seeded in the lowlands (an amount roughly equal to 2 hectares), more labor is expended than most families can supply, and the wages and costs of feeding and transporting hired labor rapidly erode returns to larger scale. The negative returns to scale shown in Table 1 are based on the assumption that all farmers sell corn at the prices prevailing at harvest time and thus conceal the fact that some who farm on a large scale can afford to wait until later in the season to sell at a more advantageous price. As Mountjoy concluded (1988, p. 53), "Profitable large scale production in the lowlands requires a large capital investment **and** the ability to retain the crop until prices rise later in the season." But in both zones, capital expenditures were indispensible. As a result, many poorer Zinacantecos no longer have the means to farm unless they borrow money, whereas wealthier compatriots with cash to spare from other enterprises do.

Farming now also requires less labor. Fields that used to take two weeks to hoe can be sprayed clean of weeds in a few days. In 1987 families provided most of the labor, but given the prevailing price of corn, tending the milpa remunerated families very poorly relative to prevailing wage rates. Certainly returns to farming milpa do not justify paying prevailing wages to fieldhands, and therefore few of the latter are hired.

A Zinacanteco household of average size consumes about 60 almud (900 metric liters, 650 kilos) of corn in food. Under normal conditions, a family would have to farm 2.34 tablones in the highlands to secure this much corn after paying for the costs of farming. Of the 22 men represented in Table 1, 10 farmed in excess of this amount in the highlands alone, but 7 farming only in the highlands worked less acreage. Thus some Zinacantecos farm enough to feed themselves and more; others do not and must join the growing number of landless in obtaining food in other ways.

WORKING FOR FOOD VS. WORKING FOR MONEY

Corn, as the quintessential food, has been central to what it means to Zinacanteco men and women to live together in households. But as productive relations in farming change, and as Zinacantecos turn increasingly to wage work and use cash earnings to purchase commodities -- including foods -- other than corn, those very concepts have been subject to challenge and to change.

For the older generation of Zinacantecos, living together in households meant, above all, sharing in the production and consumption of corn. Although Zinacantecos distinguish different kinds of foods by roots of the verbs for eating (/ve'/[6] for corn-based foods; /ti'/ for meats; /lo'/ for fruits, etc.), the generic concept of food was and is that of corn (_ve'_). Regardless of how household members contributed to household production, by cooking, planting, hoeing, and even working for wages, they were conceived as working for and having a stake in the corn supply from which a household ate and funded its ongoing production. Whether or not families worked "together" was described in terms of whether or not they ate together. When households split, they divided stored-up corn in proportion to members' contributions to it. The right to inherit hinged on whether or not heirs supported elderly benefactors, by lodging and feeding them if they had the need.

---

6. The verb roots are in a phonemic transcription in which the character ' is a glottal stop.

When families were too poor to feed themselves, their members might "seek food" in work for others; and an important responsibility of Zinacanteco employers was to provide them food and lodging. Thus employers used to pay workers in corn. Today, although some Zinacantecos still "seek food" in work, many seek money instead. And while some Zinacanteco employers board their workers, many simply pay cash wages, as do most non-Indian employers.

Zinacantecos hire field hands when they farm on a scale that requires more labor than the members of their households working "together" can supply. During the 1950s and 1960s, most Zinacantecos who farmed rented lowland tracts on a large scale contracted workers from neighboring Chamula on a seasonal basis to work for them. Zinacantecos would work alongside their employees and supervise them. Chamula workers expected their Zinacanteco employers to cover the costs incidental to their work, transport and food. Generally, Zinacantecos paid Chamula workers not in cash at the time of work but in corn from the future harvest delivered to their homes. Some poor Zinacantecos also worked for other Zinacantecos in this manner during the 1950s and 1960s. In Apas, those who worked as field hands for other members of the community also farmed milpa of their own, but they were poor, predominantly of the lowest quartile of wealth.

With the greater proletarianization of the 1970s and 1980s, a much larger proportion of the population of Zinacantán has taken up wage work for others as field hands. At the same time, employment practices have shifted markedly toward the payment of cash wages. Seventy-four percent of the quartile of poorest men do some work as field hands, and in the middle quartiles the percentages are thirty-six and twenty-nine percent respectively. As in the past, many of these men also farm corn in their own right -- but they also now work as unskilled laborers in construction, in commerce and so forth. As in the past, Zinacanteco employers pay field hands' transport costs, but employment need not entail the provision of workers' food. Although many employers and workers negotiate for the worker to be fed at a discount on wages (for example, in 1987, being paid 1500 pesos per day plus food instead of 2000 pesos per day without food; or in 1989 being paid 42-45,000 pesos plus food per week instead of 55-60,000 pesos without food), some employers do pay straight cash wages. Today, workers have become accustomed to being paid in cash weekly or semi-monthly rather than awaiting payment in corn at the time of harvest.

Men's work outside of agriculture usually involves relations with non-Zinacanteco employers in unskilled construction jobs or other work in distant urban places. In such employment, workers generally receive all-cash wages and purchase their own food. Some members of the community do, however, work for others in non-agricultural jobs, as chauffeurs of trucks, as vendors in market stalls, in construction of homes in Apas. It is true that Zinacanteco employers commonly feed such workers as well as paying them; but they do not pay them in corn. Thus working men, today, work for wages rather than for food.

Many women, by contrast, still work for food. Women from households that experience shortfalls in food -- typically women from poor households, or women from households that lack men to head up farming -- "seek food" by taking up piecework for other women. They may make tortillas and hardtack for other families, using the latter's corn but supplying their own firewood, and accepting as pay an amount of corn equal to that which they process.

Some Zinacantecan women, predominantly those who are elderly, poor, and/or widowed, also work as remunerated field hands, especially in milpas close to home in the highlands, and in the harvest. Generally these women are "seeking food," rather than "seeking money," and receive pay in kind with an option of cash. For example an elderly widow and her daughter harvested a younger couple's beans in a milpa close to Apas and received a standard measure of 4 dry liters of shelled beans for each sack of unshelled beans they harvested; but the daughter asked for the cash equivalent of beans -- $5000 pesos -- for one of the bags she had harvested. In addition, some women who weave for others are paid in cash; others work for corn; and many women simply trade weaving to take advantage of one another's different weaving skills or embroidery abilities.

The differences in the meaning of work and its relation to livelihood are thus gendered as well as generational. Young men, above all, who have matured in the contemporary world of work for wages, are bringing changed meanings into the lives of their elders and their womenfolk, who did and do live in a world of work for food. In contrast to those who once were fed by their employers, young workers expect to feed themselves in construction work and other employment, just as their self-employed Zinacanteco counterparts who run market stands or engage in trucking in distant lowland cities and towns. They relish being able to try out foods other than corn. And, ever attentive to style, they experiment with popular clothing, music, and electronic wares.

As they bring new consumption home in the form of non-corn foods, faddish clothes, and even changed house construction, youthful Zinacantecos are altering concepts of living together in ways that challenge meanings held by the older generation and by women of their own generation that center on shared production and consumption of corn. The conflict over changing meanings emerges poignantly in marital disputes. In airing quarrels with their husbands, many women take their mates to task for spending their wages in unessential consumption rather than on inputs for the production of corn or on the provision of corn and beans for their families. In disputes that pit young wives against their in-laws, the wives seek resolutions in terms of setting up independent households through the division of corn supplies, even when their husbands earn most of their income in wagework and commerce. For their part, young men are likely to counter charges of neglect by reference to new goods they have provided -- such as the different kinds of footwear they have bought for their children (tennis, sandal, boot). And they try to resolve disputes through cash settlements. Living together, for them, does not center on provisioning their homes with corn, but rather with commodities bought from earnings.

LABOR AS A COMMODITY

Wealthy Zinacantecos whose trucking, vending, or construction contracting businesses give them cash to spare resort increasingly to prepaying workers at a discount to contract for their future labor. Zinacantecos who are desperate for cash and cannot secure loans (see below) resort to selling their labor early, placing themselves at the disposal of their employer to call upon them when their labor is needed throughout the following agricultural cycle. In recent years, as wages have risen to adjust for inflation, the prepayment for future labor early in the agricultural cycle has been at about half the rate of wage that prevails by the close of the cycle. For the employer, prepaying wages at a discount brings the wage down closer to the poor rate of return that milpa farmers receive on their own family labor (refer to Table 1), making it feasible for the employer to substitute hired labor for family labor. Such employment forces the worker to accept a low wage and strips him of discretion to work for other employers later in the season except with the consent of the employer to whom he is indebted. The worker may even find himself assigned by his employer to work for someone else. His work has become a commodity.

NEW MEANINGS FOR OLD LAND

Zinacantecos continue to acquire land primarily by inheritance and not by purchase. Ejidal land, by law, passes from the head of household to whom it has been assigned to a single designated heir -- usually from father to son. Tracts of communal farmland generally pass from parents to sons; settlement land passes to all children. By Zinacanteco custom, children legitimate their right to inherit by supporting parents in their old age and burying them properly. Heirs who are willing to support elderly kin can thwart alienation of land from the line of descent, for example if a parent endeavors to sell a parcel of communal land. Although some Zinacantecos have managed to purchase land, especially settlement land, farmland continues not to be a freely marketed commodity. It should be borne in mind that demographic growth has negated the effect of the distribution of ejido land on inequalities in land tenure (refer to Figure 1); as in 1939, just before the distribution of land in the Ejido of Zinacantán, half of Apas's married men lacked land in 1989.

At the same time, ownership of land has shifted over the years to reflect the growing power of youth vis-a-vis their elder kin. When farmland was surveyed in 1967, 56 percent was in the hands of men over 45 years of age and only 35 percent was held by men aged 25-44 years. The distribution reflected the relative power that elder Zinacantecos held over youthful heirs. By virtue of the marriage system, that indebted youth to them, and by making respectful obedience a precondition for the distribution of a household's productive assets, elders used to control the productive labor of offspring well after children's marriage. Today, by contrast, elder Zinacantecos control only 44 percent of the land, while men aged 25-44 hold 49 percent. This shifting of ownership to young men is related to changing age structure of the population, but it also mirrors their increasing economic independence and the concomitant advantages they have in transacting relations with elder kin. Today's youth can marry without incurring debt. Many are unafraid to challenge parents and in-laws in the realm of public politics. And young adults can command earlier distribution of inheritable assets as the price of supporting their parents in old age, rather than having to demonstrate the right to inheritance through respectful obedience.

While land itself has not become a commodity to be bought and sold, the use of land has become so, to a substantial degree, in ways that also reflect the growing economic power of Apas's younger adults. Firewood once was free for women to gather anywhere in the ejido or communal lands, but today Zinacantecos treat woodlot fuel as a private good to be bought and sold. Rental of highland parcels for cultivation has also become more widespread.

Zinacantecos of means who own land do not give out their fields in rental. For example, a trucker, who was also a farmer with land, criticized his half- brother as foolish for having rented out land for others to use. His brother should have kept it fallow for his own use in another year if he was not going to farm it at the time, he said. But his half- brother was happy to rent out fields that he could not farm himself because he could not afford chemical inputs. Zinacantecos generally pay one another rent in kind (three of the average eleven to thirteen bags of corn harvested for each hectare rented), and the half-brother was happy to receive the corn.

Now that highland farming requires capital expenditures, poor families with non-liquid land assets more readily turn land over in rental to those who have capital. During the 1987 farming season the majority of those who gave land in rent were single or widowed women "seeking food" in the form of rent in kind, and poorer married men who made most of their living from work as field hands. Those who farmed rented land were wealthier young adults, many of whom derived substantial income from skilled wagework and commerce and who thus could afford fertilizer, weed sprays, and even the cost of laborers to farm for them.

Renting farmland is one of the many alternatives, furthermore, in which Zinacantecos with cash can invest their assets flexibly. Rented land need not entail a long term commitment of renter to landowner. Thus a wealthy merchant and truck owner rented enough Apas farmland in the 1987 season to employ as many as 25 field hands at a time to work those fields for him, but in 1989 he rented not at all in the highlands, having decided to farm land he had rented near lowland Villaflores, where he owns and runs his fruit and vegetable business. Such employers may be too deeply involved in activities other than farming to be able even to work alongside and directly supervise their workers. They may leave supervision to a dependent, or they may trust their employees to work on their own. One Zinacantec who works full-time in commerce simply contracted the harvest of his milpa to three Zinacantecos as piece work to be paid a set amount regardless of how they organized the work.

LENDING AND BORROWING: "LETTING MONEY WORK" FOR NEW ELITES

The character of lending and borrowing in Zinacantán has changed as productive relations have become more class- based and capitalist. Zinacantecos have always borrowed from one another for the expenses of curing, ritual cargos, and funerals, but often from kin or ritual kin (*compadres*) without interest. The giving of loans was one of the ways in which the powerful could obligate others through generosity. This is not to say that borrowing was always without the payment of interest: Zinacantecos did pay interest on loans taken out for production of milpa. Today, members of the community still expect not to pay interest on loans taken for ritual, but loans taken at interest for production have proliferated. Some poorer women make production loans as a way of "seeking food." But most rich lenders, men and women, now loan for the purpose of "making money" by letting money "work," rather than as a way of building personal followings through generosity.

Lending and borrowing have become more prevalent in the sphere of production as Zinacantecos need more cash than ever before to pay the costs involved in producing corn. But cash is also required to earn a living outside farming. Merchants need funds to purchase their inventory and cover transport and living expenses while on selling trips. Local people who invest in such capital equipment as trucks or corn mills may resort to banks and government agencies for credits, but they also borrow from compatriots.

Those Zinacantecos who have rights in the Ejido of Zinacantán or who own communal tracts of land have been eligible for credit from the state , through Banrural for the purchase of fertilizer with crop insurance from ANAGSA. Farmers have sometimes used these credits, especially if they lacked cash in June when fertilizer must be applied, but they have felt penalized by having to repay credits in February at harvest time, when crop prices are at their seasonal low. It is frequent for local people to borrow from one another, even at higher interest rates than those offered by the Banrural, in order to avoid the paperwork involved in obtaining official loans and the unfavorable date of maturity at harvest time.

Tzotzil distinguishes two kinds of loans that Zinacantecos make to one another: those used to pay for future delivery of a crop by buying it while it is still "green," and those that bear interest. Loans against future delivery of a crop simply purchase the crop at a discount -- for example in June at half the market price anticipated at the time of harvest and delivery the following January or February. Interest-bearing loans involve payment of an agreed-upon rate, typically 10 to 20 percent per month, over a specified term; and interest is not compounded. Rates of interest are roughly similar to the returns Zinacantecos earned to cash inputs in milpa farming in 1987 after inflation (refer to Table 1), suggesting that loans and farming are comparable investments for those who have capital to spare.

Seven women, all of them never-married, separated, or widowed heads of households, give out loans in the form of the purchase at a discount of corn to be harvested in the future. Most of these women are elderly and poor. Most are following a subsistence strategy in which corn purchased early at a substantial discount is used both for food and for fodder for pigs and chickens. A woman will fatten pigs from part of the harvest received in January or February, retaining corn for her own consumption; she will sell the pigs in June or July and use the proceeds to give out loans against next year's harvest to farmers who lack the cash needed to buy fertilizer and weed killer. These women are said to be "seeking food" rather than "seeking money," in contrast to the relatively wealthy women who provide loans at interest and to the wealthy men who give out both kinds of loans.

In Apas, eight of the 29 men considered to enjoy the highest incomes give out loans of one or the other kind. Except for three older men who earned their wealth long ago in milpa, all derive substantial income from activities other than farming milpa, activities in which cash assets play an important part. They are said to be "seeking money" by letting their money "work" for others for a price. Some are young truck owners (two of the four who make regular runs to Tuxtla Gutierrez and San Cristobal markets); others are middle-aged merchants who own and run lucrative market stalls in lowland towns. Another received a windfall of cash as indemnity when the government closed down the reforestation program in which he worked. Two of the ten who give out loans also run stores in Apas, and two operate corn grinding mills. All are married heads of households.

Through lending, these wealthy Zinacantecos are living in substantial measure from the product of others' work in a manner that used to characterize only non-Indian usurers. Their advantaged position enables some of them to explore new ways of living and working. One, for example, who is 32 years old, works less hard as a trucker today than when he ran both a truck and a van, since he now earns interest on the money he made when he sold his van. He is reputed to have 20 million pesos out in loans. Unlike elders of yore who gathered followings by making loans to common folk, he lends only to men of substantial means. And althouth he told me that he could easily earn one million pesos per month by running his truck every day, he only does so on the weekdays that give him the most lucrative business, because he earns so much income from interest.

TRANSPORT AND POLITICS

In the 1950s, Zinacantecos walked to their milpas and packed tools, food, and harvested crops on horse or mule. Wealthy members of the community might own five or six beasts of burden that they would rent out to local farmers in harvest season and to some who engaged in long-distance trading. As roadways spread into the Grijalva valley during the 1960s, Zinacantecos began to hire motorized transport to reach fields rented in more distant zones than before (cf. Cancian), and some living along major roadways invested in trucks. Today, wealthy residents of Zinacantán own a fleet of trucks and vans, undertaking the majority of shipping paid for by other members of the community, and the *Camioneros* (Truckers) have emerged as the dominant elite in the region.

To engage in commercial transport of passengers and their produce, truck or van owners must affiliate with associations that obtain route concessions from the state, and in practice they are thereby beholden to the party in power, the Partido Revolucionario Institucional (PRI). There are three such associations in Zinacantán, one for the fleet of Zinacanteco- owned vans and two for truckers. A man from Navenchauk, the hamlet on the Pan American highway that developed commercial flower trading in conjunction with trucking, founded the larger of the two truckers' unions several years ago. His union represents over sixty truck owners, most (but not all) Zinacantecos. When a competitor from Apas attempted to form a rival union with some twenty trucker members about six years ago, while he was still associated with an opposition party, state authorities made it clear that the union would not receive its route concession until he reverted to the PRI, which he did. Most truckers in both unions consequently are *priistas*, who are thereby referred to as Camioneros, although there are some truckers who form part of the opposition to the PRI in Zinacantán, as well as many priistas who are not owners of trucks.

Zinacanteco-owned transport has become increasingly important to Apas milpa cultivation as logging roads have opened up the ejidal and communal lands to truck transport since 1982. Transport had always been a major cost of milpa production, especially for those who farmed on distant rented lands in the lowlands. After the economic crisis of 1982, when the state began to cut fuel subsidies and to raise gasoline prices, the cost of transport to and from the lowlands became prohibitive for many Zinacanteco farmers; and this change, coupled to the opening of nearby highland tracts to motor transport, contributed to the shift of Apas milpa cultivation from the lowlands to the highlands as Zinacantecos returned from wagework to milpa after the 1982 crisis. Zinacanteco trucking has also made it easier to transport new fruit and garden crops to market and more comfortable for the monolingual -- especially women -- to do so.

It would seem that transport costs account for much of the variation in prices local people receive for their harvest. Zinacantecos who sold corn at harvest in February 1988 received about 258.50 pesos per kilo, as compared to the 310,000 peso per ton guaranteed price which they might have received if they had paid to deliver the crop to a federal warehouse. In December, 1989, when the guaranteed price had risen to 435,000 pesos per ton, farmers were receiving 360 pesos per kilo at the site of harvest, about 390 pesos per kilo after transporting corn back home, and about 420 pesos per kilo if they hauled it from Zinacantán to San Cristobal to sell -- differences largely attributable to the cost of transport. A trucker speculated that the price per kilo might be higher than the guaranteed price in distant Villahermosa, perhaps as high as 500 pesos per kilo, but that the cost of transport did not justify transporting to this market of high demand.

The cost of transport is not, however, set by free market conditions. The Apas truckers hold a monopoly on transport from the hamlet to the Tuxtla and San Cristobal markets by virtue of their route concessions. As the Zinacanteco truckers' unions meet regularly to coordinate and set transport fees they protect one another from pressures from clients to compete in shipping fees. Truckers demand -- and receive -- cash on the line for transport, whether the product is hauled from field to home for consumption or is destined for sale in the market. As almost all produce from Apas lands sold into regional markets is transported by Apas truckers, they are in a position of power that could be expected to wrest advantage from any increase in the market value of products.

Ritual and politics also generate passenger business for truckers. Fares from Apas to the ceremonial center, Jteklum, where cargo-holding families perform ritual and where the municipal court and other municipal offices function, are 2400 pesos each way per passenger. A litigant seeking to settle a dispute outside his or her hamlet must also foot the bill for transport of spokespersons and witnesses to the municipal court. Therefore the cost of transport is an important weapon in political disputes; and truckers, who can provide transport, hold an important political asset.

THE DILEMMA OF HIGHER PRICES

In the past, Zinacanteco public life was founded upon stratification based on rank. Politics revolved around the personal followings of men of the generation who were beholden to the PRI for distribution of ejido lands during the land reform. Political leaders -- often brokers for the programs of the state -- were those who, in the manner of elders, orchestrated kin and followers to help them fund prestigious careers as cargo holders, thus gaining the prerogative to speak for others.

Today, the politics of Zinacantán have become increasingly class-based. Camioneros (Truckers) affiliated with the PRI are the dominant faction. In opposition to them stand the Campesinos (Peasants), so-called despite the fact that many of them are semi-proletarians who depend heavily upon wagework for their livelihoods. Even though the PRI encompasses peasants and workers, as well as the wealthy truckers, while the semi-proletarian Campesinos may be led by newly wealthy, the opposing groups do nevertheless conform roughly to the emerging class structure of Zinacantán.

As the Campesinos have sought support in the larger political arena, they have turned to various interest groups within the PRI, to the opposition Partido de Acción Nacional (PAN), and --in the case of the hamlets of Apas and Nachih -- to the Partido Revolucionario Democrático (PRD), as new *cardenistas*. They have lambasted the Camioneros as corrupt power holders who have used public resources for personal gain. And they have held forth the promise to their followers that opposition parties, if they are brought to power, will improve the lot of peasants -- even poor peasants or semi-proletarians -- by raising the prices paid to primary producers of corn and other staple crops, which have recently been extremely low.

The hope of these poorer Zinacanteco farmers is that with higher crop prices, they can offset to some extent the rapidly rising cost of cultivation and thus forestall their further marginalization within the context of an increasingly capital-intensive corn farming environment. There is no doubt that low producer prices hurt such people and that higher prices are essential elements in any strategy to protect small farmers. Nevertheless the overall picture is a complex one indeed. In a context like that of Zinacantán today, it is the Zinacanteco entrepreneurs, who have capital to deploy at will in commerce, trucking, and farming -- wealthy men of the PRI as well as young, newly wealthy upstarts among the cardenista opposition -- who stand most to profit. Those who stand most to lose are the growing number of people in Zinacantán who have no recourse but to buy food in the market.

Once a peasant society stratified by rank, Zinacantán was a place where the disadvantaged -- young, or poor, or female and widowed -- could count on the generosity of elders and leaders who relied upon them for their own standing. They could count on others for their basic livelihood, corn food, as long as they were willing to work in others' corn production. But corn food, and its production for subsistence, is being displaced from its once-central place in Zinacanteco life by the making of money and the consumption of commodities. Ironically, this is increasingly so, even as Zinacantecos have returned to farming corn -- as capitalist enterprise -- in the post-1982 era of economic crisis.

Chapter 6

THE REMNANTS OF COMMUNITY: MIGRATION, CORN SUPPLY AND SOCIAL TRANSFORMATION IN THE MIXTECA ALTA OF OAXACA[1]

Raúl García Barrios and Luis García Barrios

The life chances of rural people in Mexico are shaped not only by their access to natural resources, but also by the quality of mutual support which can be mustered through family and community structures. In this book, a continuum of rural social integration running from areas of strongest communal organization, with greatest capacity to provide for the needs of all local inhabitants, at one pole, to areas where local human and physical resources are least sufficient to maintain a minimum degree of solidarity or level of livelihood, at the other, would begin with Plan de Hidalgo, Veracruz (discussed in chapter 4c), and end in San Andrés Lagunas, Oaxaca. The cases taken up in other chapters would fall at various less extreme points along the line.

San Andrés is a Mixtec Indian community[2] whose inhabitants have been dramatically affected by three interrelated processes underlying the general rural crisis in Mexico: a) the outmigration of poor peasants, accompanied by increasingly strong dependence in the communities of origin on external income and resources, both of which are unstable and unreliable; b) the transformation of traditional forms of valuing basic grains, as well as the collapse of incentives which once provided a political, as well as an economic, stimulus for surplus corn production; c) the disintegration of local systems of authority and reciprocity which determine the rights and obligations of producers and encourage collective action and participation.

Permanent emigration, which gradually reduced the population of the village and undermined its farming potential, began far earlier in San Andrés than in most other rural areas. By the 1980s, this community could be studied as an unusually clear example of a rural remittance economy, in which corn was grown entirely for subsistence and there was virtually no incentive to rehabilitate the local agricultural economy. The contrast with a situation like that just described for highland Chiapas, in chapter 5, could not be more marked. In Zinacantan, a struggle is under way for control of an important corn-producing region, where those with sufficient capital make money and control the market. There is a surplus of labor and a serious shortage of land to be farmed. In San Andrés, on the other hand, there are not enough able-bodied inhabitants to expand production beyond very narrow limits; and capital and labor are the limiting factors of livelihood, not land.

It is useful to consider how a situation like that of San Andrés developed and to understand the dynamics of this kind of remittance economy. In the following pages, special attention will be given to the historical development of rural markets (whether free, discriminatory, or forced; see Bhaduri 1983), as this has formed the basis for the massive proletarization of the local population. Changes in the distribution of resources that are directly mediated by political struggle among villagers themselves, or between peasants and

---

1. This paper is based on research undertaken within the framework of the Program of Science, Technology, and Development, at El Colegio de México, and financed by the International Development Research Center (IDRC) of Canada.

2. The municipality of San Andrés Lagunas, in the center of the Mixteca Alta (or highlands) of Oaxaca, covers 5,111 hectares within the district of San Juan Teposcolula. The area encompasses two small valleys with partially dessicated lakes, 2,100 meters above sea level, and is bordered on the east and west by two long mountain ranges with peaks reaching 2,700 meters in height. The climate is temperate and partially humid, with summer rains. According to the municipal census, there are 445 hectares of excellent rainfed farmland, containing residual moisture, 1,866 hectares more of rainfed farmland without residual moisture, and 2,799 hectares of pasturelands and hills, most of which are eroded and deforested.

other agrarian agents will not be considered here, nor will corrolary phenomena related to distribution and dispossession of agricultural land.

ECONOMIC TRANSFORMATIONS: CORN AS A CURRENCY
AND THE BASIS OF A MORAL ECONOMY

During the nineteenth century there was enough fertile land in the valleys and mountain range now forming the municipality of San Andrés Lagunas to allow for the development of a group of rich indigenous agriculturalists, who dominated the local economy until land was distributed during the agrarian reform of the 1930s.

The power of these wealthy agriculturalists rested on two economic activities: raising goats and producing corn. Each activity had a characteristic logic and a dynamic of production which differed radically from the other. From the sixteenth century onward, goat raising constituted one of the most important economic activities of indigenous groups in the Mixteca Alta, first because it could be reconciled with the scarcity of labor brought on by high mortality among the Indians in the wake of conquest, and later, during the seventeeth, eighteenth, and nineteenth centuries, because of the expansion of regional, national and international demand (Pastor 1987). From the beginning, goat production in San Andrés was linked to monetized regional markets; and it soon became the most important means by which the wealthy could accumulate monetary resources, as long as they could control the norms and arrangements for collective management which otherwise might restrict their use of communal lands. Once this goal had been achieved, goat production was guided by a typical logic of extraction, involving rapid, competitive and unregulated accumulation. This set the stage for deterioration of the lands on which the animals grazed, in an early example of what is now often termed "the tragedy of the commons" (Hardin 1968).

The reasons why the elite of San Andrés farmed corn, and the organizational strategy they employed to produce it, were quite different from those involved in raising goats. Corn had two economic functions in the local economy: it served as a means of payment in an interlinked market of credit and labor; and it formed the basis of the moral economy which established the rights and obligations of all members of the community. The majority of the indigenous people in the region were clients of the local elite. The rich advanced corn to the poor as a form of credit in exchange for a promise of future labor. The system was mediated and reinforced by a structure of reciprocal obligations, in which the moral prestige and political leadership of the wealthy rested on their capacity and willingness to respond to the demands of families which could not meet their consumption needs. In other words, communal rules protecting the poor were translated on the economic plane into mechanisms which ensured (through an interlinked market of credit and work) that there would be no involuntary unemployment. The wealthy had to utilize sufficient land and labor to attain communal food self-sufficiency and to satisfy any basic needs of the population which had not been covered.

It is evident that this system of corn production bestowed considerable economic and political power on the wealthy. In the first place, it awarded them control of an abundant supply of labor -- a control reinforced by the fact that the poor of indigenous communities were at the time (and in some cases still are) subject to intense social and economic discrimination outside their villages. Thus the rich gained monopoly power within local employment markets and reduced the terms of trade for labor and corn to the point of severe exploitation of the local work force. (In fact, at the beginning of the twentieth century, a day's wage was paid with a liter of corn; today it is the equivalent of eight liters of corn paid in cash.) The prevailing system also permitted the indigenous elite to expropriate land from producers who were unable to pay their debts or meet other obligations. Finally, it endowed the rich with extensive political and moral power based on their role as organizers of collective work and guarantors of community subsistence; and this authority increased their control over the communal lands used to pasture goats.

Evidently, the economic and political benefits of corn production were greater than its costs, and thus the rich were willing to marshall their resources in order to attain community self-sufficiency. At the same time, however, the excessively high costs of transporting corn constituted a disincentive to increase production of grain beyond a subsistence level, in response to regional and national demand (Pastor 1987). Because transport was so problematic, corn production, as opposed to that of goats, did not develop its own market in the Mixteco highlands until the twentieth century; and owing to restrictions on the effective demand for corn, the maximum limit for local production was set at the point where community self-sufficiency was ensured. Since this also marked the minimum acceptable level for production, population increases and concentration of land were the systematic determining forces of corn production.

LAND REFORM, THE SHORTAGE OF LABOR, AND THE DEVELOPMENT OF A MONETARY ECONOMY

With the advent of land reform, those who received new rights to communal land gave priority to working their own parcels; and the rich had to divest themselves of some of their own property, since they were unable to find laborers who would work under the conditions which had been accepted in the past. In consequence, the richest production units in the community broke into various family holdings, each with much less economic capacity; and this shift in the pattern of land distribution eventually altered earlier standards for the organization of the local economy. The nuclear family became the fundamental unit of production, income, investment, and consumption; and its objectives, whether of a subsistence or profit-oriented nature, began to govern economic processes. Although communal property was formally recognized, most arable land was distributed among families in private usufruct. Collective usufruct of water, forests, and pastures was reestablished, since given the small size of most productive units in San Andrés, collective property was the only way to maintain private access to the resources which were necessary to sustain some of their fundamental options, such as goat production and collecting firewood. The exploitation of these communal resources is nevertheless carried out strictly by family groups, and there is no institutional system to regulate their use.

With the atomization of production, traditional mechanisms of protection and security for the poor ceased to exist. A few years after land was distributed, it became clear that production within individual families could not satisfy the minimum consumption requirements of the majority of the inhabitants of San Andrés. Bad agricultural years took on catastrophic proportions and threatened the very existence local people, none of whom had the economic capacity to organize collective production or sustain others. Since there were now no complementary options, which reduced risks, such as those previously inherent in the nexus of labor, credit, corn and goat production created by the indigenous elite, this new system of private family production was extremely unstable. The inhabitants of San Andrés therefore had to look for opportunties outside the community.

Massive migration from San Andrés began in the 1930s. At first, people migrated to Tlaxiaco (a major trading center in the highlands) and to the coast of Oaxaca to search for temporary employment, supporting themselves by selling baskets made of palm leaves. Traditional temporary migration to the sugar cane producing regions of Veracruz was simultaneously intensified. With the inauguration of the Panamerican Highway in 1945, however, migration was channeled toward Mexico City and Puebla, where national industry was developing. In both cities, those who arrived first formed groups helping later arrivals to find work and/or providing support for compatriots who came to study. The majority of these migrants settled permanently in cities and swelled the ranks of the urban proletariat. Still, they maintained close ties with family and friends in San Andrés; and their remittances strengthened the productive capacity of the village economy, thus permitting those who did not migrate to subsist as farmers, artesans, small tradesmen or simply as family dependents. From the 1930s onward, the livelihood of those who remained in San Andrés was intimately linked to the development of the national economy and to the fortunes of the urban working class.[3]

Although the migration and proletarization of many inhabitants of San Andrés was, perhaps, initially driven by the immediate need to reassign family or community resources, the process implied unexpected structural consequences over the longer run: a) the depopulation of San Andrés, accompanied by a change in the composition of the remaining rural population, implying reduction in the labor force required to farm the land; b) an increase in local monetary income and the formation of a predominantly monetary economy; and c) the abandonment of work on community infrastructure, the degradation of traditional agricultural practices and consequent ecological deterioration. Let us first analyse the first two types of transformation in the local economy of San Andrés, before turning at a later point to the economic and ecological consequences of abandoning infrastructure and agricultural land.

FIGURE 1

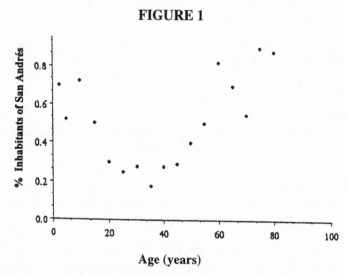

**Proportion of all people born in San Andrés who lived there in 1984 - 1985
by age category (from García Barrios, García Barrios and Alvarez Buylla, 1991)**

Depopulation

While thirty years ago the municipality had a population of about 5,000 inhabitants, in 1985 there were only 920 people in San Andrés. In other words, seventy-six percent of the people living in the community thirty years ago were no longer there. As a result, average family size has been reduced from eight to only four. Figure 1 shows that less than 50 percent of all people between 15 and 45 years of age who were born in San Andrés actually lived in the community during the period under study and that more than 32 percent of the family units in the village were made up of couples over sixty years old. Of the thirty households surveyed in detail (about 15 percent of those living in San Andrés), 70 percent had only one member (generally

---

3. Migration from San Andrés to the United States has been minimal, and generally of a temporary nature.

a male older than 13) capable of carrying out or supervising agricultural work. Thirteen percent of the family units contained no male worker.

Monetization of the economy

At the same time that family units are limited by a reduced labor force, excessive migration has caused an increase in the monetary resources of those still living in San Andrés who receive remittances from relatives. In 1985, money transfers from migrants totaled 24 million pesos, or 38 percent of the gross annual external income of the community. This figure is itself quite large, but the importance of remittances increases when its percentage of net annual external income is taken into account (that is, gross external income minus monetary outlays for goods and services obtained external to the community).

Table 1 gives details of outside income and expenditure for the most important economic activities of the inhabitants of San Andrés during the agricultural year running from September 1984 to September 1985. With the exception of remittances, all other sources of income ultimately required expenditures for inputs purchased outside the community. This outflow reduced the overall size of the monetary economy through lessening the scope for internal transactions and thus narrowing opportunities to generate income within the community.

Table 1
Income and Expenditures Associated with the Principal Monetary Income-Generating Activities of San Andrés Lagunas for the Agricultural Year 1984-1985

Activity	Income	Expenditure
Crops (corn, wheat, beans, rye, fruit)	2,493,600	498,200
Livestock (goats, draught animals)	29,083,900	9,237,100
Palm-weaving	4,640,500	1,608,200
Commerce and services	390,000	8,498,100

The relative importance of each economic activity in generating net external income can be measured utilizing the following formula :

$$\text{Importance of sector in the generation of net income} = \frac{\textit{gross external income of i - external expenditures of i}}{\textit{total gross external income - total external expenditure}}$$

Applying this formula to monetary remittances from migrants, one finds that those remittances make up 58 percent of the total net external income of the community. Thus the people of San Andrés are heavily dependent on income generated outside their village; and in fact a considerable proportion of the inhabitants could not subsist without remittances and the multiplier effect on income which they provide.

Resources provided by migrants now sustain the system of social security of the community. Local people do not have confidence in their own ability to get through bad agricultural years or other disasters. They continually seek outside assistance, which is provided by their urban relatives; and because this assistance is forthcoming, it is not necessary for families in San Andrés to have recourse to potential sources of local credit (like that which might be offered by merchants) in order to survive. Thus remittances have impeded the formation of forced markets of labor and goods as well as the development of patterns of accumulation based on usury and the concentration of land in a few hands. Of the 30 family units surveyed, only one (made up of a woman over sixty years old with no children to support her) had recourse to financing consumption through loans -- and those loans were made by close relatives. One other family had given a small piece of land (less than ten percent of the total worked by the family) to a creditor to be used until a debt could be repaid.

Outside assistance is even necessary to organize and maintain the political and religious life of the community. Migrants are often the honored hosts (*mayordomos*) who pay for public celebrations; and in one case at least, a migrant has been elected municipal president. Although the traditional system of political and religious offices or *cargos* has been maintained in San Andrés, the opportunity costs of dedicating scarce local labor to meeting such obligations are very high. This, together with the disintegration of the traditional system of authority and prestige, has begun to generate a tendency for work on behalf of the community to be paid for in money -- a system underwritten in part by the migrants. Finally, the economic dependence of those remaining in San Andrés on their urban relatives has created strong ties of identification with the urban world. Because symmetrical institutions to ensure subsistence and protection have not been forged in the village, the inhabitants of San Andrés must play the role of younger siblings, dependent on their urban relatives.

The foregoing suggests that monetization of livelihood in San Andrés was caused by the interaction of two processes: the reassignment of local resources during a period of increasing labor scarcity; and changes in patterns of consumption growing out of closer contact with urban environments and national culture. In this paper we will analyze only the former process.

Our hypothesis is the following: as migration led to an overall reduction in the population of San Andrés, both consumption requirements for agricultural products and the productive capacity of families declined. Nevertheless, productive capacity contracted more rapidly than consumer needs: it was usually the younger and stronger who migrated and the more dependent members of the family who stayed behind. Besides, when family size diminishes, there are changes in the division of labor, and output per capita is likely to be reduced. Finally, while in activities like agriculture, hunting and gathering, production requirements do diminish to some extent as the size of the population is reduced, this is not the case for certain other activities, such as those linked to religion or politics, which make strong demands on a shrinking pool of community labor.

Both sources of pressure on the family work force induced local people to reduce their effort per capita in agricultural activities (and with that their consumption of their own agricultural products) or to increase their demand for non-family labor when it was necessary in order to keep from falling below a certain minimum level of production for family consumption. In the second case, the weakening of institutions which had traditionally facilitated the reciprocal exchange of labor among families made it more and more difficult to meet the demand for non-family labor through non-monetary means. Only access to monetary income could allow families, first, to reduce pressure on their consumption by allowing for acquisition of basic food staples from the regional market and, second, to gain access to labor markets or technical substitutes (a team of draft animals or a tractor) which could meet production requirements.

Analysis of the present system of corn cultivation in San Andrés provides us with an excellent example of how the sphere of production has been reorganized in response to labor scarcity and how demand for money has consequently increased. Because they lacked sufficient family labor, residents of the community depended to a great extent on hired hands to carry out agricultural work during the 1984-1985 farm year. Twenty of the thirty families surveyed at that time paid for more than 25 days of hired help, surpassing the figure set by Schejtman (1982) as the limit separating a peasant enterprise from a capitalist one. In fact, during the 1983-1984 and 1984-1985 agricultural cycles, each family in San Andrés paid the equivalent of 52 days of hired labor per cycle; and 100 percent of the tractor service was paid for with money. Almost all families purchase the implements they need for farming, usually from local artisans who make hoes, parts for plows, goad-sticks, digging sticks and so forth.[4] In sum, agricultural production is strongly dependent on monetary transactions, which themselves generate new sources of income for those in the poorest fifth of the population who derive more than 60 percent of their monetary income from working as agricultural laborers in the pay of other peasant families.

FIGURE 2

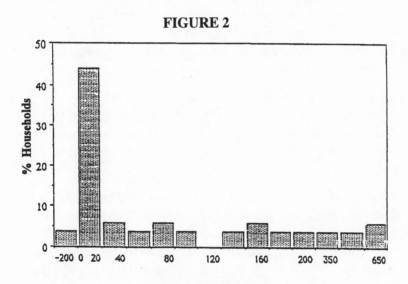

Income Received from Migrants
(thousands of pesos)

Distribution (% Households) of remittances received by 30 families of San Andrés during the period September 1984 - September 1985. Only one family sent money to relations outside of the community. The average remittance was 99,700 pesos (with a standard deviation of 31,851 pesos).

Given the importance of remittances in the economy of San Andrés, an important fact should be highlighted. The majority of the migrants who provide those remittances have been incorporated into the urban working class or form part of the unemployed or underemployed population of large urban areas. These social groups dispose of very limited means and must consume almost all of their income in order to satisfy their own needs. Therefore the margin of savings from which they can draw to provide support for their relatives still living in rural areas is generally small and unstable. As Figure 2 illustrates, the level of contributions from those who have migrated to the cities is usually very low; and their ability to stimulate

---

4. Up to now, none of the producers in San Andrés Lagunas uses chemical fertilizers. In 1980, during the short-lived SAM program, small cultivators were persuaded to buy chemical fertilizers using agricultural credit; but the following year they did not purchase that input because of what they termed bad management in Banrural and the National Agricultural and Livestock Insurance Company (ANAGSA). It appears, however, that their decision was also influenced by the fact that the cost of fertilizer is too high to be compatible with the economic logic of subsistence corn production and the considerable risk of crop damage in the region.

productive capacity in rural areas is therefore very slight, especially when a considerable part of those contributions must be spent by rural people to satisfy urgent consumer needs. Although migration and the resulting symbiosis between proletariat and peasantry have provided a basis for the survival of the village of San Andrés, for many of the families involved the outcome has been just that: survival.

CORN IN THE FORMATION OF MONETARY INCOME

During the 1984-1985 agricultural year, 60 percent of the families surveyed in San Andrés received more than 70 percent of their income from one economic activity and 93.3 percent from two or less. It is therefore possible to classify the population of the village according to the economic activity from which families obtain the major portion of their income. Six groups can be identified, one of which contains three subgroups: i) traders; ii) dependents of migrants; iii) women who weave palm baskets (*tenateras*); iv) local agricultural laborers; v) livestock producers (small, medium, and large-scale); and vi) agricultural laborers who work in neighboring communities.

The local population can also be divided into income categories. Despite its generalized poverty, San Andrés is not a homogeneous community: its inhabitants are differentiated by levels of monetary income, consumption and production outlays, and savings. Figure 3 will serve to illustrate the unequal distribution of access to resources within the population. It can be seen that in 1985 the richest family of the village earned thirty times more than the poorest.

These two ways of differentiating the families of San Andrés (by major source of income and by wealth) do not produce correlated orderings. With the exception of the traders and palm weavers, who are the richest and poorest of the community respectively, the levels of income of members of other groups do not differ according to occupation. Furthermore, neither of the two modes of differentiating families correlates with the amount of land they manage or the corn they produce. In more general terms, neither the level of income nor the way income is obtained depends directly on the amount of resources dedicated to agriculture. In fact, there is no socioeconomic group in San Andrés which generates monetary income from agricultural production to any significant extent, and this is especially the case for corn cultivation. Thus the cultivation of corn and other plants differs substantially from all other economic activities undertaken by the peasants in this community.

To understand the economic significance of the foregoing, it is necessary to analyze two aspects of corn production in San Andrés and to compare them with similar aspects of other economic activities: i) the type of labor force required, and ii) the rate of return on monetary outlay. Such an analysis requires the construction of a social accounting matrix (S.A.M.) for the 1984-1985 agricultural cycle (see Table 2). The latter traces monetary flows (in 1985 pesos) among the four principal aggregated productive sectors, three productive factors, diverse agents of the local economy (including the social groups defined previously and the local government) and the rest of Mexico. Therefore it constitutes the monetary aspect of dual accounts within the San Andrés economy.

As is customary in this type of table, the element "aij" represents the monetary flow directed from the account in column j to the account in row i, such that an expenditure for the first is income for the second. The income and expenditure registered in the table represent only monetary flows and do not include different types

FIGURE 3

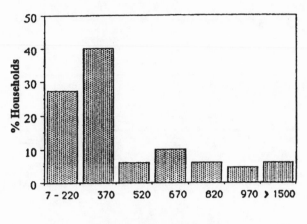

Total money income

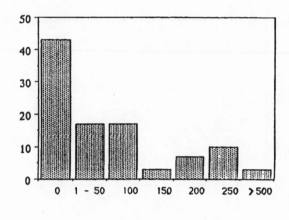

Savings

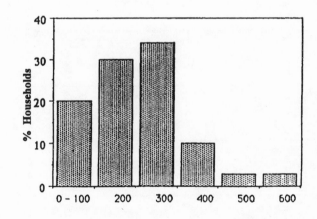

Expenditure of non-durables

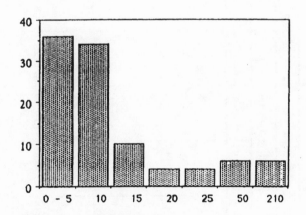

Productive expenditure

(x-axis figures are thousands of pesos)

Distribution (% Households) of relative frequencies of total money income, savings, expenditure on non-durable goods, and productive expenditure for 30 families of San Andrés, September 1984 - September 1985. Average income = 475,190 pesos (Sd = 495,100; 70,000 - 2,987,000); Savings = 77,940 (Sd = 115,340; 0 - 798,800); Expenditure on non-durables = 215,170 (Sd = 118,260;35,962 - 515,600); Productive expenditures = 204,050(Sd = 204,050; 8,730 - 2,100,000).

Table 2 Social Accounting Matrix for the Monetary Economy of San Andrés, September 1984 - September 1985

	Productive Activities				Factors			Socioeconomic Groups				
	Agric	Livestock	Palm-w	CommSvc	NonfamL	Animals	Tractor	MerchSer	Migrants	PalmW	LocDayL	LgFrmr
Productive Activities												
Agriculture	73900	164250	0	0	0	0	0	8700	538100	138450	52000	341950
Livestock	0	300000	0	0	0	0	0	0	0	0	0	0
Palm-weaving	0	0	0	0	0	0	0	0	0	0	0	0
Commerce & services	0	0	0	0	0	0	0	1413450	2321500	253700	662500	2327800
Factors												
Non-family labor	6183700	0	0	0	0	0	0	0	0	0	0	0
Draft animals	592200	0	0	0	0	0	0	0	0	0	0	0
Tractor	1528500	0	0	0	0	0	0	0	0	0	0	0
Socioeconomic Groups												
Merchants & Service providers (n=9)	79300	1892800	252000	4112350	120950	0	0	0	0	0	0	0
Migrants (n=38)	-3869500	-819400	553900	250000	58050	0	0	0	0	0	0	0
Palm weavers (n=15)	-152700	236250	440100	0	181400	0	0	0	0	0	0	0
Local day laborers (n=15)	86200	85500	114950	0	2657900	0	0	0	0	0	0	0
Better off farmers (n=30)	85800	10837950	202500	130000	1654600	0	0	0	0	0	0	0
Middle farmers (n=53)	-118200	6494700	1226600	0	1233700	177650	0	0	0	0	0	0
Small farmers (n=37)	-244000	1152000	327150	0	251600	355300	0	0	0	0	0	0
Day laborers outside village (n=7)	-111300	-197250	15000	0	25400	59200	0	0	0	0	0	0
Accumulated Savings	0	0	0	0	0	0	0	0	0	0	0	0
Institutions												
Local government	0	0	0	0	0	0	0	189050	356600	25550	98700	189000
Capital												
Savings (incl. investment in durable goods)	0	0	0	0	0	0	0	3518500	1332300	18100	970800	4190900
Education	0	0	0	0	0	0	0	62500	150000	27000	75000	3061500
Rest of Mexico												
Migrants' remittances	0	0	0	0	0	0	778500	0	0	0	0	0
External productive resources	498200	9237100	1608200	8498100	0	0	0	2670150	6631700	666000	1299300	4764650
External consumer goods	0	0	0	0	0	0	0	0	0	0	0	0
Debt service and capital payments	0	0	0	0	0	0	750000	0	0	0	0	0

Table 2, continued   Social Accounting Matrix for the Monetary Economy of San Andrés, September 1984 - September 1985

	Socioeconomic Groups			Accumu-lated Savings	Institution	Capital		Rest of Mexico			
	MedFrmr	SmFrmr	OutDayL		Local govt	Savings	Educ	Remit	Ex tRes	Consumer	Debt
Productive Activities											
Agriculture	503500	242500	75000	0	0	0	0	0	0	2493600	0
Livestock	0	0	0	0	0	0	0	0	0	29083900	0
Palm-weaving	0	0	0	0	0	0	0	0	0	4640450	0
Commerce & services	3598200	1510650	612600	0	0	0	0	0	0	390000	0
Factors											
Non-family labor	0	0	0	0	0	0	0	0	0	0	0
Draft animals	0	0	0	0	0	0	0	0	0	0	0
Tractor	0	0	0	0	0	0	0	0	0	0	0
Socioeconomic Groups											
Merchants & Service providers (n=9)	0	0	0	1450000	0	0	0	-45000	0	0	0
Migrants (n=38)	0	0	0	0	0	0	0	15157500	0	0	0
Palm weavers (n=15)	0	0	0	75000	0	0	0	423750	0	0	0
Local day laborers (n=15)	0	0	0	600000	0	0	0	138750	0	0	0
Better off farmers (n=30)	0	0	0	750000	0	0	0	1365000	377250	0	0
Middle farmers (n=53)	0	0	0	750000	0	0	0	3399450	0	0	0
Small farmers (n=37)	0	0	0	0	0	0	0	3123750	0	0	0
Day laborers outside village (n=7)	0	0	0	0	0	0	0	465000	1950000	0	0
Accumulated Savings	0	0	0	0	0	0	0	0	0	0	0
Institutions											
Local government	390900	205500	40000	0	370300	0	0	0	0	0	0
Capital											
Savings (inc. investment in durable goods)	533200	421900	6500	0	0	0	0	0	0	0	0
Education	1144500	196500	232500	0	0	0	0	0	0	0	0
Rest of Mexico											
Migrants' remittances	0	0	0	0	0	0	0	0	0	0	0
External productive resources	0	0	0	0	750000	0	0	0	0	0	0
External consumer goods	7370900	3138800	1239600	0	375000	0	0	0	0	0	0
Debt service and capital payments	0	0	0	0	0	0	0	0	0	0	0

of in-kind flows between the elements of the accounts. This differentiates the S.A.M. from a conventional amplified input-output matrix. Moreover, the income-expenditure relations between sectors, factors and agents cannot be utilized to compute aggregate value since the factor transactions here considered are only those occurring outside the family, and value is not imputed to family resources. In some cases, family income derived directly from productive activity can be interpreted as a payment to family resources involved in that productive activity, but only when family consumption is marginal or non-existent, as in cattle production, palm weaving or trade. This is clearly not the case in agricultural production, where a considerable proportion of output is indeed for family consumption.

The labor force

Different types of labor are utilized for different kinds of productive activity. In San Andrés there are some agricultural practices (such as handling a team of mules, running a tractor, planting and harvesting) for which a young male labor force is indispensible. Generally, the scarcity of young men in the village forces farming families to hire day laborers to do such work. Thus when a family decides to produce corn, it is chosing an option which will require it either to utilize that part of the family labor force with the highest opportunity cost or to invest in its monetary equivalent. This differentiates corn production from other economic alternatives like trade, livestock raising or weaving, which can be carried out by women and children. As is shown in the S.A.M., labor is never hired to carry out the latter activities.

From this information it is clear that the composition of the family labor force can limit access to certain income generating activities. For example, women in San Andrés cannot sell their labor, and their income generating options are reduced to weaving palm baskets and caring for goats. Only those women who receive considerable monetary remittances can undertake agricultural activities which require hiring men to work in the fields. In other words, the scarcity of a male labor force can be alleviated, generally at high production and transaction costs, if other sources of income are available. And in this sense, the cost of production establishes fundamental limits on access to diverse economic activities.

Rate of return

Peasant enterprises differ from capitalist businesses, among other things, because they make use of family resources that are not accounted for in monetary terms and because those who engage in production directly consume part of the output. Calculation of the rate of monetary return of a sector can thus be of only indirect use when studying peasant societies, since such a concept is designed to relate monetary outlay with the monetary surplus obtained from productive activity within the sector. In the case of San Andrés, one must attempt to understand rates of return within two different contexts: trade, palm weaving, and livestock raising are not activities undertaken to produce goods for family consumption, but to obtain money; while agricultural production is the only activity in which self-provisioning is of considerable and systematic importance for all social groups.

In the case of the first type of activity, monetary surpluses (profits) are a notional payment that families make to their own resources (including labor and money) invested in production. This payment can vary considerably depending on the activity in question. For the sake of example, we take the cases of trade and palm weaving, which are comparable because in both activities the only family input is labor, and principally female labor (see the S.A.M.). In 1985, family labor dedicated to the sale of groceries and articles for domestic use produced an average return equivalent to 30 percent of the minimum wage for the state of Oaxaca, although one trader in the village obtained a daily return of about 1.5 times the minimum wage. The rate of return on monetary outlay, as distinct from remuneration to labor invested, was approximately 54 percent. Palm weaving, on the other hand, provided those who worked at it with 12 percent of the minimum wage paid in the state, but the rate of return on capital invested was 189 percent. This apparent contradiction can best beexplained by the very low relative monetary costs for palm weaving and the very high levels of family labor exploited in this activity.[5]

Unlike monetary income from other economic activities, income from the sale of agricultural products must be considered as only partial payment for resources invested by the family, since the major part of all output is consumed within the household. As shown in the S.A.M., agricultural production is the only activity in which return on monetary investment is low in relation to expenses and thus systematically shows a monetary deficit.

Let us take corn as an example. In San Andrés Lagunas, all families with rights to land cultivate corn, but no household bases its income formation strategy on corn farming. In 1984, only 7 percent of the population produced a surplus of corn. This surplus represented slightly less than 12 percent of total production and generated only 7 percent of total monetary income in 1985. Furthermore the production of a corn surplus did not correlate with the income level of producers. In other words, families with greater productive capacity were not those who had surpluses. In general, the income obtained from corn farming was insufficient to cover the monetary costs of the crop, which in fact had to be subsidized by other productive activities. This explains why there is no correlation between peasant income and the amount of land they work.

All the economic activities undertaken by the families of San Andrés, with the exception of agricultural production, have something in common. When engaging in any of the other activities, local people try to generate the greatest profit and the largest income possible in order to finance famly consumption and productive investment; they are not oriented by a goal of self-sufficiency. In this sense, the productive logic underlying the cultivation of corn and other basic grains is the exception and not the rule.

THE MICROECONOMY OF FOOD SELF-SUFFICIENCY

Over the last hundred years, the purpose of corn production in San Andrés has evolved from ensuring community self-sufficiency to supporting family self-sufficiency. Corn is no longer a means of prepayment of salaried labor nor does its production and distribution provide the moral underpinning of the society. At present, in fact, there is practically no reciprocal exchange of corn in San Andrés. And even though the development of the regional road network has eliminated earlier restrictions on the effective demand for corn outside the village, corn is not produced commercially and its cultivation is limited to covering family consumption needs. Income is generated by other economic activities.

To produce only for consumption is indicative of a particular economic logic. In San Andrés, the situation cannot be attributed to attitudes which might value autarchy for its own sake, or defend practices in harmony with nature. The people of the community accumulate wealth when they are able to; and the manner in which they breed goats does a great deal of damage to the environment. A better explanation would seem to be that, as in the case of the pre-reform production system, an upper and lower limit of rational corn

---

5. The high level of return on monetary outlay provided by basket weaving, and the very low level of return to labor, explain three facts: a) taking advantage of the possibility to generate some income without having to invest much money, all social groups in San Andrés engage in palm weaving in order to obtain complementary income. However, since this involves a great deal of effort and high levels of exploitation, it is usually only a secondary occupation, generally carried out while tending the animals or the store, or in the evenings; b) only women living alone, who receive very small remittances, are full-time basket weavers; and c) in other communities of the Mixteca Alta where there is scarce land and local agricultural potential is practically nil, regional traders providing fibers to weavers and marketing the finished product enjoy extraordinary profits (personal communication, Teresa Ramos).

production exists, and at present both are in the range of family self-sufficiency. Any surplus is produced under conditions which provide extremely low returns both to labor and to monetary investment.

Before moving on to explore this explanation further, we must discard a possible alternative hypothesis: lack of land as a determining factor in the absence of a marketable surplus. In San Andrés scarce land clearly does not explain the low level of corn production. With the migration of entire families, much arable land has been abandoned: approximately 40 percent of the 400 hectares of top quality land in the central valley falls into this category, and an even greater proportion of poor quality land (far from the center of the municipality, on slopes or of low fertility) has been deserted. A part of the abandoned land has been occupied by local residents through loan contracts and sharecropping arrangements; and because of this, the average amount of land in the hands of each family has increased from 2.89 to 4.91 hectares. During the 1984 and 1985 agricultural years, 43 percent of the corn produced by villagers was in fact grown on borrowed or sharecropped land. During those years, 50 percent of all households obtained more than half of their grain from land which did not belong them, and twenty percent obtained almost 100 percent of their corn supply in that manner. This was made possible by the fact that relations between residents and migrants facilitate cultivation of abandoned lands. Much land nevertheless remains deserted; and families still residing in San Andrés are not motivated to cultivate it in order to produce a crop for the market.

A process of substitution of better land for worse has also been under way for some time, as many households residing in San Andrés abandon their own land to take up cultivation of better-quality parcels belonging to others. Then, when a certain limit is reached, families will go no further, as demonstrated in the following simple regression based on information provided by the households surveyed.

$$\text{Average hectares not cultivated per family during the 1984-1985 agricultural cycles} = .22 * Z - 0.4$$
$$R = 0.7744, P < 0.0001, n = 30$$

where Z is the sum of land families have in private usufruct and lands occupied through loans and sharecropping. This behavior is the product of what will here be called a "corn resource trap," because resources that exceed those necessary to attain family self-sufficiency are utilized for other production or income options. When these options do not exist, resources are simply disregarded or utilized inefficiently, as is the case with the land. In 1984, families of San Andrés did not work about 13 percent of their lands.

The appearance of a corn resource trap is the result of a particular system of restrictions and stimuli that govern the production decisions made by peasant households. In San Andrés average soil productivity is low. In 1985, a year considered to have been good for agriculture, yield per hectare was 600 kilograms of corn. Grain production per day of work invested was approximately 20 kilograms, a figure well below the 150 kilograms per day produced in other regions of Mexico where corn is cultivated on irrigated lands, using machinery (Parra 1989). At the same time, the monetary costs of agricultural production are, as previously noted, relatively high for the farmers of San Andrés, given low productivity and scarce available labor.

Although this cost varies according to the system of cultivation and the level of mechanization,[6] the investment of money required to produce a liter of grain averaged 25 pesos in 1985 (S= 28 pesos, n=30 families).

Since the consumer price of corn at that time was approximately 43 pesos per liter, local families realized significant savings by producing their own corn. Those savings vanish, however, when we consider the costs of family labor utilized in the production process. If we assign an opportunity cost equal to the local rural wage to each day of family labor invested in farming, the cost of a liter of corn increases by 14 pesos (S=150 pesos, n=164 parcels); thus for the period under study and in real terms, the approximate average cost of one liter of corn was 39 pesos. In other words, if we base our determination of the relative value of corn cultivation on a comparison of production costs with the cost of purchasing corn in the market, it seems incomprehensible that the people of San Andrés continue to produce corn. Why would a group of people whose economy is highly monetized and semiproletarianized, and who are highly averse to taking risks, opt to grow corn at all under these circumstances?

The answer is to be found in the method of valuation employed. The argument just presented is based on calculations which suppose that inputs and outputs (costs and benefits) of production have a value equal to their market price. The people of San Andrés have recourse to such logic, however, only when calculating the value of their surplus production. To calculate the value of production for family consumption, they use a very different system for determining personal benefits. In other words, the social valuation and the personal one only coincide in the case of surplus grain which remains after family self-sufficiency is assured.

Peasant families value their cornfields highly because they obtain many useful consumption goods from them -- the majority of which have no wider market and therefore no monetary value. When the peasants produce corn, they supply themselves with grain that is superior to that available in the local market. The damaged ears and corncobs feed their pigs and poultry; the dry stubble and tassels are virtually the only feed available for draft animals from December to May when pastureland is dry. In fact, some of the areas planted in corn are primarily intended to produce fodder.

As already discussed in other chapters of this book, the cornfield or *milpa* constitutes a very rich and complex agroecological system. Squashes, various types of beans, dry peas and chiles are grown there, along with a wide variety of other plants used as food, medicine, forage or for traditional rituals. Birds and mammals make their home in the milpa, and can be hunted; and hornets and beetles produce larvae which are collected as well. The subproducts of the milpa, some to a greater and some to a lesser extent, play a fundamental role in the peasant economy, providing an important dietary complement and thus reducing monetary outlays for animal and human consumption. The importance of these subproducts increases during the period between June and October-November, when complementary crops are abundant in the cornfields and the monetary costs of feeding the family sink to only about 50 percent of what they are the rest of the year.

The milpa is also an integrated agroecological system, in the sense that the production of each of its components depends on the others as inputs. This kind of integration can imply a very efficient use of both

6. The people of San Andrés have three systems for planting corn: in rainfed areas, where the seed is planted in the furrow and then covered using the foot (*tapapié*); on land with residual moisture, where holes are dug, the seed is planted, and a half glass of water is added; or on land which floods every year, using the "cajete" method (for a detailed description of these systems, see García Barrios, García Barrios, and Alvarez Buylla, 1988). During the 1984-1985 agricultural cycle, the cost of planting tapapie was 5,684 pesos per hectare (S=11,800 pesos, n=87 parcels), or 9.25 pesos per kilogram of corn (S=$230). On land with residual moisture, production costs were 9,980 pesos per hectare (S=$9,300, n=44 parcels), or 12.50 pesos per kilogram produced. Finally, in flooded areas, the cost was 6,398 pesos per hectare (S=$6,800, n=35 parcels) or 9 pesos per kilogram produced (S=$120). These monetary costs of production are negatively correlated -- and this explains the fact that when all three systems of cultivation are considered together, the total cost of a person/day of work increases.

labor and money. The system also lends itself to a sophisticated exploitation of the multiple productive possibilities inherent in microenvironments. The impressive number of corn varieties planted in San Andrés (8 pure and 26 mixed races), as well as the diversity of systems of cultivation developed over the centuries, allow inhabitants to tailor corn production to specific constraints in different arable areas. For example, local families can use early varieties of corn, with short growth cycles, for environments which are flooded for a part of the year, or varieties with long growth periods for areas with residual moisture. Under conditions of production in rainfed mountainous regions similar to those in San Andrés, there is no other crop which can compare to corn in its capacity to adapt to different environments, and thus to shield farmers from production risks.

Benefits like these, related to questions of provisioning and self-sufficiency, determine the high personal value rural people place on cultivating corn. The marginal benefits of this activity remain high until self-sufficiency is attained and, for the majority of the producers, compensate for high average costs. The marginal value that peasants assign to the milpa falls rapidly, however, when cultivation surpasses the scale of production which is strictly necessary for family self-sufficiency and begins to produce a marketable surplus. This is the case due to two set of factors:

(1) From the perspective of potential producers of surplus, the local economy does not contain mechanisms which confer sufficient value on surplus grain. As opposed to what happened in the period before land reform, when the economy was managed by an elite of wealthy indigenous cultivators, production of a surplus no longer provides the benefits of prestige and power which were once associated with control of the moral economy and the labor force of the community. Now, effective demand for corn on the part of members of the community is scant and unstable, and tends to be further reduced by competition from Conasupo and the ease with which the local population can gain access to stores in larger towns and cities. For both these reasons, those with the capacity to produce a surplus (about 50 percent of the community) cannot maintain the kind of local oligopoly which would be necessary to increase the value of the surplus to a remunerative level.

(2) The family itself generates the only demand for the majority of all products from the milpa, since for most of these there are no economic agents willing to undergo the risk and expense involved in attempting to establish a market. Only corn is valued in markets outside the community and can in consequence be sold, although often without any adequate recognition of differences in quality of grain. The personal valuation of such sales depends upon the value (once the risk premium has been discounted) that households assign to any net monetary income they receive. In San Andrés that income is about zero, or even negative, given the low price of grain and the very high opportunity costs of producing corn surpluses. Under these conditions, the production of surpluses is simply a waste of resources.

In such a situation, corn production by families with different quantities of resources will evolve as described in Figure 4a. Families who have insufficient monetary or labor resources cannot attain self-sufficiency even though they dedicate considerable efforts to cultivating corn. When families reach a certain level of resources, however, they can attain self-sufficiency; and at that point, production stabilizes and the proportion of resources destined to produce corn begins to decrease. The latter may be used in other income-generating activities or simply abandoned. In other words, the "corn resource trap" appears, in which the decision to produce corn is not immediately influenced by a change in resources at the disposal of a family.

All the households of San Andrés fall into one of the two categories described above; they show permanent deficits or maintain a strategy of strict self-sufficiency, only occasionally producing a small surplus. In the first case, it is not insufficient land but rather scarce family labor and an insufficient monetary income which prevent the attainment of self-sufficiency. It is nevertheless evident that these two conditions do not exhaust the theoretical possibilities of the analytical scheme under discussion. As is also shown in Figure 4a, after attaining a certain level of access to resources, resulting economies of scale can reduce average costs of corn production enough to make marketed surpluses profitable in comparison to other options.

Figure 4b illustrates the differential effect of an increase in the producer price of corn. For the majority of farmers producing at a level of self-sufficiency, a change in price, unless it is considerable, does not affect their level of production or standard of living. A price rise will bring about an increase in production and in levels of living only in the case of families which already produce a surplus for the market or in the case of families producing for self-sufficiency but able to gain access to sufficient resources to make corn profitable when compared to other income-producing options. Finally, households which habitually run a deficit respond to price increases like any other consumer; they reduce their demand for purchased corn, which in their case means increasing their own production. For this group of families, about 25 to 30 percent of the population of San Andrés, a price increase would mean a reduction in living standard. Moreover, it is probable that such a reduction would not be compensated by the limited expansion in employment opportunities created by a small increase in local surplus production, if in fact there were such an expansion when prices increased.

In conclusion, under present conditions and if no complementary measures are taken, of a kind to be analyzed below, an increase in the producer price of corn would stimulate both deficit and surplus producers to increase corn production; but their reasons for doing so would be very different and their wellbeing would be affected in opposite ways.

REDUCING COSTS AND INCREASING PRODUCTIVITY: INSTITUTIONAL BOTTLENECKS

As opposed to what occurs when corn prices increase, a reduction in production costs improves the living standard of all families, irrespective of the amount of resources they control. With a reduction of costs, families producing at a deficit can increase their production with fewer resources, and families which are self-sufficient in grain can release resources for other more profitable production options. What are the institutional factors which determine the very high local costs of corn production in San Andrés and how can those factors be modified to increase net benefits and overcome the "corn resource trap?"

From our standpoint, two problems condition all others: a) high transaction costs; b) the failure of economic institutions which should stimulate and regulate cooperation in the management of natural resources. Together, these two factors have determined the pattern of technical change and the management of natural resources within local agriculture -- and as a consequence, the unsatisfactory evolution of the productivity of labor and land.

In San Andrés, peasant households do not have relations with Banrural, nor does any other source provide them with the kind of credit they would require to increase productivity. Remittances finance the widespread rental of tractor services, necessary to offset the shortage of labor. Chemical fertilizers are too expensive to justify systematic utilization. One state-financed effort to construct a drainage system for flood-prone areas of the municipality failed because there were errors of design, as well as from lack of repair and maintenance by local people. In other words, very limited public investment has not generated the local supply of complementary resources which would be required to promote economies of scale and reduce production costs.

FIGURE 4

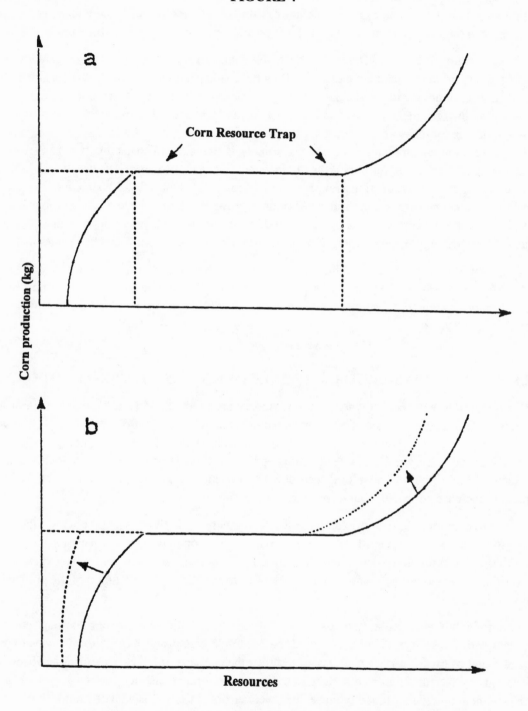

(a) Hypothetical evolution of corn production as productive resources to
peasant families vary; (b) hypothetical response as corn prices increase.

There is also a serious flaw in the cooperative response of residents when confronted with the need to manage and conserve local agricultural resources. It is evident that this lack of response has generated serious ecological problems, including erosion and flooding, as well as reduction in fertility of most arable land, all of which increase agricultural production costs. For example, in spite of the very high degree of erosion in the area and the fact that 40 percent of the humid soils of the municipality are clogged with infertile sand, the reforestation initiatives of individual producers have not been adopted by the majority of the population. Moreover, no agreements have been reached to regulate collective management of pasture land or to build terraces on communal or abandoned land.

Obviously, such weakness or absence of collective response reflects the serious institutional problems created by the loosening of community ties, the atomization of production and the growing scarcity of family labor. In the pre-reform community, collective participation was regulated by the indigenous elite. And in addition to vertical relations of power, there were horizontal relations which facilitated collective work. Relatives and friends with close personal ties (*compadres*) coordinated activities at a lower transaction cost and played a supervisory role in the collective work process. In other words, traditional systems of reciprocity and authority were the determining factors in the technology of cooperation in San Andrés. With the distribution of land and subsequent decrease in population associated with migration, these systems collapsed, provoking both a reduction in the exploitation of labor and an acute institutional crisis, and drastically increasing the costs of collective activities.

At the same time, reduction in the size of the local labor force has taken its toll on traditional agricultural technology. Traditional farming practices, which are labor intensive and require a high degree of cooperation, have deteriorated significantly or, in some cases, have been abandoned altogether. Ideally, it should be possible to hire laborers to replace family members in the fields, and thus to maintain good farming practices. But contracting hired labor requires important supervision, since traditional agriculture is artisanal in nature and the quality of work is crucial in producing a good harvest. Unsupervised workers, putting in minimum effort, produce very little in relation to the investment required to hire them. And the income of most local families is too low to permit large expenditures on labor.

CONCLUSIONS

Although the people of San Andrés participate actively in defending the "corn culture" of Mexico, then, they do so by practicing a profoundly deformed traditional agriculture in which producers lack both the innovative impulse that has characterized Mexican indigenous agriculture and the interest and ability to deal with the deterioration of the environment. Although migration provides families with additional resources, it also reduces the work force and has weakened the institutions which support agricultural production. Similar situations can be found not just in Mexico but also in the Middle and Far East, as well as in the Andean region of Colombia and Peru (Blaikie 1985).

A particular pattern of rural development has made the goal of stimulating productivity and conserving the environment unattainable for families like those in San Andrés. Developing an institutional strategy for reversing this trend requires a profound change in this pattern of development.

The establishment of policies to stimulate productivity and conservation requires, first, increasing the ability of peasant communities to compete for their own labor through developing a sustainable agriculture. This does not means attempting to find -- at whatever cost -- forms of employment and income to resolve problems of poverty. Rather it means encouraging a profitable and healthy agriculture based upon the conservation and rehabilitation of local natural resources.

An increase in the price of corn could be an effective instrument in such a process of rural development if it were implemented in conjunction with programs of investment which increased productivity and provided productive resources of a kind which ensured that an increase in corn prices would not result in a reduction of the living standard of the poorest members of the community. Detailed studies of the nature of the "corn resource trap" in different rural contexts could assist in anticipating the effects of a price increase and other economic policies on production and rural employment.

Traditional resource management systems must be carefully studied in order to find adequate ways to stimulate increased productivity across large areas of the Mexican countryside where these systems are now under severe pressure. In particular, it is incumbent on policymakers and researchers to abandon the idea that an unlimited supply of labor is available in all peasant communities. When innovations or technological adaptations are being developed, priority must in many cases be given to those that are labor saving and permit small-scale conservation of the environment.

The only viable way to ensure the conservation of natural resources in mountainous regions of rainfed agriculture is to improve the livelihood and productive potential of small-scale cultivators. This is a fact which must be understood by the entire society, if policies favorable to rural development are ever to be implemented. At the same time, democratic peasant organizations must play a leading role in creating and supporting the kinds of rural institutions required to respond to this challenge.

Chapter 7

THE ECONOMIC AND ENVIRONMENTAL CONTEXT OF CORN PROVISIONING IN ALCOZAUCA, GUERRERO

Carlos Toledo, Julia Carabias and Enrique Provencio

During the last several decades, the mountainous regions of the state of Guerrero, like the majority of all peasant areas in Mexico with subsistence economies, have suffered a rural crisis characterized, among other things, by a relative decline in corn production. The erosion of local provisioning capacity has been determined by both economic and political factors, as well as by problems of a technological and ecological nature.

Under present circumstances, there is only a limited likelihood that the situation will improve. Governmental programs for rural areas give priority to regions which have the highest potential for increasing production in the short run; and areas like the the mountains of Guerrero, which have low productive potential, are clearly marginal to these efforts. The latter thus receive very limited funds to promote production, little support from extensionists or for training, and very low levels of longer-term public investment.

Regions catalogued as areas of low potential are to be aided through special programs to counteract extreme poverty. While they provide some support for basic services, such efforts grant little attention to promoting productivity. Therefore it seems probable that integrated programs of rural development, which both stimulate production and underwrite social services, are destined to remain a pending item on the national policy agenda.

Many groups throughout the country are nevertheless working jointly with rural people to encourage new efforts at integrated resource management, as well as new forms of organization which can meet some of the most pressing livelihood needs of local families. One of the latter is to ensure a regular supply of corn at relatively stable prices; and this is the topic to be discussed below, first as it is conditioned by problems of production in agriculture and then as it is related to the nature of the regional grain market.

GENERAL CHARACTERISTICS OF THE REGION

The northeast corner of the state of Guerrero contains a mountainous region covering 8,670 square kilometers, where some 250,000 people currently live. Given its geological origins and thus its rough terrain, the region is characterized by a remarkable degree of ecological diversity. Altitude ranges from 750 to 3,100 meters above sea level and climate varies across a range from hot and dry to hot and subhumid, then to warm, semi-temperate, humid-temperate, and subhumid temperate zones. Within this setting, one finds low tropical forests, as well as oak and pine forests, and in areas with limestone there are junipers. It has been estimated that the region contains over 600 higher plant species.

There are marked differences between seasons: a rainy period between June and October, a dry cool season between November and February, and a hot dry period from March to May. In addition, rainfall varies widely throughout the region from one year to the next, and this has a significant effect on agriculture.

The municipality of Alcozauca, with an area of 550 square kilometers, lies in that part of the region between 1,300 to 2,900 meters above sea level where the slopes of the Southern Sierra Madre mountain range descend to the Balsas river valley. There are very few roads in Alcozauca, most of them in poor condition, and they are impassable during the rainy season.

In spite of its extraordinary biological and cultural wealth, the region is marked by the extreme poverty of its inhabitants and the rapid deterioration of the environment. In 1985, the government of the State of Guerrero estimated that seventy percent of the gainfully employed population of Alcozauca had an income below the prevailing minimum wage. Ninety percent of its more than 15,000 inhabitants (distributed in 21 communities) are of the Mixteco Indian group, and sixty percent of the latter speak only the Mixteco language.

Most of the land in the municipality is held within the context of the traditional indigenous community, although there have been considerable transformations in some areas as a result of the increase in small private holdings, especially around the urban center of the municipality, as well as in more general response to population growth. The latter has encouraged the founding of new communities, and thus the fragmentation of the larger and older villages.

Adherence to traditional patterns of communal land management continues in most most cases to be strong in Alcozauca; and in this respect, the situation prevailing there is markedly different from that in San Andrés Lagunas, discussed in the chapter by Raúl and Luis García Barrios. Livestock and forestry are developed on a communal basis, while agriculture is carried out on family parcels which are designated by the village council or by the agrarian authority, if it exists. Only nine of the 21 communities are legally recognized by the agrarian reform ministry of the Mexican government. The others have land titles granted in the nineteenth century, or even earlier; but these titles have not been confirmed by the designated national authorities.

The principal economic activity in all communities is subsistence farming of corn, beans, and squash. Secondary activities include small-scale goat production and the poorly paid weaving of straw hats. During the dry season, from 30 to 40 percent of the heads of family in the municipality, and throughout the mountains, are driven by lack of local opportunities to migrate on a temporary basis to the northern and central states of Sinaloa, Morelos, and Mexico, and even to the United States. There has, however, not been the massive and permanent exodus which is characteristic of areas of the Mixteca Alta of Oaxaca, discussed in the preceding chapter, nor is there the degree of social disintegration which can accompany permanent emigration.

CORN FARMING IN ALCOZAUCA

Between 3,450 and 3,600 hecatares are devoted to agriculture in Alcozauca, on which approximately 2,760 peasant families produce between 2,750 and 5,300 tons of corn, depending on the vagaries of climate and changing conditions of access to needed resources. The average household farms about 1.25 hectares, the smallest average holding of any analyzed in this book.

The heterogeneity of the environment has forced local people to diversify their farming techniques. They rely in large part on traditional technology, developed over centuries of cultivation within specific ecological niches; but they have also adopted some elements of modern technological packages --most particularly chemical fertilizers -- introduced into the region in the 1970s by SARH and Banrural.

Nine corn production systems, with an even larger number of variations, can be distinguished. Three are irrigation systems (on mountain slopes, in fertile lowlands and in partially irrigated areas); and six are adapted to dryland farming according to different lengths of the growing season, different seasons of the year, and different ways of preparing the land for cultivation. Yields vary from 500 to 1,600 kilograms per hectare in rainfed areas, but they can reach 2,000 kilograms when irrigation is available (Gonzalez et al. 1989). Only one-tenth of the agricultural land of the municipality is irrigated.

One of the factors limiting agricultural production in the mountains of Guerrero, and particularly at higher elevations like those predominating in Alcozauca, is the difficulty of finding level surfaces within the rough terrain. It is estimated that 82 percent of the area has steep slopes (above 20 degrees) and only 3 percent is level (between 5 and 20 degrees) (Obregon 1989). Therefore the majority of the holdings are on gentle to steep slopes, which creates two serious and interrelated problems. First, very shortly after land is cleared for planting, it begins to produce lower yields; and as a result producers must let these areas lie fallow to recuperate their natural fertility. Then the lack of plant cover on abandoned areas causes serious erosion -- a problem heightened by the fact that goats graze over the wild vegetation that does begin to grow during the fallow period.

PRICES AND CORN PRODUCTION IN ALCOZAUCA

As illustrated in the previous chapter, when there is an overall situation of deficitary grain production, as there is in many rural areas of Mexico, the level of the official support price for corn affects small-scale cultivators in complex ways. A systematic decrease in the producer price negates any effort to increase local production, unless farmers have simultaneous access to subsidies which lower production costs. An increase in the support price, however, also causes problems for the majority of peasant families, who are net buyers of grain.

In remote areas where poverty is endemic and conditions are similar to those in Alcozauca, the pricing dilemma is further complicated by two sets of phenomena: the lack of competition in local and regional grain markets, where there is a tendency to reduce the prices paid to small scale producers and increase the price of corn which they need to purchase; and the very marked effect that the time of year and variation in rainfall have on grain supply.

The municipality of Alcozauca is self-sufficient in grain in years when the climate is favorable, but when there are droughts or other crop damage, it runs a considerable deficit. During bad years, there is an urgent local demand for purchased grain even though the monetary resources of the inhabitants, obtained from making straw hats and seasonal migration, are very limited. Paradoxically, however, the area continues to export a small amount of corn even at such difficult times, since the majority of all producers must sell small lots in order to obtain the monetary resources necessary to satisfy other needs. Moreover, there are some farmers producing under relatively better ecological, technical, and economic conditions who systematically sell small quantities outside the region.

Given the very limited development of the official grain marketing infrastructure in the region,[1] most trade (including both local retail services and the purchase of corn from peasant holdings) is handled by private owners of small and medium sized stores located in communities of between 500 and 1,500 inhabitants. The latter maintain relations with wholesalers in the regional market center of Talpa, who supply the merchants of Alcozauca with key retail commodities like soft drinks and beer. Tlapa wholesalers also constitute the

---

1. Of about 500 communities in the mountains of Guerrero, only 87 have a retail Conasupo store; and the Ejido Marketing Program known as PACE has never operated there.

principal link connecting the grain market of Alcozauca, and surrounding municipalities, with consumers in the nearby state of Puebla, where a drier climate creates high demand for purchased corn.

As shown in Table 1, there is a significant difference between corn prices in the municipal center of Alcozauca and in the Tlapa market; and this margin permits intermediaries to make considerable profits both in times of scarcity and in good agricultural years.

Table 1

Corn Prices in Alcozauca and Tlapa, Guerrero, and Transport Costs between Alcozauca and Tlapa (current pesos/kilogram)

Year	Support Price	Corn Price Alcozauca	Corn Price Tlapa	Transport Costs
1987	120-140	250-300	120-140	60
1989	370	250-300	500-550	130

NB: Transport costs for vehicle owners are in fact less than the figures noted here, which assume that transport is hired.

1988 was a relatively good year in terms of rainfall in the Alcozauca region, while in Puebla a drought affected the harvest and generated a high demand for corn. Therefore during July and August 1989, when corn was scarcest, the price on the local market of Alcozauca ranged from 250 to 300 pesos per kilogram, well below the support price (370 pesos per kilogram). In Tlapa, on the other hand, prices fluctuated between 500 and 550 pesos per kilogram, as wholesalers bought grain to send to Puebla.

During years of poor harvests in Alcozauca, the situation is reversed. 1986 was marked by little rainfall and thus corn was very scarce in 1987. Local prices in Alcozauca rose notably during the first half of the year, reaching 250-300 pesos per kilogram while the support price at the time was 120 to 140 pesos per kilogram. The latter prices were in effect in Tlapa, since Conasupo imported large volumes of cereals into the region.

To deal with the provisioning crisis which arose in Alcozauca during 1987, the state government provided a loan of ten million pesos at an annual rate of interest of 20 percent, channeled through the Agricultural Promotion Fund, which permitted the town council to set up a Corn Bank. Some 200 tons of grain were brought into Alcozauca by the bank and sold at 125 to 175 pesos per kilogram. These prices were sufficient for covering transportation costs, repaying the entire loan, including interest, and even making a modest profit for the newly established organization.

The Corn Bank was well managed by the municipal council, a representative body made up of elected municipal commissioners, indigenous representatives and other community delegates. The experience demonstrated that public participation in the provisioning process could constitute a viable alternative to private speculation. Unfortunately, however, the policies of the state Agricultural Promotion Fund were modified; and in spite of fact that the loan had been entirely repaid on time, funding for the program was not renewed. A permanent bank could have effectively resolved the serious supply problems which inevitably appear during bad agricultural years, while providing an advantageous marketing outlet for local corn when harvests are relatively good.

In sum, this brief analysis of variation in corn prices demonstrates the high level of dependence of local families on oligopolistic grain markets. Even during a period when grain was scarce in neighboring regions, and prices therefore relatively high on the private market, producers in Alcozauca who sold some corn were paid 20 to 30 percent less than the official support price. And in a poor agricultural year, when there was a serious deficit of grain for local consumption, the households of Alcozauca would have had to pay double the official price to supply their needs if it had not been for the work of the Corn Bank. The importance of efforts to increase the presence of public institutions, and to support the work of other organizations which have the capacity to diminish the vulnerability of a poor and isolated population, is obvious.

SUPPORT PRICES, CREDIT AND THE ECONOMICS OF CORN PRODUCTION

Although most of the corn produced in Alcozauca is consumed by local households without ever entering the market, and thus is never formally valued in monetary terms, both the official support price and regional prices influenced by the former constitute basic indicators of the level of advantage or disadvantage assigned to rural people within regional and national economies. The support price represents (though hypothetically) the value that is given to their principal product, and therefore to their labor.

For many years, that value has been exceedingly low. Table 2 shows that if a price (equivalent to the local rural minimum wage) is assigned to the labor expended in corn cultivation, which is almost always provided by families themselves, income obtained from the crop (valuing total production at the support price) exceeds production cost in only one of the four years under consideration -- and then only when yield per hectare was unusually high. Given this situation, corn cultivation continues to be carried out in part because there are no employment alternatives offering higher income which can absorb the labor force, and in part because if we subtract the cost of family labor which is not in fact remunerated, it is less expensive to grow corn than to buy it. In addition, in Alcozauca as in many other villages throughout Mexico, the life of the community rests on cultivating corn, and thus the grain has a non-monetary value which makes it worthwhile to defend corn production even in a context of economic disadvantage.

At first glance it appears illogical to talk about credit in a context of economic deficit like the one just analyzed. Nevertheless, farming families in areas like Alcozauca must have access to credit in order to be able to purchase fertilizers for their depleted soils and to defray household expenditures until harvest time. Although the local credit system was once almost entirely based on usury, this is no longer the case. Both the entry of official institutions and seasonal migration have provided alternative sources of financing to those traditionally offered by intermediaries and local shopkeepers.

The credit program implemented by Banrural in Alcozauca from the early 1980s onward, although providing a useful counterweight to local moneylenders, proved unable to meet the community's needs. Poor management of the program was reflected in increasing debt, as many loans went unpaid year after year. A number of factors contributed to the failure of the endeavor, including complicated requirements to qualify for a loan, constant increases in the cost of credit, the inefficiency of the official insurance program, and problems related to delivering fertilizers at appropriate times, among others.

Table 2

**Economic Aspects of Corn Production
in the Mountains of Guerrero, 1985-1988
(in current pesos per hectare)**

Item	1985	1986	1987	1988
Loan debt[a]	11,000	15,000	31,700	180,000
Interest rate (%)	10	30	40	58
Fertilizer price[b]	10,825	12,000	24,400	93,604
Daily minimium wage	861	1,611	3,542	6,638
Local daily wage	600	1,500	3,000	5,000
Total costs[c]	83,000	195,000	391,700	780,000
Estimated yield (kg)	1,600	900	1,250	1,400
Support price[d]	53,500	96,000	245,000	370,000
Gross income	85,600	86,400	306,250	518,000

Indices:

	1985	1986	1987	1988
Income/cost with actual yields	1.03	0.44	0.78	0.66
Income/cost with high yields	1.03	0.79	1.00	0.76
Income/cost with low yields	0.58	0.44	0.56	0.43
Support price/cost	0.64	0.49	0.63	0.47
Productivity[e]	13.33	7.50	10.42	11.67

(a) The only collateral required by this credit program was the producer's promise to repay the loan.
(b) For the dosage 80-40-00.
(c) 120 work days at the prevailing local wage, plus the cost of credit.
(d) Pesos per ton for the spring-summer corn cycle.
(e) Yield (in kilograms) divided by number of work days.

Sources: González et al. (1989); Conasupo; interviews and direct observation.

NB: Since systems of cultivation in the region are extremely heterogeneous, adapting both to environmental variation and to the specific characteristics of farming families, an exercise like this one can only be based on a hypothetical average case. The figures provided here refer to dryland plow agriculture.

In 1984, the state government attempted to provide an alternative to Banrural through initiating a new credit program which eliminated many of the steps formerly required to obtain a loan. The new system, known as _crédito a la palabra_, was based on trusting the producers and their organizations to repay their debts. It initially offered subsidized interest rates and did not require paying an agricultural insurance premium, since it was argued that the inefficiency of the insurance company made any such payment economically indefensible. The high proportion of repayment within this program during its first year of operation contrasted markedly with the performance of the Banrural program in other areas of the state, and for the moment seemed to support the conclusion that the new arrangement could be highly effective.

The following year the program was extended and, responding to a request from the municipal government of Alcozauca, began to operate in that region. Some of the residents of the municipality who wanted to join the new credit program began to develop a union of ejidos and indigenous communities which would eventually be legally empowered to manage their credit operations. Until legal standing for the new organization could be obtained, they received financing through the intermediation of the municipal government itself. Meanwhile, another group of more or less the same size, affiliated with the Independent Peasant Confederation (CCI), continued to receive Banrural credit.

During 1985, corn farmers working within the framework of the new program incurred debts which were on average 25 percent below those registered with Banrural, because the former obtained a lower interest rate and did not pay an insurance premium. Weather conditions were good that year and almost 95 percent of all loans made within the experimental program were repaid. Average yields were about 1.6 tons per hectare in that year, and the income/cost index was just slightly above unity (see Table 2).

Nevertheless the program began to disintegrate after 1985 as uninsured borrowers were hit with a series of bad agricultural years, and also as the components of family income were further affected by recession and adjustment. Very low corn prices were one element in this equation, as were rising costs of inputs. Figure 1 shows the behavior of three indices of income/cost and of support price/cost for the system under analysis. The first of the three indices is calculated utilizing estimated yields for each year, which were of course influenced by climate. The other two indices are calculated using constant yields, one when yields were highest (1985) and one when yields were lowest (1986). By eliminating the effect of variation in the weather, the latter indices illustrate the impact of economic factors; and the same is true for the support price/cost index.

As is immediately evident in the graph, the current system of corn production in Alcozauca operates in chronic economic deficit: the area covered by the index of constant yields, within which the index of real yields oscillates, is below one in all years. The survival of such a system can only be explained by the exploitation of family labor and does not allow for any possibility of commercial production. Furthermore, on balance, conditions worsened during the four year period. The fall of the income/cost index during the last year (1988) was the result of a marked increase in the price of fertilizers and very high interest rates, neither of which was compensated for by an improvement in the support price.

Since the new credit program did not have an insurance component, it was of course particularly vulnerable to the impact of bad weather. In 1986, a serious drought reduced yields sufficiently to bring on a loan repayment crisis, to which the Agricultural Promotion Fund of the state government responded by restructuring debts. In Alcozauca, SARH issued a decree establishing a grace period of two years, during which neither interest nor late payment charges were levied. Given the rate of inflation at that time, such a policy in fact represented a cancellation of the debt.

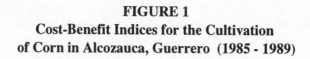

FIGURE 1
Cost-Benefit Indices for the Cultivation
of Corn in Alcozauca, Guerrero (1985 - 1989)

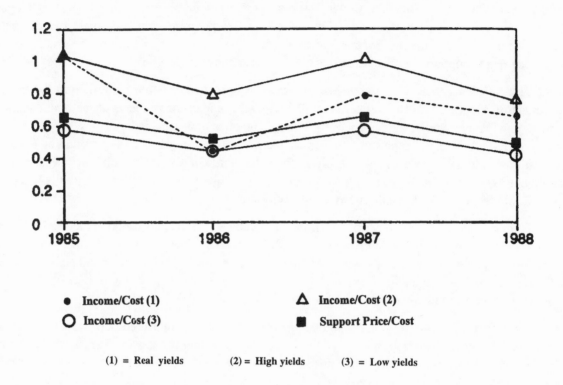

In succeeding years, policies of the experimental credit program began gradually to approximate those of Banrural. Interest rates increased significantly and conditions which had to be met to qualify for credit became stricter. During 1987 drought again reduced yields; and although the SARH emited a new decree, it was not recognized by the state Agricultural Promotion Fund, which took a tougher stance toward the borrowers. After a significant delay, it was possible to renegotiate both the outstanding debt and terms of credit for the following year, but under very unfavorable conditions for the producers. In addition to setting high interest rates, the agreement conditioned new loans to the purchase of insurance from ANAGSA.

In 1988, although the rains began late, harvests were generally good. Nevertheless, the producers of Alcozauca were disillusioned with the credit program and disheartened by its costs. They decided to default on their loans so that they could use their money to purchase fertilizers -- a strategy that was 40 percent less expensive than paying off their loans. As a result, 1988 was the last year in which this program operated in the municipality.

A number of conclusions can be drawn from this experience. In the first place, it should be noted that many of the innovations introduced as part of the experimental credit initiative were positive; but the lack of an alternative insurance strategy constituted a fundamental flaw. After the 1986 drought, municipal officials and local producers presented a proposal to the state government to create a mutual self-insurance program which could transcend the deficiencies of ANAGSA; but their proposal was not acted upon by the authorities. It is possible that a plan of this type, even if highly subsidized, might have resulted in considerably smaller losses than those actually incurred.

Second, it is obvious that even within subsistence agriculture, such as that practiced in Alcozauca, national policies which determine the cost of fertilizers, the support price, and interest rates have an impact on local livelihood. The level of farm and off-farm wages also affects the provisioning capacity of these families, since loans to purchase fertilizer are not repaid with profits from the sale of corn (which is sold in very small lots, if at all), but with remittances from migrant workers.

Finally, it is clear that a long term solution to the dilemma faced by the corn producers of Alcozauca will not be found in a simple increase in the support price of grain nor in simple efforts to expand the use of chemical fertilizers, subsidized or unsubsidized. In a region with a production deficit, increasing the cost of grain without complementary measures which will lead to a significant improvement in average yields simply extracts scarce income from consumers.

Similarly, although experimental results show that an adequate use of fertilizers could increase production in the short run, intensifying cultivation through fertilization over the longer run implies serious hazards. Strategies which rely too heavily on chemical fertilizers eventually encourage soil depletion and contribute to the further deterioration of the environment.

As previously noted, the majority of the agricultural systems in Alcozauca allow the soil to lie fallow in order to recover its fertility; but when fertilizers are applied, land can be cultivated even after its natural fertility is exhausted. Soils are overutilized and then abandoned in worse condition than before, since fertilizers increase the availability of nutrients but do not improve other aspects of fertility, such as the structure and content of organic matter in the soil. Moreover, prolonged use of fertilizers intensifies erosion. Eventually the use of chemical fertilizer creates an addiction: it has to be applied in larger quantities and, since it modifies the conditions in which seeds are selected, local corn varieties adapt to the new input and do not produce well without it.

For these reasons, the introduction of fertilizers must be accompanied by other measures, including soil conservation and crop diversification, which contribute to improving all aspects of soil fertility; just as higher support prices for corn must be accompanied by a range of efforts to improve the economic viability of agriculture.

INTEGRATED RESOURCE MANAGEMENT: AN APPROACH FOR DEALING WITH POVERTY AND ENVIRONMENTAL DETERIORATION

A policy of increasing prices to corn producers like those in Alcozauca could become a powerful instrument of rural development only if it were part of a set of activities encompassing the entire chain of production in an integrated manner: developing appropriate agricultural technologies, respecting environmental conditions in order to avoid depleting natural resources, and introducing mechanisms of crop finance, insurance, marketing and grain provisioning to support the overall effort.

The program of applied research in integrated natural resource management of the National University (UNAM) is attempting to build such strategies in a way which permits them to be adopted by peasant organizations and institutions, and thus to influence rural development policies. After studying the natural resource endowment of Alcozauca, and the way those resources are being used, and after experimenting with ways to improve agricultural practices and repair environmental damage, an action package has been designed and implemented on a pilot basis to increase and diversify production, create an infrastructure for soil and water conservation, and restore depleted areas. The activities undertaken are the following:

1. To increase productivity: improve the use of present farming inputs and incorporate new inputs; rotate and diversify traditional crops; incorporate new commercial crops; establish family gardens; and construct simple aquaculture tanks.

2. To conserve soil and water: construct consecutive terraces, small dams to store water, and small-scale irrigation projects; using plants as barriers, protect the course of rivers.

3. To restore the environment: reforest with useful native species.

In addition to encouraging a more sustainable pattern of land use, these activities have the potential for increasing yields significantly. In fact, productivity has already improved on holdings where the package of recommendations (including modifications in dosage and type of fertilizers and pesticides utilized, and changes in plant density) has been applied. Table 3 summarizes the difference between present yields and those which are feasible under the new regime. Table 4 illustrates the way the resulting increase in corn production alters the balance between consumption needs and availablity of grain in both good and bad agricultural years. Corn production could be manifestly better than it is at present, could cover local provisioning requirements and usually allow for a surplus to be marketed. In bad years, a small amount of corn would have to be imported.

Such an alternative model requires a sound and self-sustaining financial system which can promote production. This becomes feasible if there is a strategy which both improves the price paid for corn and assures the complementary production of other crops with a high market value. At the same time, such measures must be accompanied by a program of ecological improvement supported by well-justified and efficiently utilized subsidies. Since local labor would be employed in these projects, an immediate improvement in local standards of living could be encouraged. A strategy of this kind would not imply an onerous outlay: on average the required expenditure on infrastructure can be put at 3.5 million (1991) pesos per hectare, or roughly 1,150 US dollars. Governments across the northern hemisphere have invested a great deal more than that in protecting the livelihood of small farmers and reversing processes of severe environmental degradation.

The alternative model must also encourage the creation of more stable, less oligopolistic provisioning structures. Here the experience of communities across the mountain divide of Guerrero, toward the coast, is extremely instructive. Armando Bartra examines this aspect of integrated rural development in the following chapter.

Table 3

Present and Potential Yields of Corn in Alcozauca
(tons per hectare)

System	Area	Actual Year		Potential Year	
		good	bad	good	bad
Irrigated	300	2.00	2.00	3.00	3.00
Dryland plow	2,750	1.60	0.70	2.50	1.30
Winter	450	0.80	0.50	1.90	1.20
Average yield		1.47	1.07	2.47	1.83

Source: González et al. (1989)

Table 4

Provisioning Requirements Compared to Present and
Potential Levels of Corn Production in
Alcozauca, Guerrero (in tons)

System	Actual Year		Potential Year	
	good	bad	good	bad
Production	5,360	2,750	8,630	5,015
Needs[a]	5,304	5,304	5,304	5,304
Difference	56	(2,554)	3,326	(289)

(a) Average consumption requirement per family times number of households in Alcozauca(1990). Family provisioning requirements were estimated taking into consideration present dietary patterns (Casa and Viveros 1987), as well as need for forage and seeds. This gives a figure of approximately 1.6 tons per family per year.

Chapter 8

ON SUBSIDIES AND SELF-MANAGEMENT: LESSONS FROM PROVISIONING EXPERIMENTS ON THE GUERRERO COAST

Armando Bartra

Guerrero is one of the poorest states in Mexico, and its rural areas -- with their precarious small-scale farming, peasant communities and entrenched political bosses -- are among the most depressed. The southern Sierra Madre mountain range sets natural boundaries between an inland region, running from the mountains to the Balsas River basin, which contains the municipality of Alcozauca, discussed by Toledo, Carabias and Provencio in the preceding chapter, and a coastal region running from the mountains toward the sea. The latter is known to the northwest of Acapulco as the Costa Grande, and to the southeast as the Costa Chica.

The rural provisioning experiments to be analysed here took place in these two coastal areas -- subregions with similarities and differences which are useful for comparative analysis. The first similarity is simply an institutional one: in both cases, organized provisioning efforts developed within the framework of the Diconsa program, and the supply system has therefore been structured around a regional warehouse, supplied by Diconsa and distributing to dozens of community stores. On the Costa Chica, the warehouse is located in Ometepec and is the hub of a network of 66 stores that extend throughout the municipalities of Azoyú, Cuajinicuilapa, Igualapa, Ometepec, Xochistlahuaca and Tlacoachistlahuaca. On the Costa Grande, the warehouse is located in Alcholoa, just a few kilometers from the municipality of Atoyac de Alvarez. It supplies 50 stores, and its sphere of influence extends from Atoyac to the neighboring areas of Benito Juárez, Coyuca de Benítez, and Tecpan de Galeana.

The two zones have similar climates, hot and sub humid, and share a rugged terrain: steep slopes meet a narrow coastal strip, so that only about 10 percent of the land is level and 70 percent is such rough terrain that cultivation is difficult. In the aftermath of a late agrarian reform, implemented at the end of the 1930s, most land in both subregions is held in ejidos, fragmented into small holdings. Corn is the crop most widely cultivated, using a digging stick or a team of animals and a plow. Farm machinery is rarely utilized.

Within this traditional agrarian setting, some specifically market-oriented activities have developed. Although both areas produce copra -- a crop which can be found along the entire coast of Guerrero -- each is distinguished by reliance on a different combination of marketable goods. Cattle are the principal source of income on the Costa Chica, although only the well-to-do can engage in livestock raising, and corn production is the most widespread moneymaking activity for smallholders. On the Costa Grande, in contrast, coffee growing is the principal commercial activity for both small and large landholders, followed by a far less important dedication to cattle raising. The fortunes of the rich on the Costa Grande have been amassed by producing, processing and marketing coffee, while the best way to become rich on the Costa Chica is to buy future corn harvests of small producers at bargain prices or to undertake extensive cattle production.

These contrasts can be further refined. In the six municipalities of the Costa Chica, approximately 50,000 hectares of corn are cultivated with yields of about one and a half tons per hectare and a total production of almost 80,000 tons -- in principle, enough to meet the consumption needs of the 130,000 inhabitants of the region. In the four municipalities of the Costa Grande, the same area of corn is cultivated; but yields are lower and the average of 60,000 tons of grain harvested annually is insufficient to satisfy the consumption requirements of some 200,000 inhabitants.

In summary, while the system of rural stores of the Costa Chica, centered on Ometepec, can be said to operate in an area which is potentially self-sufficient in corn and may even produce a surplus, the subregion serviced by the Alcholoa warehouse is clearly deficitary. Such a generalization is, however, of only modest use in understanding local provisioning problems, since marked local differences exist within each region.

For example, to affirm that the six municipalities of the Costa Chica are self-sufficient in corn is to take a simple arithmetic approach which omits some crucial information. In fact, more than half the local harvest is shipped out of the region between October and December, to be replaced between April and September by a large quantity of imported yellow corn. These significant and perhaps unnecessary extra-regional flows are related to the fact that although corn is a basic element in the diet of almost all the inhabitants, only six out of every ten families actually produce it; and to the further fact that the region lacks the kind of physical infrastructure, as well as the commercial and financial mechanisms, which would be required to organize a more or less direct exchange between the group of corn farmers who harvest much more than they consume (some 60 percent of all corn producers), on the one hand, and local families who must buy a part of their grain supply on the other.

Looking still more closely, it is apparent that the approximately 20,000 producers of corn on the Costa Chica are divided into two groups. One is to be found at high altitudes, working parcels on steep slopes with slash and burn techniques and obtaining yields insufficient to meet the needs of their families. The other group farms relatively flat lands with deep soils which are situated at mid- and low altitudes and permit much higher yields. With irrigation or the use of residual moisture, corn can be harvested twice a year on such land. Therefore it is the latter group which can produce a genuine surplus and should in principle be considered a net seller of grain. But even that statement is a simplification. Families frequently incur debts during the growing season and must sell a part of their harvest to repay them. In consequence, they sell more of their crop than they would like, even though they know that afterwards they will pay higher prices to buy the grain they need for home consumption.

As far as the four municipalities of the Costa Grande are concerned, one can put forward the general assertion that the shortfall of corn is of the same order as the volume of the harvest. But this obscures the fact that Coyuca produces a surplus, while communities along the mountain peaks, as well as those in the coffee producing area of Atoyac and in the cattle-raising area of Tecpan, produce little or no corn.

All of this subregional variation means that even within an area which is virtually self-sufficient in corn, like the Costa Chica, there is localized and sometimes severe scarcity for four to five months each year, and for an even longer period in certain high altitude zones. On the other hand, in the Costa Grande, where there is an overall deficit, it is possible to find areas which have large surpluses. Contrary to what general statistics show, then, the problem in the Costa Chica is not simply to find a buyer nor is the problem of the Costa Grande to find a seller: in spite of their different socioeconomic settings, both regional marketing systems confront the same task of articulating local supply and demand, and promoting regional self-sufficiency insofar as it is technically and economically possible by facilitating more or less direct dealings between producers and consumers.

But to translate such a provisioning problem into a challenge, the question must be taken up and confronted in concrete ways by local people. Thus it is necessary to look for a moment at the evolution of popular organizations in the two regions.

The origin of provisioning networks in both the Costa Chica and the Costa Grande can be traced to the late 1970s, when Conasupo-Coplamar initiated a program which not only provided a concrete service but also created an organizational structure for popular participation: supervision of local stores was entrusted to village committees, and a regional consultative group made up of one elected representative from each community had the right to request and receive information concerning the functioning of the central warehouse. Although the intention of this effort was laudable, its legacy has all too often been organizations which exist only on paper. When effective participation on the part of local beneficiaries is lacking, management rests with those in charge of the stores and the warehouses, and in the final analysis in the hands of the state and federal bureaucracy of Diconsa, the department of Conasupo which took over the program when Coplamar was disbanded in 1983.

Such was originally the case on the Costa Chica, following inauguration of the program in 1979. The lack of community participation in fact led to corruption in the administration of both the local stores and the warehouse, and eventually created food shortages and financial deficits. The situation changed, however, after 1985, when the local committees and the Council were renewed at the initiative of members of the Regional Union of Ejidos for Production and Marketing on the Costa Chica (URECCH).

Founded in 1981 by the Regional Coordinating Center of the National Indigenous Institute, the URECCH was another organization which existed only on paper until a group of bee keepers revived it in 1984 by designing a series of regional development projects, including one to reactivate the moribund community provisioning system. At first the Union played an adversarial role within the local provisioning committees and the regional Council; but by 1985, it began to shift toward a more open dialogue with Diconsa, making demands on the system but showing greater willingness to share responsibility. By 1987, organized consumers defined the direction management would take within the provisioning program of the Costa Chica; they chose administrative staff, established direct contact with suppliers other than Conasupo, and promoted unorthodox programs like the Corn Bank, which sought to reconcile the interests of producers and consumers in a system of direct exchange which eliminated the need for intermediaries.

It should be stressed that democratic reform of the supply system on the Costa Chica was not the work of rural consumers qua consumers, in isolation, but formed part of a larger effort on the part of URECCH to assure adequate provisioning of basic goods through rethinking all aspects of regional production and marketing. In this sense, the effort to ensure local control over community stores and over the warehouse in Ometepec was simply one episode in a wider battle waged by rural people to take control of their economic and social destiny.

The central role that wide-spectrum regional peasant organizations can play in the structuring of self-managed provisioning systems is even more evident in the case of the Costa Grande, where the Diconsa program was first introduced in response to mobilization by small-scale coffee producers belonging to the Union of Ejidos Alfredo V. Bonfil.

Although the Alcholoa wholesale warehouse and surrounding network of retail stores are more recent than those on the Costa Chica, they in fact have longer experience with democratic self-management. Since their initiation in 1983, the village councils and regional committee of the Costa Grande have been engaged in an authentic dialogue with Diconsa concerning how best to make use of scarce resources during a period of austerity, increasing budgetary restrictions and a continual battle to obtain basic supplies. Beginning in 1986, their goal became that of introducing complete self-managment and obtaining legal ownership of retail and wholesale operations.

The conditions for this transformation were established over the course of the coming two years. By 1988, the communities had completed repayment of all capital previously loaned by Diconsa to the retail stores; and the wholesale warehouse, whose administration was now closely linked to the users' organization, was financially solvent for the second year in a row. In November 1988, Diconsa transferred the Alcholoa installations to the regional council and the United Coffee Producers of the Costa Grande; and from then on, these organizations have had the sole responsibility for running the community provisioning system of the region.

THIRTEEN LESSONS ON SELF-MANAGED RURAL PROVISIONING

There is no doubt that given certain organizational conditions, local cooperative management of this kind is not only possible but necessary. It forms part of a more general process in which regional peasant organizations formulate projects of integrated rural development, and in which civil society replaces official institutions as the center of efforts to improve levels of living in rural areas. The transition toward locally managed provisioning systems nevertheless implies confronting a series of difficulties inherent in rural provisioning. Some of these are of course of a largely local nature and depend on the peculiarities of the region in question. But even though the process of change is disorderly and diverse, there are common problems which should be defined and discussed, and lessons to be extracted. The first and most general of these has to do with the nature of rural markets and the role of the state within them.

LESSON 1. *Self-management and subsidies are not incompatible, nor is self-management a substitute for governmental support.*

There is at present an underlying supposition within the government that the devolution of managerial responsibility to groups of organized citizens in the countryside can be equated with privatization: in this interpretation, the state is involved in turning over its enterprises in rural areas to the private sector. Therefore a condition for transferring state functions and enterprises to rural people is that the enterprises in question show themselves capable of operating profitably, so that future services can be rendered by local organizations without requiring subsidies.

This is, however, an erroneous approach. The task at hand is not to eliminate the role of the public sector in rural provisioning, but to redefine it. Although old fashioned paternalism is increasingly anachronistic, compensatory and redistributive programs continue to be indispensable. The provisioning of low-income rural families is not a money- making operation; and local self-management of businesses with high costs and low margins cannot be equated with private businesses. In fact, efforts like those just described on the Costa Grande must soon come up against the problem of how to reconcile provision of a much-needed service with attempting to balance the books.

Rural supply systems cover the areas of the country which have the highest marketing costs, they serve the poorest of the poor, and they are expected not only regulate prices in regional and local markets, but in many cases to operate where private commerce is virtually nonexistent. Thus social enterprises are assigned to carry out tasks which to commercial capital seem unprofitable and which are in the best of cases performed precariously by small merchants through applying very high margins to sales. In fact, one could say that the function of the peasant supply systems is to compensate for forces within the market which ensure that the part of the population with the lowest income must pay the highest price for consumer goods. In such a context, it is illogical to require that local provisioning networks be oriented by the rationale of the market, when their task is precisely to counteract the natural tendencies of the latter.

Participatory and democratic management can control excessive spending, motivate people to provide voluntary services and ensure a more rational deployment of underutilized resources. It cannot, however, compensate for certain basic comparative disadvantages nor can it make subsidies unnecessary. To be viable, rural supply systems presuppose preferential financial and commercial treatment on the part of the government -- not to cover up inefficiency, but rather to facilitate, in the most effective way possible, the redistributive and compensatory functions of the government.

Thus the gradual assumption by rural organizations of responsibility for managing provisioning networks cannot imply surrendering rights to obtain subsidized basic products. Furthermore, it is important to consider whether such programs can operate in many areas without access to subsidies which go beyond the maintenance of low prices on consumers goods. A subsidy which is transferred to the consumer cannot cover the costs of providing necessary but unprofitable services, or establish a basis for capital accumulation.

In sum, promoting self-management does not eliminate the need to provide subsidies, nor should the redistributive function of state-run programs be curtailed as local people organize to assume a greater role in regional supply systems.

LESSON 2. *Real control over provisioning is more important than formal autonomy.*

When the experiences of the Costa Grande and the Costa Chica are compared, it is clear that greater advances in self-management have been made in the former than in the latter, both in formal and in real terms. But the difference in degree of local control and participation is due less to the fact that the installations of Diconsa were transferred to organized citizens on the Costa Grande than to the effect of mobilization on public awareness. As we will see, formal transfer of ownership has not modified the internal functioning of the system in any qualitative way. While it is true that new challenges and new opportunities have surfaced, post-transfer tensions are similar to those of the previous phase.

Moreover, it has at times been useful to renounce certain aspects of formal autonomy in order to benefit from association with the Diconsa system. Thus, paradoxically, while groups which have not asserted their independence from Diconsa often engage in efforts to promote direct purchases from suppliers, the provisioning system of the Costa Grande, now free to purchase on its own, is considering the advantages of triangulating purchases through Diconsa, in order to obtain more favorable prices and conditions of payment.

In sum, formal autonomy is less important than real control over provisioning. In the case of the Costa Chica, it has been possible to improve retail services, and to enlarge the sphere of participation and initiative of organized consumers, without a change in ownership. It seems clear that a step toward formal independence which precedes organizational maturity may actually lead to setbacks.

LESSON 3. *It is difficult to strike a balance between the need for specialization and the need for integration within multipurpose organizations.*

Participatory provisioning systems tend to be associated with broader, multipurpose organizations operating at the regional level, in some cases because the former were first established at the initiative of the latter and in others because the mobilization of consumers promotes further efforts in the field of collective action.

On both the Costa Chica and the Costa Grande, the councils which supervise and monitor provisioning activities of regional warehouses are closely related to a more comprehensive regional union or coalition of ejidos. Thus they are enmeshed in a double strand of relations: a hierarchical provisioning network which runs from local stores through warehouses to the national offices of Diconsa; and a crosscutting regional network of organizations involved in promoting various productive activities, facilitating credit and the sale of crops.

In such a situation, the dynamics of provisioning -- even though it has its own logic -- cannot be separated from broader organizational processes.

The number of associations operating at the local level can be large. In the case of the Costa Grande, for example, rural stores, now run entirely by consumers themselves, coexist with a wide variety of other organizations: there are collective work groups of local corn and coffee producers, of beekeepers and of women; credit committees; health committees; as well as Rural Provisioning and Marketing Committees (CRAC). There are also different second-level entities, including not only the Administrative Council of the Integrated Regional Marketing System, but also the United Coffee Growers Society of the Costa Grande, the Credit Union, the Legal Services Office and others.

Although such diversity reflects an organized response to real needs and provides new options for meeting those needs, it also creates a risk of dispersion and fragmentation within local communities. Multiple first- and second-level groups are not usually compartmentalized; in fact the various areas of regional organization are ultimately integrated under a single leadership, and community groups cooperate relatively closely with each other. Nevertheless, the multiplication of local organizations is a problem, since it frequently leads to duplication of effort and places a considerable burden on the time and resources of community activists.

The division of labor can also be illogical. In the provisioning sphere, for example, and continuing with the example of the Costa Grande, it does not make sense for the local CRACs to be made up predominantly of men, when it is obvious that problems of domestic consumption fall within the traditional domain of women; nor is it logical for the CRACs to be operating independently of collective work groups for women, and of health groups in which women also constitute the majority.

This is a problem of compartmentalization which was created because associative forms of provisioning were originally generated from above. First Conasupo-Coplamar and then Diconsa envisioned their clientele as a network of consumers, isolated conceptually and practically from other aspects of rural life. The problem has been compounded by a real need for specialization: provisioning services require particular organizational forms, like stores and warehouses, as well as technical, administrative and accounting support from second-level organizations which must also provide specialized services.

Multi-purpose regional organizations integrate the wide range of community groups administratively and promote coordination. But a union or coalition of ejidos must be more than the sum of its grassroots groups and secondary level apparatus. Although specialization and division of labor is inevitable at higher levels of the system, at the community level it is irrational to promote new groups, especially when such dispersion is initiated from above and does not necessarily respond to the needs of grassroots organizations.

The community, like the rural family, has a noteworthy capacity for integration; and despite internal cleavages of numerous kinds, both institutions can provide a strong counterbalance to divisive tendencies generated within the larger society. For a peasant family, producing, buying, selling, consuming food or obtaining credit are all facets of a single search for a better life. Regional organizations must build on this unity of purpose, without ignoring the requirements for specialization which are part of survival in the modern world.

LESSON 4. *Although supportive interaction between rural provisioning programs and other rural development efforts is essential, it creates accounting difficulties and requires careful management of funds.*

The chances of success of rural provisioning programs are greatly improved if they form part of broader efforts to develop regional and local economies. The creation of greater management capacity and the promotion of democratic participation, as well as the generation of new sources of local income, depend not only upon collective efforts in the field of provisioning but also upon efforts of other kinds. Therefore it is not surprising that regional supply systems tend to establish fairly close operational links with other programs of support for rural livelihood.

In the cases which concern us here, regional networks of rural stores play a role in parallel efforts to develop marketing structures for local corn. They support coffee production through providing local coffee growers with the basket of basic products which the latter make available to hired laborers at harvest time. Their infrastructure of transport and storage facilitates the sale of agricultural inputs within other programs. From an organizational point of view, this suggests a predisposition toward integration and concerted support on different livelihood fronts; and from an economic vantage point, it makes possible a more efficient and intensive use of resources and implies potentially significant economies of scale. But seen strictly in financial terms, such mutual support conceals economic transfers among different enterprises, and these flows are not always adequately captured in accounting terms.

The horizontal and vertical integration of programs and enterprises managed by multipurpose regional organizations requires sophisticated programming. Precisely because integration among programs is close and systematic in the two regions under consideration, and especially in the Costa Grande, it is particularly easy to see the risks involved. The first of these is a lack of financial and accounting transparency, since the administration of each program and enterprise is in itself a complex task, and pinpointing visible or invisible transfers is even more difficult. It would seem that the solution to this problem entails design of an overall economic strategy, within which separate records could be kept for each program, without sacrificing the financial autonomy of any of the latter.

Another hazard grows out of the possibility that failures on one economic front could have very harmful secondary effects. When, in an attempt to resolve a critical situation, all available resources are channeled to the program in jeopardy, there is the risk that the entire structure of economic activity will be undermined; and thus a problem which could have been isolated and dealt with separately may be responsible for destroying a regional development effort.

Here it is important to note that the domestic economy of the peasantry is oriented more toward ensuring stability over the medium and long term than toward optimizing immediate returns. In this sense, the survival strategy of rural families can serve as a lesson to regional organizations, which should give priority to developing a diversified but integrated economy, and protecting it from sudden shocks.

LESSON 5. *Continuous work on provisioning can counterbalance the marked seasonality of other activities in the countryside.*

Because the consumption of food staples is a daily activity, provisioning requires more or less permanent attention; and in this regard, it contrasts notably with other activities such as purchasing inputs, working in the fields, harvesting, processing and marketing, each of which requires concentrated effort at specific times during the year. Perhaps it is precisely the seasonality of productive activities which makes them stand out in the daily life of rural communities, while work in the realm of provisioning is less visible but steadier.

The viability of any process of popular organization at the regional level depends in large measure on combining permanent efforts with more immediate responses to the challenges of the moment; and a common weakness of many producers' organizations is precisely their tendency to engage in sporadic activism. Subject to the whims of agricultural and economic cycles, these organizations combine periods of idleness with phases of intense activity in a way which undermines their stability. Work in the field of provisioning can significantly offset such difficulties: on both the Costa Chica and the Costa Grande, it is evident that although the village supply councils and the regional warehouse committee almost never play a leading role in the overall process of regional organization, their presence lends stability to the latter.

LESSON 6. *Attention to provisioning issues broadens the social base of regional peasant organizations and meets the most general needs of the population.*

The consumption of basic food staples is obviously a universal necessity, and provisioning is thus a topic of general interest. Although the most remote communities and the poorest sectors of the population suffer most intensely from provisioning problems, all rural people, whether ejidatarios, private smallholders, or day laborers, whether organized or disorganized, are interested in ensuring adequate access to basic consumers' goods. The all-inclusiveness of organizations of rural consumers contrasts strongly with the relatively more exclusive nature of other forms of regional association -- even those such as the union of coffee growers on the Costa Grande and the union of corn producers on the Costa Chica, which may be stronger and develop larger programs but cover less of the population.

It is often the case that programs designed to facilitate access to credit and manufactured agricultural inputs, and to promote the marketing of farm products, favor the slightly better off within any rural population and thus provide some impetus to existing trends toward polarization. Programs of basic food supply, on the other hand, have different effects, since they favor not the somewhat better off but the poorest groups of rural inhabitants, who live the daily drama of provisioning with greatest intensity. Therefore on both the Costa Chica and the Costa Grande, the promise of assistance in the field of basic provisioning can generate organizational efforts in small communities and settlements with weak economies, where there are no producers organizations and where the latter would be very difficult to establish. In the process, regional organizations broaden their social base and fulfill their obligations to promote social justice by turning their attention to the most disadvantaged sectors of the population.

LESSON 7. *Community stores can benefit from important economies of scale, since they are supplied through modern commercial networks, but they still confront an inherent contradiction between operating profitably or providing an essential service to their clientele.*

If up to this point we have attempted to understand how rural provisioning programs fit into broader efforts of regional development and how they are related to governmental agencies like Diconsa, it is no less necessary to understand a series of problems which arise within the rural supply network itself.

As noted at the outset of this discussion, associative enterprises operating in the field of rural provisioning confront an inevitable dilemma: they cannot function profitably, as a private enterprise would do, and still provide the service to local consumers which is their raison d'etre. Serving poor consumers living in relatively remote areas is not a good business proposition; and for this reason, most rural people are dependent upon precarious networks of small stores run in an artisanal fashion by local families. The latter manage to survive despite their high costs and the slow rotation of their stock because in many cases they operate at a subsistence level and, above all, because they transfer their high costs to the consumer.

Rural stores associated with the Diconsa system cannot pass these costs on to their clientele without betraying their mandate. Peasant provisioning systems exist precisely in order to sell goods at low prices in places where selling is an expensive proposition. Also unlike small private merchants, whose commercial activity takes place within the context of a domestic economy, associative rural stores form part of large networks which function within a modern administrative and financial framework.

It might seem that since the latter can benefit from important economies of scale, generated through the Diconsa system, it should be possible to resolve the contradiction between providing a much-needed service and covering costs. This is partially true, but the advantage should not be overestimated. If rural storekeepers offer services which are unsatisfactory and expensive, this is not so much because small merchants are inefficient as because they operate within a setting which is not easily adapted to the business strategies employed by large commercial chains. In fact, there is a real danger that networks of cooperative rural stores may attempt to copy systems utilized by large-scale enterprises, in a market where these procedures are not viable. Community supply programs have at least as much to learn from small merchants as from modern corporations.

LESSON 8.   *To function efficiently, associative enterprises must manage their greatest resource-- the labor of their members--with care.*

One of the ways to deal with the contradiction between operating at a profit and providing a necessary service to low-income rural people is to utilize subsidies efficiently. Another, of perhaps greater importance, is to mobilize the labor and creative energy of consumers. Cooperative rural stores have one advantage over private businesses: consumers are not just a market, creating an abstract demand for goods, but human beings capable of participating in a common effort to improve the provisioning system.

We are not referring here to voluntarism -- a useful resource but one that is quickly exhausted -- but rather to the creation of an objective human resources economy. It is a fact that communities construct stores, maintain roads, unload merchandise and generate resources through any number of collective and individual activities. Elected representatives fulfill managerial functions, evaluate work and formulate proposals. All of this is vital for the survival of the project, even though it is not expressed in monetary terms.

To take full advantage of the human resources at their disposal, associative enterprises must create a dual accounting system, in which value is expressed both in monetary terms and in terms of non-salaried contributions of labor. The resources accounted for within the latter framework are in fact the more valuable and must be rigorously managed, since they have a finite limit and can be exhausted. If monetary outlays that are not recovered lead to bankruptcy, community efforts that are not paid back with better service lead (sooner rather than later) to social disarray.

LESSON 9.   *Rural supply networks transfer resources within regions, from more profitable central areas to less profitable peripheral ones, and this implies a form of internal subsidy.*

Private commerce in both regions under study is structured in concentric circles, so that in the center of the system, around the principal towns of each region, there is a high level of activity and a diversified commercial structure, offering prices which are not much above the national average; while in the periphery, with its scattered and sparsely populated communities, stores are few, poorly stocked and expensive. The logic of private commercial capital favors the center over the periphery, concentrated over dispersed demand, accessible communities over those which are difficult to reach, areas with high to medium buying power over sectors with very low income.

The spatial logic of alternative provisioning systems is precisely the inverse. In networks of peasant stores, the greatest effort is made in the periphery, where the need for service is most acute, and the system is of relatively less importance in larger towns. Obviously, the peripheral market, with its long supply routes, implies higher operating costs, less volume and slower rotation; but this cost differential is not reflected in consumer prices, which are the same in all stores.

Giving priority to service over profits, and to the periphery over the center, is made possible by the fact that resources can be transferred from stores in the larger regional centers, where operations are more profitable, to those in small settlements. Thus we see that a system of internal subsidies exists within the regional provisioning structure and that this mechanism plays a significant role in the operation of the program.

LESSON 10. *Conflict of interest between local stores and the regional warehouse is inevitable. The structural roots of this conflict should be clearly understood and the benefits of dialogue recognized.*

Regional supply systems are networks made up of dozens of stores and one warehouse. At the heart of this apparatus is a central administration, located within the warehouse, which deals with suppliers and with Diconsa, manages regional storage and transport facilities and oversees the distribution of merchandise to local stores. The central administration also handles all accounting, for each store and for the warehouse.

There are many tensions and contradictions within this framework, and all too frequently these are seen in personal or narrowly institutional terms. When supply systems continue to be associated closely with Diconsa, conflict between local stores and the warehouse management is interpreted as a struggle of local people against the government bureaucracy. When the entire system belongs to organized consumers, as in the case of the Costa Grande, disagreement between community groups and the central warehouse can be seen as a legacy from the past.

There is some truth in this, but the root of the problem is deeper. In essence, each kind of institution pursues a specific goal: 1) stores are community organizations which must attempt to meet the needs of specific local consumers; while 2) the central administration of the warehouse serves a wider group of consumers and attempts to maintain the financial equilibrium of the system. Each of these sets of interests is legitimate.

It is important that local groups come to understand the problems of the entire system; but the widening of their perspective cannot imply that community organizations will no longer put forward a defense of their own interests. The fact that warehouses bargain with stores, and that there is criticism from below of those above, constitutes a demonstration of vitality and provides one way of judging the legitimacy of the central administration. Although they may sometimes seem particularistic and irrational, the positions of the local committees are an expression of grassroots sentiment and counterbalance an inevitable tendency on the part of the central administration to adopt an unresponsive managerial stance.

LESSON 11. *Rural provisioning systems have different functions in different rural contexts.*

Rural provisioning systems, whether government-run, consumer-owned, or mixed, were not created for the purpose of replacing private commerce, but to protect local livelihood by regulating prices through competition. It is above all this regulatory function which justifies the existence of peasant stores in medium and large towns, where private businesses are dominant and cooperative stores are marginal in terms of the percentage of all demand they meet. Under such circumstances, competition among merchants themselves tends to reduce the likelihood of oligopolistic price setting. Nevertheless cooperative stores do play an important role in the regulation of the price of grain and other staple products in these towns, since it is through such channels (as well as through local corn mills) that subsidies are transferred to the consumer.

In the smallest and most distant settlements, in contrast, the rural provisioning system significantly complements private trade and sometimes replaces it. Here the principal function is not to regulate prices but to offer a service that otherwise would not exist.

Finally, there are places on the extreme periphery of the system where creating a permanent retail outlet is not rational, no matter how much the regional network might subsidize the least profitable stores. Here the periodic delivery of rations or food packets to organized consumers is likely to be the most effective and cost efficient alternative.

LESSON 12. *Since rural consumers must meet a constant need for basic products with an irregular annual income, networks of rural stores must confront the challenge of organizing demand as well as supply.*

Tensions within rural supply systems are expressed not only in spatial but also in temporal terms. One of the most significant dilemmas of rural life is precisely the lack of correspondence between the annual flow of income, which is sharply seasonal, and a constant need for consumption goods throughout the year. Therefore rural households often resolve pressing needs for money, agricultural inputs or other goods through recourse to strategies which impoverish them. Loans from usurers, purchases made on credit and the pre-harvest sale of crops are the options most commonly available; and these are also the traditional mechanisms through which small-scale capitalists are able to make money.

One of the immediate objectives of any rural development program is the elimination of these ruinous arrangements, whether through improving access to income or to basic production and consumption goods. It should be obvious, then, that rural provisioning systems must go beyond organizing supply. The real challenge is not simply to make certain products available to the consumer at reasonable prices, but to organize demand, so that an irregular flow of income can be made compatible with an annual distribution of needs.

More than an efficient network of warehouses and stores, a rural provisioning system is an organization of consumers whose most basic unit is the household. Organizing supply is a technical problem that can be resolved by a few people; but consolidating and programming demand is a complex socioeconomic problem which requires the participation of all families and implies confronting some of the deepest dilemmas of village life. It cannot be accomplished without linking organization for provisioning with organization for production, since income and expenditure are inseparable within the domestic economy.

From this perspective, the most important and strategic provisioning experiments carried out during the past few years on the Costa Grande and the Costa Chica have been those which integrate consumption and production through programs like corn banks; the barter of consumer goods or their delivery for payment in kind; the delivery of food baskets at harvest time to areas where wage laborers are concentrated, or to remote villages which have no commercial infrastructure at all.

LESSON 13. *Corn banks can constitute a central element in the network of regional provisioning enterprises, but it is unrealistic to think that they can operate effectively without financial subsidies which offset the high cost of interest.*

For most rural families of the Costa Grande and the Costa Chica, corn is the central element of livelihood. Farmers view their grain as a product of their work and as a guarantor of family consumption, much more than as an investment or source of profit. Therefore they have not the slightest doubt that their most rational strategy is to conserve grain for family consumption, marketing only what may remain after household needs have been met. Selling the family supply of corn, only to buy it back later, is an absurdity that is only justified under extremely difficult economic circumstances.

Reasoning along the same lines, some regional organizations have set themselves the task of protecting family consumption by creating a community corn fund or "corn bank" which makes it easier to avoid excessive "exports" and "imports" of grain. At first glance, such projects appear to be technically feasible and economically impeccable, since they not only lower transport costs, but also protect both producers and consumers in a market which is proverbially prone to offer very low purchase prices and very high consumer prices for corn. A corn bank can minimize losses which affect both producers and consumers and ensure, furthermore, that local families have access to grain from their own region, which is far preferable in both taste and texture to imported yellow corn.

In practice, however, corn banks have been difficult to run. There tend to be systematic shortfalls in meeting reception quotas for grain and complying with scheduled sales; there are grain storage problems; and financial costs skyrocket. It is as if the logic of self-provisioning, when applied to a regional rather than a domestic context, becomes inoperable. Yet the same rural organizations which have had difficulties managing corn banks find it easy to handle short-term mercantile operations like those practiced by private traders. Through associative enterprises of the latter kind, small producers are able to retain the profits what would previously have gone to middlemen.

Does this mean that storing corn for future consumption is rational only from the perspective of a peasant family, while on a larger scale, the only viable alternative is to follow the example of private merchants, accelerating the movement of grain and capital by buying and selling as often as possible?

In part, yes. On a domestic scale grain can be stored without an expenditure of money, so that for peasant households, keeping their corn does not entail any evident financial costs nor does it compete with more profitable investment options. In contrast, running a corn bank for an entire region does entail considering the cost of purchasing, storing, conserving and redistributing grain, as well as the financial costs that are involved in "freezing" capital invested in grain for several months. And that is where the real problem begins, for although the difficulties posed by purchasing, storing, and selling corn are not insuperable and these costs can be amortized without significantly increasing the price of the grain, financial costs are disastrous, particularly given the present level of interest rates.

Thus storing corn is a viable premercantile activity but impractical as a commercial operation on a regional scale, unless its financial costs are subsidized. And would such a subsidy be legitimate? Again the answer is yes, for the simple reason that governmental intervention in the purchase, importation, storage and distribution of corn already implies macroeconomic subsidies which are as large as they are justified and indispensable to the process of regulating the national supply of grain.

Although corn, like almost all agricultural products, is a seasonal commodity, it is consumed on a permanent basis, and therefore it must be conserved over a certain length of time. Stocks of grain rotate slowly, so that from a strictly mercantile point of view, prices should be high and, with seasonal variation of supply, should fluctuate dramatically. In order to avoid such undesirable distortions in the market, the government must engage in some regulatory activity, providing subsidies of a financial nature at the very least.

If peasant enterprises are to collaborate in purchasing, storing and redistributing corn, in order to avoid excessive and costly movement of grain and to facilitate a more rational system of regional and micro regional exchange, those enterprises must realistically assume the technical costs of the operation (purchasing, storage, conservation and redistribution). But it is imperative that they receive financial subsidies from the state in the form of low-interest credit which can be applied to working capital.

In the sphere of basic provisioning, the state (utilizing subsidies to pursue social goals, but excessively centralized, bureaucratic and inefficient) and private business (providing profit for traders, but extremely onerous terms for the majority of all producers and consumers) are not the only options. Associative enterprises are a third modality through which social goals can be furthered without bureaucratic management and at a reasonable cost. Subsidies which encourage inefficiency and conceal corruption are incompatible with the development of economic enterprises in the social sector, but this development is unthinkable without some financial compensation to counteract the speculative effect of high interest rates.

Chapter 9

TRANSFORMING FOOD POLICY OVER A DECADE: THE BALANCE FOR MEXICAN CORN FARMERS IN 1993

Kirsten Appendini

In 1991, a decade after the onset of economic crisis in Mexico, official statistics registered over 2.4 million rural producers -- 10.4 percent of the gainfully employed population of the nation -- cultivating corn during the spring-summer season. These farmers were spread throughout the countryside, where corn was being grown on 48 percent of the total crop area, including 59 percent of all rainfed and 28 percent of all irrigated land.[1]

Ninety percent of the 2.4 million producers worked landholdings of 5 hectares or less. Their small plots accounted for 67 percent of the harvested area during the spring-summer season of 1991 and contributed 56.5 percent of its output. Even though over half (51.9 percent) of the corn harvest on plots of 5 hectares or less was destined to household consumption, 3.5 million tons (21 percent of the total 1991 corn harvest) entered the market. For smallholding families, corn thus continues to be very important both as an element in a strategy of local food security and as a means of obtaining a cash income. The volume of marketed corn produced on small plots is also important within the national food system, since it still amounts to double the average volume of imported grain.

In the early 1990s, small corn producers are, like the majority of Mexico's farmers, facing even greater challenges than they were at the outset of the crisis. Restructuring has implied the dismantling of public institutions charged with implementing agricultural policy, but not the creation of alternatives that can ensure the recovery and development of a stagnant and crisis-ridden agriculture. Furthermore, the expectation that deregulation of rural markets would attract private investment has in large part proved illusory.

In addition to the early challenges posed by restructuring during the 1980s -- including the reform, reorganization and/or liquidation of agricultural credit institutions, marketing agencies for inputs and crops, agricultural extension services and research -- Mexican corn farmers now face two more: the creation of a new option to privatize ejido land, as a result of the reform of Article 27 of the Constitution in 1991; and advancing trade liberalization, associated with the implementation beginning in 1994 of the North American Free Trade Agreement (NAFTA) between Mexico, Canada and the United States.

How will producers of corn in Mexico deal with this new economic environment, in which they will gradually be obliged to compete with foreign producers, particularly their counterparts in the grain belt of the midwestern United States? Will the former be able to survive at all? Is it important that they survive? What

---

1. Figures are taken from the National Survey of Corn Profitability and Productivity (*Encuesta Nacional de Rentabilidad y Productividad del Maíz, P.V. 1991, DGE-SARH*), cited in SARH (1992). Eighty-eight percent of all corn produced in Mexico is grown during the spring-summer season, when rainfed land and smallholdings are cultivated. The remaining grain is grown during the autumn-winter season, on irrigated land containing commercial farms in very specific areas of Mexico (especially the state of Tamaulipas, which accounted for 38 percent of the autumn-winter harvest in 1989-90).

pressures will be unleashed in domestic and foreign labor markets, and what forms of rural-urban and transnational migration will develop, as uncompetitive producers are pushed out of the Mexican countryside? What arrangements will constitute the future bases for food security in Mexico -- at national, community and household levels? Will Mexico become more and more dependent on corn imports, or will food security based on domestic output still be on the national agenda? In the latter case, how will agricultural policy be shaped to ensure higher levels of productivity and competitiveness in the Mexican countryside? These are some of the central issues in the current debate on the future of rural Mexico, as the country moves toward free trade and privatization.

Previous chapters of this book have shown how different kinds of corn farmers in very different parts of the country were affected by changes in agricultural policy during the 1980s, and how -- up to 1990 -- they attempted to redesign their livelihood strategies. The purpose of this closing essay is, first, to leave the reader with a retrospective summary of major policy changes during the decade just ended and then to provide up-to-date information on recent developments which are of central importance in understanding the policy and institutional framework shaping the life chances of small corn producers in 1993. As the Mexican economy becomes increasingly more integrated into a North American economic region, transcending its national boundaries, patterns of production in the Mexican countryside are bound to change still more than they did during the 1980s in both spatial and social terms, and so are the livelihood options of the rural population.

THE EVOLUTION OF AGRICULTURAL POLICY AND CORN PRODUCTION IN TIMES OF STABILIZATION AND ADJUSTMENT: 1982 TO 1988

When the contributors to this volume met in Tepoztlán, in January 1990, national agricultural statistics pointed to a deep rural crisis. As Figure 1 illustrates,[2] the output of corn in 1989 stood at a low average of 10.7 million tons, and the harvested area for that crop had dropped to 6.4 million hectares, with decreases registered for both irrigated and rainfed areas. Imports were increasing, reaching 3.6 million tons of corn and 4.5 million tons of other food and feed grains in 1989.

Figures 2 through 6 provide further commentary on the policy determinants of this crisis. Public expenditure and investment in rural areas, availability of official agricultural credit, levels of subsidies on interest rates for rural loans, and real support prices had by 1989 reached the bottom of a downward trend which began with the contraction of public resources in 1982, but which accelerated from 1986 onward.

As noted in the introduction to this book, agricultural production -- and within it, the production of grain -- held up relatively well, even in the face of constantly contracting public expenditure, during the first years of macroeconomic stabilization and adjustment (between 1982 and 1986), until a second fiscal crisis in 1986, and then the impact of a heterodox stabilization policy (implemented at the end of 1987), created new and often insurmountable difficulties.

After a recession in 1982-1983, agricultural output in fact grew at a rate of 4.3 percent per year from 1983 to 1985. Corn output increased 3.2 percent per year and national production reached a high of 14.1 million tons in 1985, surpassed only by the record harvest of 14.9 million tons during 1981, when agriculture received unusual public support through the Mexican Food System, or SAM (Appendini 1992, pp. 123 and 231).

---

2. All figures are located at the end of the chapter.

Several factors may explain this positive performance during the first years of the debt crisis. In the first place, an initial 'shock' adjustment implemented in 1983, in order to reduce the fiscal deficit and inflation, was followed by more gradual adjustment policy in 1984 and 1985 (Ros and Rodríquez 1986, Ros and Lustig 1987). Thus although public expenditure and investment in rural areas were cut, it was possible for the government to protect rural credit, as well as real support prices, to some extent until 1986.

Corn, in particular, was relatively favored in spite of resource contraction. Though the total number of hectares with credit from the official rural bank dropped from 7.2 million hectares in 1982 to 6.0 million in 1983, and credit for corn fell from 3.4 to 2.4 million hectares, coverage for corn recovered by 1985. The number of hectares dedicated to corn cultivation with the benefit of credit increased at an annual rate of 12.5 percent from 1983 to 1985, while the total amount of land receiving official agricultural credit grew at a lower rate (8.9 percent). In 1985, 35.6 percent of the acreage receiving Banrural credit was dedicated to corn, a proportion which reached a high of 39.3 percent in 1988 (Appendini 1992, p. 109).[3]

The support price for corn also increased in real terms until 1987 (except for a drop in 1986), remaining well above world prices and above the support price of sorghum, which competed directly with corn on rainfed land. Until 1987, the price of corn was also evolving favorably in relation to changes in the price of fertilizers and certified seeds. All of these factors -- as well as good weather after 1982-1983 -- contributed to a growth of output on both rainfed and irrigated land, although the greatest source of dynamism quite clearly came from the latter (a 9.5 percent growth of output between 1983 and 1985 on irrigated holdings, compared to 1.9 percent on non-irrigated ones).

The positive trend in output ended in 1986. Adverse climate no doubt played some role in the change, but the most important element in the decline of corn production during the late 1980s was rapidly falling public expenditure and investment in rural areas. The profound fiscal crisis created by a contraction of state oil revenues encouraged new constraints on public spending in the countryside, as can be seen in Figures 3 and 4.

At the same time, the total amount of credit for agriculture contracted, although the number of hectares cultivated in corn which were covered by the official credit system actually increased slightly until 1987, as credit was spread wider but thinner. Banrural credit was destined more to rainfed than to irrigated land, thus concentrating on distributing scarcer resources to relatively less favored smallholders (Myhre 1993). But credit cost more: subsidies were reduced until Banrural interest rates reached the average cost of money in 1986.

Real corn prices also slumped in 1986, recovered in 1987, and then dropped to historic lows in 1988 and 1989. Corn farmers did not respond to the temporary price stimulus in 1987. Production decreased by 2.4 million tons between 1987 and 1988, harvested area decreased by 1.1 million hectares, and output did not recover for the rest of the decade.

The implementation of a heterodox stabilization program at the end of 1987 was the final blow to agriculture. This program was designed above all to fight inflation, and it rested on fixing the key prices in the economy -- the exchange rate, the prices of basic commodities and wages -- while continuing to reduce the fiscal deficit and encourage trade liberalization.

With a fixed exchange rate, export agriculture in Mexico gradually lost the competitive advantage previously generated by repeated devaluations, while imports became correspondingly cheaper for Mexican consumers. Importing cheap grain from the United States was of course consistent with a cheap food policy, since it contributed to reducing the public budget deficit and made it less necessary for the government to buy

---

3. For a detailed analysis of rural credit for corn see Myhre (1993).

up local grain at support prices which were double the prevailing international price. Needless to say, rising imports were also consistent with a growing commitment to trade liberalization.

Corn support prices were fixed by taking into account the officially approved movement in the general price index, but adjustment was not large enough to prevent their erosion in real terms in both 1988 and 1989, when they reached their lowest of the decade. Prices of inputs -- fertilizers and certified seeds -- had been revised upward in the months prior to the agreement to freeze prices, in order to lessen the drain of subsidies on the budget, and agricultural producers were hit by a subsequent cost/price squeeze.

By the end of the decade, the ability of agriculture to adjust to crisis was clearly weakened, and the sector entered a deep crisis. Output within the sector as a whole decreased at a rate of 4.5 percent per year from 1987 to 1989. Basic food production was 11 percent less in 1989 than in 1981, while population had grown by 9 million people; and corn output fell at a rate of 6.1 percent per year from 1985 to 1989.

Imports increased from 1987 onward, facilitated by a credit line for food imports extended to Mexico by the United States government under the Commodity Credit Corporation's GSM-102 program. In 1986, the Mexican government began slowly to liberalize import licensing requirements for corn; and the corn flour industry, as well as other industries utilizing corn in their manufacturing process were allowed to import grain on a quota/licensing basis as a complement to domestic purchases. In 1989-1990, 40 percent of all corn imports were handled directly by private industries. The traditional tortilla industry was not, however, included in this arrangement. Conasupo remained the sole supplier of cheap grain for tortillas, implementing a system of delivery quotas and continuing to control the price of this basic food product (Appendini 1991).

At the end of the 1980s, then, economic crisis had spread across the Mexican countryside. The productive capacity of farmers and subsistence cultivators was much weakened, and the organizational strength of producers had deteriorated. Mobilization to demand better support prices ended in 1986-1987. The daily struggle to make ends meet in a context of declining and expensive credit, falling prices, rising costs, and insecurity concerning the fate of public institutions had differential impacts on producers, who survived by designing the kinds of livelihood strategies described in earlier chapters of this book.

With hindsight, it can be said that the agricultural crisis enjoyed relatively low priority on the government agenda between 1982 and 1988. During the De la Madrid administration, agricultural policy seems to have been shaped more by the requirements of broader macroeconomic policy than by any explicit policy of restructuring. Crisis management was the norm, implying the resolution of immediate conflicts and response to specific demands of producers as they fought for a share of contracting public resources. This explains the government's initial positive response during the first half of the decade to the demand of peasant organizations for better support prices. Corn was given priority at the time, both through price and credit policy, perhaps as part of a political and social strategy for buffering the impact of the overall economic crisis on the countryside (Myhre 1993).

With time, however, the original goal of national food security based on self-sufficiency became inconsistent both with the fiscal crisis and with the opening of the economy to foreign trade. Food security came to be defined largely in relation to concern about consumers -- the poor urban population whose income had contracted severely during the crisis. Feeding the poor at less fiscal cost was easier with imported grain, which enjoyed low, subsidized international prices and could be obtained with cheap credit.

Structural reform within the agricultural sector was on the policy agenda before the end of the De la Madrid administration: Mexico began negotiating a structural adjustment loan for agriculture with the World Bank in 1986. But restructuring did not occur during that presidential period. Macroeconomic policy was the priority concern in the last years of this administration (1987-1988). Its heterodox stabilization policy was on trial, with strains coming from high interest rates and an increasing trade deficit (Lustig 1992). In addition, 1988 was an election year and not suitable for policy experiments.

RESTRUCTURING THE COUNTRYSIDE: MODERNIZING WHOM?

This situation changed with the advent of the Salinas administration, which initiated a profound restructuring of the Mexican economy, oriented toward improving the competitive position of the latter in the world market.

The neoliberal technocrats who now took charge of reforming agricultural policy attributed the rural crisis to excessive state intervention, which had in their view distorted rural markets for decades. State agencies had been virtually the only source of credit, inputs, extension services and, to a large extent, marketing support for medium and smallholders within the ejido sector. Large subsidies on the price of inputs and on the cost of credit, as well as guaranteed grain prices, they argued, promoted inefficient resource allocation and encouraged small producers to rely on the state instead of searching for new opportunities, investments and markets. The agrarian law, which made it impossible to sell ejido land legally, to lease it or to use it as collateral for credit, was also criticized for limiting farm investment and making it difficult to attract private capital.

"Modernization" became the slogan associated with the new Salinas program for restructuring the countryside. The term was meant to imply more efficient resource allocation, increasing productivity, and greater competitive capacity in the international arena -- in other words, adjusting the agricultural sector to the needs of a changing national economy which would base future growth on exports and would become more closely integrated into regional trading areas.

Seen from the prevailing macroeconomic perspective, the problems of Mexican agriculture were simple: while agriculture, forestry and livestock production accounted for only 7.2 percent of the gross domestic product in 1989-1990, over 22 percent of the total labor force made a living in that sector. Most rural producers held plots so small that they could not make a living from agricultural and livestock activities alone. This in spite of the fact that most food and feed grains had traditionally been protected from foreign competition and that local prices were above prevailing international levels. Since the majority of all very small holdings were not economically viable, agricultural policy aimed at reactivating production could no longer be linked with requirements to resolve the social problems of the Mexican countryside -- poverty and underemployment -- which had for many years been kept in check by subsidies to production.

In spite of a decade of reduction in public spending, there was still a strong fiscal argument in 1988 for further reduction in subsidies which, it was argued, would only support an inefficient sector. The World Bank also put forward strong arguments for market deregulation and tied its loans to progress in this area (C. Schatan 1987). And, of course, implementation of trade liberalization policies required that the prices of agricultural commodities in Mexico be aligned with world prices.

"Modernization" thus rested on the premise that the government should withdraw from its former role as intermediary and provider of services within the agricultural sector and let the market take its place. Private resources should replace public resources. The role of the state in such a scenario was to create the proper institutional framework for ensuring that private capital would be attracted to the countryside, through policy reform and the restructuring of existing public agencies.

This new agricultural strategy was outlined in the Program for Modernizing the Countryside (*Programa de Modernización del Campo*), drawn up by the Ministry of Agriculture in early 1990 (SARH

1990). In the months following publication of the document, government policy closely followed the guidelines it laid out.

The modernization program underlines the importance of trade liberalization, promoting international competitiveness and encouraging efficient resource allocation, as well as reducing state intervention in the agricultural economy. This is to be accomplished by deregulating rural markets and by relying on policy measures differentiated according to the type of producer under consideration, thus recognizing the heterogeneity of the Mexican agricultural sector.

In the field of trade deregulation, the government proceeded in 1989 to abolish most import licensing requirements previously regulating the purchase of agricultural commodities abroad. In 1990, trade in only 57 agricultural commodities still required import licenses, compared to 317 in 1985 (GAO 1991, p. 14); and by 1991, the average tariff on all imports was only 13 percent (Banamex 1991, p. 416). Corn and beans continued, however, to be protected through restrictions on imports.

The first step toward restructuring public institutions was taken when the official rural credit bank redefined the nature of its clientele. In 1988, Banrural financed 7.2 million hectares. But in 1989, it declared that credit would no longer be given to farmers with a record of outstanding debt. In consequence, Banrural credit covered 1.8 million hectares less in 1989 than in the former year, then plummeted in 1990 to 2 million hectares, followed by a further decline to 1.2 million hectares in 1991 and 1992. Interest rates were pushed upwards toward the prevailing commercial market level and crop insurance temporarily suspended. The insurance agency previously working with the official rural bank, and blamed for vast corruption, was closed, to be replaced at a later time with the new firm AGROASEMEX which operates without subsidy.

Credit policy was the first area in which differential policies were designed to take into account the markedly heterogeneous nature of the Mexican farm sector. From 1989 on, official credit institutions distinguished three categories of producers. Larger farmers with profitable operations were to obtain credit from commercial banks, which began to be privatized in 1990. These farmers could also apply for a loan from special government funds such as FIRA (the Agricultural and Livestock Investment Guarantee Trust Fund of the Bank of Mexico), FIDEC (Fund for the Development of Commerce), and Bancomext (the National Foreign Commerce Bank). Farmers defined as "potentially productive" -- able to increase their productivity and to stay out of debt -- were to remain the clients of Banrural, and to be eligible as well for credit from FIRA and FEGA (the Trust Fund for Agricultural Insurance and Technical Assistance).

Indebted farmers, excluded from access to formal credit, as well as very poor cultivators who had never been covered by the credit system at all, were to be served by a new fund, established within the anti-poverty program of the Salinas administration -- Pronasol (the National Solidarity Program). Producers of corn and beans on marginal land became eligible to receive a fixed amount of credit for up to two hectares. Repayment goes to a community fund, so that social solidarity provides an incentive to repay the loan. In essence, the program constitutes a subsidy for subsistence corn provisioning: the amount granted covers no more than one-third the cost of production, if the value of labor is included in the calculation. In 1990 648,000 small-scale corn producers obtained credit from Pronasol, applied to aproximatedly 1.3 million hectareas (Méndez, Romero and Bolivar 1992).

The official crop marketing agency, Conasupo, was restructured at the end of 1989. Support prices were abolished for all commodities except corn and beans, and Conasupo withdrew from purchasing all basic grains except those two staples. The newly deregulated prices of most agricultural commodities adjusted to international levels, which meant a sharp drop in price. A new agency known as ASERCA (*Apoyos y Servicios a la Comercialización Agropecuaria*) was then set up, not to be a direct buyer of grain, but to act as an intermediary between private sellers and buyers of all grains except corn and beans. Facing pressure from well-organized producers of crops like soybeans and sorghum, who demand compensation for very low prices, ASERCA has had to intervene recently in the commodities market, providing compensatory payments which constitute a new kind of farm subsidy, based not on a medium-term policy but on short-term, individual negotiations.

The retail distribution system of Conasupo was also modified by the Salinas administration. Large supermarkets in the cities were closed; and distribution of basic staples through the government agency was targeted more toward the low income population, through small stores in poor urban areas and rural stores in the countryside. Prices of basic commodities sold in these stores were also revised upward and subsidies were cut. In 1990, the tortilla subsidy came under review, and a new mechanism for reaching low income families in large cities was implemented. Today each qualifying family (earning the equivalent of two times the minimum wage or less, and registered with the proper authorities) receives a free kilogram of tortillas per day. Although the price of tortillas to the general public has been increased, it is still controlled in order to support the price stabilization efforts of the government.

The agro-input industry established by the government during the 1960s -- including fertilizer manufacture (by Fertimex -- Fertilizers of Mexico) and seed production (by Pronase -- the National Seed Company) -- was also placed on the privatization agenda. From 1991 onward, private companies were allowed to sell certified seeds. The fertilizer industry was privatized in 1992-1993, and imports were concurrently liberalized. Irrigation systems were also privatized, as both large and small irrigation works were transferred to producers in irrigation districts, making them responsible for financing and operating their own local systems.

In conjunction with the Rural Modernization Program of the Salinas administration, several other programs were launched to raise productivity on land dedicated to basic crops in particular regions, and involving particular target groups (e. g., the *Programa de Estímulos Regionales de la Producción* [Program for Regionally-targetted Production Incentives] and the *Programa de Maíz de Alto Rendimiento* [Program for High-yielding Corn]). These efforts to provide farmers with regionally-specific technological packages have been successful in increasing yields, but they cover a very limited area and have not been continued from one year to the next. For this reason, they must be seen more as experimental programs than as a broad-based alternative of support to basic agriculture.

In sum, the post-1988 program for modernizing Mexican agriculture was oriented primarily toward deregulating markets for farm inputs and agricultural commodities. It did not constitute a program of agricultural development, which would have required providing sustained support for producers so that they could transform production processes, rationalize cropping patterns and gain access to new technologies. It was supposed that with the reduction of government involvement in agriculture, private investment would be attracted to the countryside, resources would be efficiently allocated and there would be a return to growth. After years of survival within an adverse context, however, farmers were poorly prepared to deal with trade liberalization, falling prices and scarce, expensive credit -- much less to search for new investment opportunities and switch into new crops and markets.

If the government no longer provided credit and subsidies, who would pay the cost of modernizing Mexico's largely unprofitable agriculture? The neoliberal answer to this question is that private capital must be attracted by finding a way to make investment in agriculture -- or in some sectors of agriculture -- profitable.

The reform of Article 27 of the Mexican Constitution, which deals with land tenure, constituted an attempt to move in this direction through introducing profound modifications in the legal structure regulating access to land in rural Mexico. Half of the Mexican countryside is included within the ejido sector. This is land distributed within the agrarian reform program and --until the recent constitutional reform -- subject to strict laws limiting the size of plots, the possibility of transferring rights, and the way both individually-held and common village lands can be used. The constitutional reform, enacted in January 1992, has opened the way for privatization of ejido land, removing existing legal constraints not only on property rights, but also on forms of investment and organization for production.

Smallholders within villages which work land granted them under agrarian reform law can now decide -- after going through a rather complex legal procedure -- whether to remain as an ejido or agrarian community, or to change partially or entirely to a system of private property. They can lease, sharecrop or sell their land, and use it as collateral for credit. (In fact, leasing and sharecropping of ejidal land has been a long established practice; but before the reform of Article 27 it was illegal.) They can also legally control larger amounts of land, by buying up or leasing other plots within the ejido -- up to 5 percent of the total -- and thus overcome the restraints of small farm size. Finally, they may not only form credit unions and rural associations, as in the past, but also create shareholding firms or enter into joint ventures without governmental supervision, in order to cultivate their land, market and process their crops, obtain professional services, and so forth.

The reform creates two alternatives: on the one hand, the complete privatization of rural property; and on the other, the strengthening the ejido -- or modernization, in the official terminology -- by opening up new possibilities for investment and profitable agricultural activity, mainly through association with private capital.

Approval of the constitutional reform -- after a debate notable for its brevity, considering the profound economic and political importance of the changes -- was encouraged by linking it to implementation of a new set of development policies for the countryside. Farmers' organizations which accepted the reform without enthusiasm were assured that the government was aware of the need to provide fresh financial resources for rural infrastructure, agricultural technology, and credit, as well as to support the distribution of inputs and improve facilities for crop marketing, provide subsidies on crop insurance, and continue to work toward resolving the problems posed by the large debt portfolio of Banrural. At the same time, Pronasol developed a new program, which finances small rural enterprises.[4] Nevertheless the flow of funds has been slow, non-transparent and subject to constant negotiations. Dissatisfaction is increasing in rural areas, as will be noted below.

The intention to form a free trade area between Mexico, the United States and Canada was announced before the reform of Article 27: small farmers' organizations were already discussing the possible impact of NAFTA on their livelihood, as well as the position to be taken by various groups of producers engaged in defending their crops. The outlook for Mexican agriculture in a free trade area is ambiguous, since there are bound to be both losers and winners. The latter are producers of certain fruits and vegetables who may expand exports to northern trading partners, and the former are producers of food- and feedgrains.[5]

Farmers organized in the Corn Producers Network (*Red de Productores de Maíz*) have repeatedly demanded that the crop not be included in the trade negotiations. When this demand was ignored, it became

4. "Díez puntos para la libertad y justicia en el campo mexicano," proposed by President Salinas in November 1991; followed by "Ocho puntos para un programa integral del campo," announced by President Salinas in August 1992. Another announcement that additional resources would be provided was made in February 1993.

5. For an overview of the implications of NAFTA for Mexican agriculture, see Appendini (1993). There is a general consensus that producers of food and feed grains will lose under trade liberalization. For an overview of the estimates generated by econometric models designed to analyze the impact of NAFTA on groups of crops, see Josling (1992).

urgent for the commercial strata of corn farmers to increase their productivity and competitiveness if they were to survive at all within an agricultural sector integrated into or complementary to that of the United States.[6]

According to the terms of the agreement, negotiated during 1992 and now awaiting approval by the United States Congress, Mexican producers of corn and beans will receive some protection over the short- to medium-term. A period of gradual liberalization, of 15 years duration, has been agreed upon for these two commodities. In the case of corn, import licenses will be abolished immediately, and replaced by a 215 percent tariff which will gradually diminish. Mexico will simultaneously establish a tariff-free import quota, starting at 2.5 million tons a year and increasing 3 percent annually.

CORN AND MODERNIZATION

Very few Mexican corn producers are competitive, if we consider their ability to produce profitably at international prices. Forty percent of all smallholders have plots of one hectare or less, with average yields of 1.4 tons per hectare. The average yield on plots from 1 to 5 hectares is 1.6 tons per hectare. Even farmers working more than 5 hectares of land in Mexico have average yields (2.4 tons per hectare) of only one-third the average for the United States (7.4 tons per hectare). Relatively low productivity creates a situation in which, according to one estimate, 38.6 percent of all holdings producing corn in Mexico had costs above the support price level in 1991. Comparing costs with international prices, only 7.9 percent of these holdings could be considered profitable (SARH 1992).[7]

Nonetheless there are official projections which suggest that, with appropriate technology, Mexico can reach self-sufficiency in corn, producing enough to feed the entire population without consistent reliance on imports, even within a free trade framework. The National Institute of Agricultural and Forestry Research (INIFAP) has carried out studies which conclude that there is a range of good cropland in the Mexican countryside, with appropriate soil characteristics, on which farmers can obtain considerably higher average yields of corn (3.1 tons per hectare), increasing to an average of 5.6 tons per hectare in the near future. But only 26 percent of the harvested area of the country is adequate for the proposed technology (INFOGSPUAL, 1992, table 4); and it is the better-off cultivators on good rainfed land, as well as commercial farmers in irrigation districts, who might be able to adopt the new technological package. The problem remains that more than 2 million poor cultivators and their families do not figure in any alternative agricultural policy.

To date, the government has not confronted the challenge of designing an agricultural policy that will meet the urgent need of most farmers to improve their productivity and access to essential resources. It has, however, implemented price and trade policies which have favored corn production since 1990. Such a partial and biased policy well illustrates the enormous complexity of the current restructuring effort and the contradictions it entails.

In fact, with the deregulation of markets for most food and feed grains except corn and beans, which began in 1990, prices for the former have dropped, while the price of corn remains relatively high. Large farmers growing other grains for the domestic market therefore switched to corn when the relative price became more profitable; and in consequence corn output grew on irrigated land, as well as increasing for the autumn-winter season's harvest -- both signs that corn cultivation has been adopted by non-smallholding

---

6. A series of meetings were held by peasant organizations throughout 1991 and 1993 to discuss the situation of grain producers. See Boruconsa (1991), Comisión de Seguimiento (1991, 1992), Tercer Encuentro Nacional de Organizaciones Económicas Campesinas, Sonora (1992).

7. These estimates do not consider the subsidies implicit in international prices.

agriculture. Corn production also expanded in states like Sinaloa, Chihuahua and Sonora, where that grain had not been planted for years. In 1991 these three states contributed 14 percent of the total corn harvest of the country, while in 1989 their contribution had been only 4.6 percent. This increase of corn cultivation on entrepreneurial farms partly explains the fact that the corn harvest reached a record average level of 14 million tons from 1990 to 1992.

The outcome of such patterns of crop substitution has been contrary to the spirit of deregulation and to the stated intention of targeting any remaining subsidies toward the relatively more disadvantaged groups in the countryside. For example, Conasupo has increased -- not decreased -- the amount of corn purchased at support prices (reaching 29 percent of domestic output in 1992), and has favored the best-endowed regions in its programs. In 1992, the agency bought up 98 percent of the total corn harvest in the "new" corn regions of Sinaloa and Chihuahua, while receiving only 20 percent of the harvest in Jalisco -- the most important corn producing state of the country, and a region in which small- and medium-sized commercial farmers predominate. At the same time, the government crop agency supplied grain to buyers who were no longer supposed to have access to subsidized corn. Thus in 1992 the livestock sector received 16 percent of all grain distributed by Conasupo during that year and the starch industry 11 percent, at prices lower than those charged to the tortilla industry and to rural Conasupo stores. This meant higher subsidies for industries producing non-basic commodities than for the industry producing tortillas [8].

Thus for the past few years, Mexico's self-sufficiency in corn is explained by a reversal of "modernization" policy, and not by the success of the model which has been formally proposed. Farmers have turned to a secure crop still enjoying a support price, instead of investing in new crops, such as vegetables for export, which would have been the desirable response within a model of development favoring an export orientation. Switching to export crops involves high transaction costs and implies participation in risky markets (Runsten 1992).

Although there was an upturn within the agricultural sector of Mexico in 1990 (with positive growth of 3.4 percent for agriculture, livestock and forestry combined, and 5.1 percent for agriculture alone), optimism faded when the sector grew only 0.5 percent in 1991 and experienced negative growth in 1992 (-4.2 percent).

From 1990 to 1992 there has been a slight increase in government expenditure and investment in the countryside, but neither has reached the level existing in 1987, when agriculture was already in the throes of crisis (see Figures 3 and 4). This slight recovery permits the government to take ameliorative action, channeling resources toward small commercial and semi-subsistence farmers in critical situations, rather than developing a consistent policy which could create the necessary preconditions for a more productive smallholding agriculture.

The recent evolution of farm credit, provided through Banrural, is not favorable in this regard. In 1992, official credit from this source covered just 1.2 million hectares -- some 6 million hectares less than in 1988-- including only 362,000 hectares of corn. Corn's share of the area financed by Banrural fell from 45 percent to 30 percent between 1988 and 1992. An estimate of Pronasol coverage for the poorer smallholders is about 2.5 million hectares, mainly dedicated to corn, but at a per hectare loan amount several times lower than that assigned to corn by Banrural and wholly inadequate for the financing of high-yielding technologies.

---

8. Private industry has been importing grain since 1987 at market prices. In order to clear stocks in 1992, Conasupo had to sell to these industries at the prevailing international price (383 new pesos per ton). During the same year, corn was sold to the tortilla industry at 554 new pesos per ton, to the corn flour industry at 750 pesos per ton and to Diconsa -- the rural stores of the Conasupo system -- at 595 pesos per ton (SARH 1992, p. 27).

Similarly, although support prices increased in real terms in 1990, they again fell to the lowest level of the past ten years in 1992. The cost of agricultural inputs and credit has increased at rates above those of support prices, creating an untenable situation for many commercial farmers. The fact that corn -- on which many producers lose money -- remains more profitable than other crops only illustrates the depth of the crisis for the commercial sector.

In fact, the trend in output of other basic crops since 1989 suggests that farmers now have difficulties competing with imported sorghum, soybeans, rice and wheat. Production of these commodities in Mexico has fallen and imports have grown. During 1991-92, sorghum imports increased 50 percent, soybean imports increased 47 percent, and wheat imports rose 144 percent (Bancomext 1993, p. 407).

By mid-1993, the Program for the Modernization of the Countryside showed signs of failure.[9] A wave of inconformity swept the rural areas of the country, uniting not only small and medium-sized dryland commercial farmers but -- significantly -- also some of the better-off farmers of the more prosperous agricultural regions, in a rising tide of protest. Producers were most concerned with resolving the debt crisis, since both Banrural and private banks have threatened debtors with foreclosure.[10] Farmers demanding a debt moratorium, credit restructuring and access to new money took to the road. The central square of Guadalajara, Jalisco, was occupied for over two weeks by farmers and their tractors; 800 smallholders affiliated with the Democratic Peasant Union (*Unión Campesina Democrática*) also camped for more than two weeks in the main square of Mexico City, outside the presidential palace (*La Jornada*, September 1, 1993). At the national level, the Permanent Agrarian Congress (*Congreso Agrario Permanente*, or CAP), which includes the majority of all smallholders' organizations, began to press the Finance Ministry for a solution to the problem of rural indebtedness; and the National Peasant Confederation (*Confederación Nacional Campesina*, or CNC), meeting at its national congress during August 1993, presented a long list of suggestions for solving the problems of farmers -- accompanied by a promise to support the official party in the 1994 presidential elections.

In effect, the "potentially productive" and "productive" farmers to whom the modernization program had been addressed were pressing for the kind of agricultural policy reform which would allow them to become competitive -- or at least to survive -- within the current context.

The Salinas administration responded with a new rural program (Procampo), announced in October 1993. For over a year, the policymaking team of the Ministry of Agriculture, committed to the modernization program, had been considering the possibility that the Mexican government could replace all remaining support prices and agricultural subsidies with direct payments to farmers, of a kind which would not countervene NAFTA and GATT regulations. Direct income subsidies would be justified by the fact that the basic crops of Mexico compete on the international market with commodities which are highly subsidized,[11] so that payments to farmers would be required to compensate them for loss of income due to trade

---

9. A document presented by the Forum of Rural Producers of the State of Sonora describes the situation as follows: "For the first time in the history of the Mexican countryside, we witness a crisis in which all rural activities are depressed simultaneously: fruits and vegetables; extensive and intensive cattle raising; pork and chicken farms; milk producers. There is a crisis in irrigated as well as rainfed areas -- a crisis which, in sum, questions the liberal economic model as a whole." (*La Jornada*, September 5, 1993).

10. Farmers' debts to private banks reached 2,607 million new pesos, and to Banrural 1,222 million new pesos, in August 1993 (*La Jornada*, September 5, 1993).

11. In 1991, the United States dedicated 35 billion dollars to agricultural subsidies, and the European Community allocated 84 billion dollars to that purpose. Since Mexico lowered subsidies for corn, sorghum, soybeans and wheat substantially in 1989, and for rice in 1990, it had by 1991 a lower subsidy for sorghum, wheat and rice than the United States and the European Community. The Mexican subsidy for corn and soybeans was lower at that time than in the European Community (SARH 1992).

liberalization. The importance of grain production in the rural economy of Mexico and the number of producers involved also has been utilized as an argument for instituting direct income subsidies.[12]

When the final decision on income subsidies was made, the level of compensation fell far short of any meaningful support for farmers attempting to transform their operations into businesses competitive on the world market. The new subsidy does, however, constitute a welfare payment of some significance for lower-income rural people; and it implies an enormous fiscal expenditure for the Mexican government (about 3.5 billion dollars during 1994).

All farmers who have grown basic crops during the last three years are eligible for the program, whether or not they have marketed any of their output.[13] This represents a fundamental departure from the way benefits were distributed through subsidized support prices, since in the latter case benefits could only be obtained if grain had been marketed. Each farmer will have the right to be paid for the number of hectares he holds in basic crop production; but once it has been proven that declared land has indeed been dedicated to the required crops, the subsidy is not tied in future to continued cultivation of any particular crop. Producers will be free to choose whatever land use seems most convenient.

Some 3.3 million producers are eligible under the scheme, which -- if it is comprehensive in its coverage -- will require the government to distribute 3.3 million checks throughout the Mexican countryside. It will also require a concurrent phasing out of the support prices still in effect for corn and beans, while sustaining direct income subsidies over a period of fifteen years (SARH 1993).

The program will begin during the autumn-winter cropping season of 1993-1994. The support price for corn initially will fall from its current level of 750 pesos per ton to 650 pesos, and the additional income subsidy payment will be 330 pesos per hectare (***Excelsior***, October 5, 1993). The net gain for a corn producer with average yields is therefore likely to be about 130 pesos per hectare. This is not an incentive to increase grain output, either by favoring basic crops relative to other rural activities or by providing the resources required to increase productivity. Furthermore, beginning with the 1994-95 autumn-winter cropping season, support prices will be eliminated, thus resulting in declining incomes for producers who are net sellers of corn, except in the unlikely event that subsidy payments are raised enough to offset the expected price decrease.

CONCLUSIONS

During the past few years, corn farmers have done better than other producers of grain, but they are nonetheless subject to the constraint of falling prices and rising costs, plus the uncertainy which is generated by the expectation that there will be further policy changes in the near future. Under NAFTA, import licensing and support prices for corn will be abolished; and Conasupo will no longer purchase corn in the countryside. The future of corn farmers under these circumstances seems rather bleak. Crop prices will decline immediately, and -- as just noted -- the direct subsidy provided by Procampo is irrelevant as an incentive to grow corn. Unless productivity increases are seriously promoted through new programs of credit and extension services, Mexican producers will not be able to compete with imported grain.

It is probable that large commercial corn growers will drop the crop when protection ends and will restructure their pattern of cultivation to conform to the new possibilities created by NAFTA: searching

---

12. See SARH (1992), Salcedo, García, and Sagarnaga (1993), Hibon et al. (1993).

13. Basic crops include corn, beans, rice, sorghum, soybeans, wheat, cotton and rye.

particularly for private investment -- foreign and domestic -- in the export crops that are expected to expand with greater access to the markets of Canada and the United States.

The survival of medium-sized farmers -- including the "potentially productive" -- will depend not only on the evolution of tariffs and income subsidies, which are of a short- and medium-term nature, but also on the commitment shown by the government to developing a viable, modern and productive agricultural sector, provisioning the internal market. In order to become more efficient in its use of resources and to increase productivity, this group of farmers needs technical assistance, tailored to regional and local circumstances (Hibon et al. 1993); they need cheap and secure credit, and reliable access to the market.

For medium- and small-sized commercial corn farmers, the situation might be improved if there were a deregulation of the price of tortillas, allowing the manufacturers of that basic product to raise their prices, and thus to rely less on cheap imported yellow corn and more on higher-quality Mexican white corn -- much preferred by consumers of tortillas (Appendini 1991). As noted earlier in this book, however, such a policy change involves weighing the costs and benefits to urban and rural consumers of maintaining an artificially low price for a basic staple in the diet of low-income consumers.

The group of "potentially productive" farmers is especially vulnerable at present, since the recent reform of Article 27 makes growing indebtedness -- related to a severe cost-price squeeze -- more risky than ever before. Since ejido plots can now be used as collateral for loans, default may lead to a temporary or permanent loss of land. Changes in the land tenure law do mean, however, that some of the better-off farmers in the group will be able to work larger holdings, joining small plots together and increasing productivity through the creation of new economies of scale.

The majority of the smallholders in the Mexican countryside will at best remain poor and marginal, and will be able to grow their own food on their milpa. Whether it is possible even to maintain subsistence activities will depend on the evolution of "social" programs like the Pronasol credit (*crédito a la palabra*) and the Procampo direct income payments, as well as on the real effectiveness of such payments in marginalized and isolated rural areas. These programs buffer pressure on the labor market and may lessen rural outmigration. But poor smallholders also face the threat of loosing their ejido land if indebtness --in this case not with banks, but with private moneylenders -- obliges them to sell their plots. Without access to a bit of land, millions of rural families can be at risk. Corn cultivation may provide only a fraction of these rural households' occupation and income, but as we have seen in earlier articles, it is the core of their livelihood strategies, and thus of food security at both household and community levels.

This is a new and serious danger, which has not been given sufficient attention in the food policy debate. For over a decade, food security has been defined largely with reference to the provisioning capacity of the country as a whole, and in relation to the degree of dependence on imports. There has been an especially marked tendency to think in these terms because the need to provide cheap food for the urban population dominated adjustment-related policy throughout the 1980s. Neither the recent evolution of agricultural policy nor the perspectives opened up within NAFTA seem to indicate any alteration in this macro-level view of food security. Yet in the 1990s, the survival of a great many people depends on reactivating domestic agriculture, reintegrating local and regional markets, and ensuring the livelihood of rural families.

Figure 1

Corn Output, Area, and Imports, 1980-1992

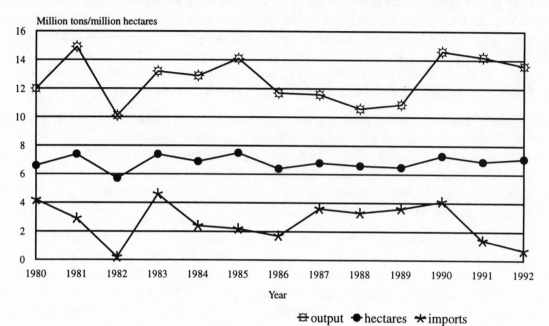

Source: Salinas de Gortari (1992).

Figure 2

Corn Support Price

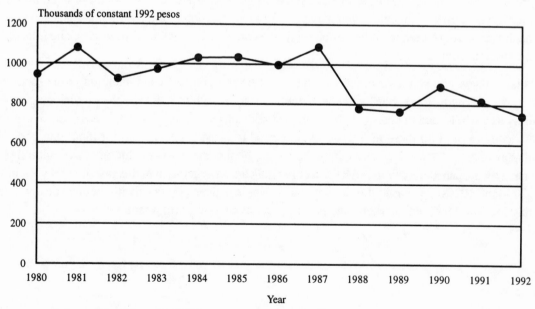

Source: Salcedo et. al. (1993).

Figure 3

Public Rural Investment

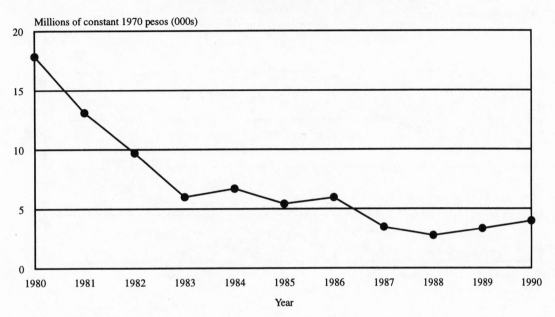

Source: SARH.

Figure 4

Public Rural Expenditure

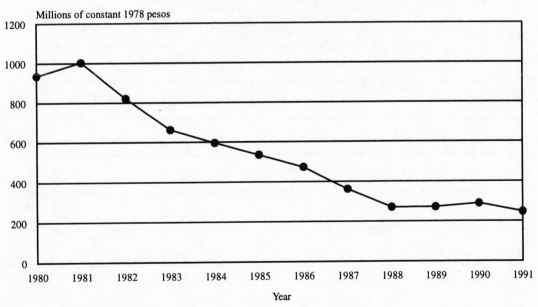

Source: Salinas de Gortari (1992).

Figure 5

Banrural Credit for Crop Production

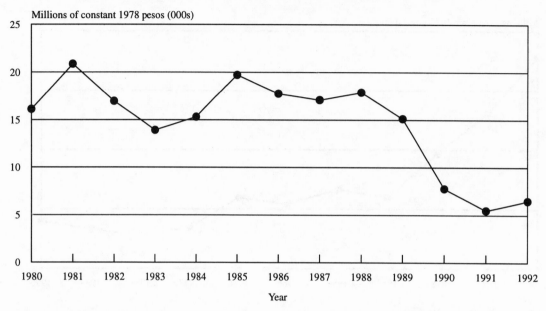

Source: Salinas de Gortari (1992).

Figure 6

Banrural Credit for Corn

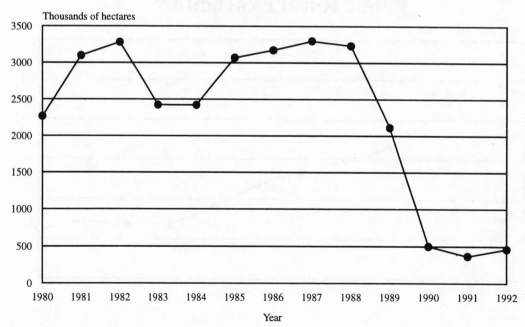

Source: Salinas de Gortari (1992).

APPENDICES

A. *Exchange Rate -- Pesos per U.S. Dollar*

Year	Pesos per Dollar
1955-75	12.50
1976	19.95
1977	22.73
1978	22.72
1979	22.80
1980	23.26
1981	26.23
1982	148.50
1983	161.35
1984	209.97
1985	447.50
1986	915.00
1987	2,227.50
1988	2,297.50
1989	2,680.75
1990	2,943.15
1991	3,074.95
1992	3,116.00
1993	N$3.19[a]
July 31, 1994	N$3.23

NB: Figures reflect exchange rates as of December 31. Because the figures do not reflect exchange rate variations throughout the year, utilizing them to convert peso amounts presented in the text to dollar amounts from 1982 onwards only yields approximate values.

[a] On January 1, 1993, the New Peso was established. 1 new peso = 1,000 pesos.

Source: Bank of Mexico, *Economic Indicators* (various).

B. *Measures of Area and Weight*

1 hectare = 2.47 acres

1 ton = 1,000 kilograms = 2,203 pounds

ACRONYMS

AGROASEMEX - Agricultural Insurance Company of Mexico
ANAGSA - National Agricultural and Livestock Insurance Company
ANDSA - National Warehouses Company.
APSN - Alliance of Producers of Southern Nayarit
ARIC - Rural Collective Interest Association
ASERCA - Agricultural Marketing Support and Services
Bancomext - National Bank of Foreign Commerce
Banrural - National Rural Credit Bank
Boruconsa -Conasupo Rural Storehouses
CAP - Permanent Agrarian Congress
CCI - Independent Peasant Confederation
CEPAL - United Nations Economic Commission for Latin America and the Caribbean
CIMMYT - International Center for the Improvement of Maize and Wheat
CIOAC - Independent Farmworkers and Peasants' Central
CNC - National Confederation of Peasants
Conacyt - National Council for Science and Technology
Conasupo - National Basic Foods Company
Coplamar - National Plan for Depressed Zones and Marginal Groups
CP - Graduate College of the SARH
CTM - Confederation of Mexican Workers
Diconsa - Conasupo Distributors
FDC - Peasant Democratic Front of Chihuahua
FEGA - Trust Fund for Agricultural Insurance and Technical Assistance
Fertimex - Fertilizers of Mexico (a state-owned company)
FIDEC - Fund for the Development of Commerce
FIRA - Agricultural and Livestock Investment GuaranteeTrust Fund of the Bank of Mexico
ICONSA -Conasupo Food Processing Company
IMF - International Monetary Fund
IMSS - Mexican Institute of Social Security
INCO - National Consumer Institute
INEGI - National Institute for Statistics, Geography, and Informatics
INI - National Indigenous Institute
INIFAP - National Institute of Agricultural and Forestry Research
Inmecafé - Mexican Coffee Institute
Liconsa -Conasupo Industrialized Milk Company
MDC - Peasant Democratic Movement
MDE - Democratic Electoral Movement
NAFTA - North American Free Trade Agreement
MINSA (later MICONSA) - Parastatal corn flour processing company
PACE - Program of Support for Ejido Marketing
PECE - Pact for Stability and Economic Growth
PAN - National Action Party
PLANAT - National Program to Support Rainfed Agriculture
PRD - Democratic Revolutionary Party
Procampo - Direct agricultural support payments program

Pronase - National Seed Company
Pronasol - National Solidarity Program
PSUM - Unified Socialist Party of Mexico
SAM - Mexican Food System
SARH - Ministry of Agricultureand Water Resources
SOCAMA - Peasant-Teacher Solidarity
SPP - Ministry of Planning and the Budget
TRICONSA - Conasupo Wheat and Bread Company
UELC - Union of Ejidos "Lázaro Cárdenas" of Ahuacatlán, Nayarit
UENCH - Union of Ejidos of Northwest Chihuahua
UGOCP - Popular General Union of Workers and Peasants
UNAM - National Autonomous University of Mexico
UPCALA - Union for the Progress of the Smallholders of Bustillos Lake

BIBLIOGRAPHY

Adelman, Irma and J. Edward Taylor. 1989. "Is Structural Adjustment with a Human Face Possible?: The Case of Mexico." Working Paper No. 500, Giannini Foundation of Agricultural Economics, Department of Agricultural and Natural Resource Economics. University of California, Berkeley.

Adelman, Irma, J. Edward Taylor, and S. Vogel. 1987. "Life in a Mexican Village: A SAM Perspective." Giannini Foundation Paper No. 843, Agricultural and Natural Resource Division, University of California, Berkeley.

Andrade, Armando N. and Nicole Blanc. 1987. "SAM's Cost and Impact on Production." Pp. 215-48 in Austin and Esteva 1987.

Appendini, Kirsten. 1990. "El marco del dilema actual sobre los precios y la comercialización del maíz: Política de estabilización en México." Paper presented at the UNRISD/Centro Tepoztlán Seminar on Corn and the Economic Crisis in Mexico. January. Tepoztlán, Morelos.

1991. "Los campesinos maiceros frente a la política de abasto: Una contradicción permanente." Comercio Exterior 41(10):976-84.

1992. *De la milpa a los tortibonos: La restructuración de la política alimentaria en México.* Mexico City: El Colegio de México/UNRISD.

Appendini, Kirsten and Diana Liverman. 1993. "Agriculture and Farmers within NAFTA: A Perspective from Mexico." Paper presented at the conference "Mexico and the NAFTA: Who Will Benefit?" of the Institute of Latin American Studies and the London Chamber of Commerce and Industry. May. London.

Appendini, Kirsten, Marielle P. L. Martinez, Teresa Rendón, and Vania A. Salles. 1983. *El campesinado en México: Dos perspectivas de análisis.* Mexico City: El Colegio de México.

Arizpe, Lourdes, Fanny Salinas, and Margarita Velásquez. 1989. "Effects of the Economic Crisis on the Living Conditions of Peasant Women in Mexico." In *The Silent Adjustment: Poor Women and the Economic Crisis.* New York/Santiago de Chile: UNICEF.

Austin, James E. and Gustavo Esteva, eds. 1987. *Food Policy in Mexico: The Search for Self-Sufficiency.* Ithaca, New York: Cornell University Press.

Banamex. 1990. *Examen de la Situación Económica de México* 66(776).

1991. *Exámen de la Situación Económica de México* 67(790).

Bancomext. 1993. "Sumario estadístico." *Comercio Exterior* Vol.43(4):402-11.

Barkin, David. 1981. "El papel del sector público en la comercialización y la fijación de precios de los productos agrícolas básicos en México." CEPAL. Document CEPAL/Mex/1051 . Mexico City: CEPAL.

1990. *Distorted Development: Mexico in the World Economy.* Boulder, Colorado: Westview Press.

Barkin, David and Gustavo López. 1990. "Migration from Small-Scale Agriculture: Can It Be Stopped?" Paper presented to the Commission for the Study of International Migration and Cooperative Economic Development.

Barkin, David and Blanca Suárez. 1985. *El fin de la autosuficiencia alimentaria.* Mexico City: Editorial Océano/Centro de Ecodesarrollo.

Barkin, David. and J. Edward Taylor. 1993. "Agriculture to the Rescue: A Solution to Binational Problems." In Daniel G. Aldrich and Lorenzo Meyer, eds., *Mexico and the United States Neighbors in Crisis.* San Bernardino, California: Borgo Press.

Bhaduri, Amit. 1983. *The Economic Structure of Backward Agnculture.* London: Academic Press.

Blaikie, Piers. 1985. *The Political Economy of Soil Erosion in Developing Countries.* Harlow, Essex, U.K: Longman.

Boruconsa. 1991. *Memoria del Encuentro Campesino de Experiencias y Alternativas para la Comercialización del Maíz; Ezatlán, Jalisco.* Mexico City: Boruconsa.

Cancian, Frank. 1965. *Economics and Prestige in a Maya Community: The Religious Cargo System in Zinacantán.* Stanford, California: Stanford University Press.

1972. *Change and Uncertainty in a Peasant Economy.* Stanford, California: Stanford University Press.

Cartas, Celso and Luz Maria Bassoco. 1987. "The Mexican Food System (SAM): An Agricultural Production Strategy." In Johnston et al. 1987.

Casas, A. and J. L. Viveros. 1985. *Etnobotánica mixteca: Alimentación y subsistencia en la montaña de Guerrero.* Mexico City: Faculty of Sciences, National Autonomous University of Mexico (UNAM).

Chávez, Paz. 1986. "El movimiento campesino en el noroeste de Chihuahua." *El Día*, Supplement on Rural Areas and Peasants. June 13.

CIMMYT. 1974. *The Puebla Project: Seven Years of Experience. 1967-1973.* El Batan: CIMMYT.

Collier, George A. 1975. *Fields of the Tzotzil: The Ecological Bases of Tradition in Highland Chiapas.* Austin: University of Texas Press.

1989. "Changing Inequality in Zinacantan: The Generations of 1918 and 1942." In *Ethnographic Encounters in Southern Mesoamerica: Essays in Honor of Evon Zartman Vogt, Jr.*, edited by Victoria R. Bricker and Gary H. Gossen. Albany, New York: Institute for Mesoamerican Studies, State University of New York.

Collier, George A. and Daniel C. Mountjoy. 1988. *Adaptándose a la crisis de los ochenta: Cambios socio-económicos en Apas, Zinacantan.* Serie: Documentos de trabajo sobre cambio en el campo chiapaneco (Documento 035-II/88). San Cristóbal de Las Casas, Chiapas: Instituto de Asesoría Antropológica para la Región Maya, A.C.

Comisión de Seguimiento, Red de Productores de Maíz. 1991. "II Encuentro Campesino de Experiencias y Alternativas Para la Comercialización del Maíz." September. Atlacomulco, Edo. de México.

1992. "III Encuentro Nacional Campesino de Experiencias y Alternativas para la Comercialización del Maíz." March. Pátzcuaro, Michoacán.

Coplamar. 1982. *Geografía de la marginación en México.* Mexico City: Siglo Veintiuno Editores.

Correa Guillermo and Rodrigo Vera. 1988. "El Pacto tronó por el lado del campo." *Proceso* 627 (November 7).

Costa, Nuria 1989. *UNORCA: Documentos para la historia.* Mexico City: Costa Amic.

Cruz, Isabel. 1990. "Las Uniones de Ejidos frente a la restructuración del program agropecuario oficial." Paper presented at the UNRISD/Centro Tepoztlán Seminar on Corn and the Economic Crisis in Mexico. January. Tepoztlán, Morelos.

de Janvry, Alain, Elisabeth Sadoulet and Linda Wilcox. 1989. "Land and Labour in Latin American Agriculture from the 1950s to the 1980s." *The Journal of Peasant Studies* 16 (3):396-424.

de Janvry, Alain and Raúl García-Barrios. 1988. "Rural Poverty and Environmental Degradation in Latin America: Causes, Effects, and Alternative Solutions." Paper presented at the conference " International Consultation on Environment, Sustainable Development, and the Role of Small Farmers" of the International Fund for Agricultural Development. October 11-13. Rome.

de la Mora Gómez, Jaime. 1990. "La banca de desarrollo en la modernización del campo." *Comercio Exterior* 40(10):943-52.

de la Peña, Moisés T. 1946. *Veracruz Económico.* Vol. II. Jalapa, Veracruz: Gobierno del Estado de Veracruz.

El Día. Mexico City daily newspaper.

Esquivel, Claudio. 1986. "Aplicación de tres métodos para la estimación del efecto del clima y de la tecnología sobre los rendimientos de maíz en temporal en el área del Plan Puebla." Mimeograph. Puebla, Mexico: CEICADAR.

Esteva, Gustavo. 1979. "La experiencia de la intervención reguladora en la comercialización agropecuaria de 1970 a 1976." In *Mercado y dependencia*, edited by Ursula Oswald. Mexico City: Nueva Imagen.

1980. *La Batalla en el México Rural.* Mexico City: Siglo Veintino Editores.

Excelsior. Mexico City daily newspaper.

Fox, Jonathan. 1990. "Organizaciones rurales de base versus 'La Ley de Hierro de la Oligarquía'." *Cuadernos de Desarrollo de Base,* No. 1.

1991. "La dinámica del cambio en el sistema alimentario mexicano: 1980-1982." In *Historia de la cuestión agraria mexicana, Volume 9 (second part)*, edited by Julio Moguel. Mexico City: Siglo Veintiuno Editores.

1992. *The Politics of Food in Mexico: State Power and Social Mobilization.* Ithaca, New York: Cornell University Press.

Fox, Jonathan and Gustavo Gordillo. 1989. "Between State and Market: The Campesinos' Quest for Autonomy." In *Mexico's Alternative Political Futures*, edited by Wayne A. Cornelius, Judith Gentleman and Peter H. Smith. Monograph Series No. 30. La Jolla, California: Center for U.S.-Mexican Studies; University of California, San Diego.

Fox, Jonathan and Luis Hernández. 1989. "Offsetting the Iron Law of Oligarchy." *Grassroots Development* 13(2).

Frente Democrático Campesino. 1988. "El movimiento campesino de Chihuahua y la lucha por el precio de garantía del maíz." In *Desde Chihuahua hasta Chiapas*, edited by Equipo Pueblo/Instituto Maya. Mexico City: Equipo Pueblo.

GAO (U.S. General Accounting Office). 1991. *U.S.-Mexico Trade: Impact of Liberalization in the Agricultural Sector*. Report to the Chairman, Committee on Agriculture, House of Representatives. Document No. GAO/NSIAD-91-155. Washington, D.C.: General Accounting Office.

García Barrios, Luis, Raúl García Barrios, and Elena Alvarez Buylla. 1988. "La tecnología de producción de una agricultura en crisis: El caso de San Andrés Lagunas." *Comercio Exterior* 38(7):578-85.

García Barrios, Raúl, Luis García Barrios, and Elena Alvarez Buylla. 1991. *Lagunas: Degradación ambiental y tecnológica en el agro semiproletarizado*. Mexico City: El Colegio de México.

González A., et al. 1989. "Los sistemas de producción agrícola en Alcozuaca y resultados del programa de experimentación agrícola." Mimeograph. Mexico City: PAIR/UNAM.

Gordillo, Gustavo. 1988. *Campesinos al asalto del cielo: De la expropiación estatal a la apropiación campesina*. Mexico City: Siglo Veintiuno Editores.

        1988b. "El Leviatán rural y la nueva sociabilidad política," Pp. 223-54 in *Las sociedades rurales hoy*, edited by Jorge Zepeda Patterson. Zamora, Michoacán: El Colegio de Michoacán/Conacyt.

        1990. "La inserción de la comunidad rural en la sociedad global." *Comercio Exterior* 40(9):803-15.

Guerrero, State of. 1987. *Programa de desarrollo de la montaña de Guerrero*.

Hardin, Garrett. 1968. "The Tragedy of the Commons." *Science* 162:1243-48.

Harvey, Alfredo. 1989. *Mexico: Políticas y subsidios agrícolas y alimentarios: 1970-1988*. Mexico City: CEPAL.

Harvey, Neil. 1990. "La lucha por la tierra en Chiapas: estrategias del movimiento campesino." Unpublished manuscript.

Hernández Aguilar, José Enrique. 1987. *En el nombre del maíz*. Mexico City: Pueblo Publishers.

Hernández Evangelina and Matilde Pérez. 1989. "El 90% del maíz se obtiene en tierras de temporal." *La Jornada*, December 12.

Hernández, Luis. 1990a. "Autonomía y liderazgo en una organización campesina regional." *Cuadernos de Desarrollo de Base*. No. 1.

        1990b. "La construcción social de la autonomía." In *De las aulas a las calles*, compiled by Equipo Pueblo. Mexico City: Equipo Pueblo.

        1990c. "Las convulsiones rurales." *El Cotidiano* 37:13-21.

Hewitt de Alcántara, Cynthia. 1978. *La modernizacíon de la agricultura mexicana.* Mexico City: Siglo Veintiuno Editores.

Hibon, Albéric, Bernard Triomphe, Miguel A. López-Pereira, and Laura Saad. 1993. "El maíz de temporal en México: Tendencias, restricciones y retos." *Comercio Exterior* 43(4):311-27.

INCO (Instituto Nacional del Consumidor). 1989. "El gasto alimentario de la población de escasos resursos de la ciudad de México." *Comercio Exterior* 39(1):52-58.

INEGI. 1990. "X Censo General de Población y Vivienda." Mexico City: INEGI/ SPP.

———. 1990. "Resultados Preliminares del XI Censo General de Población y Vivienda." Diskette. Mexico City: INEGI/ SPP.

INFOGSPUAL. 1992. *Programa Nacional de Alimentos* 3(2). Mexico City: Coordinación de la Investigación Científica, UNAM.

Instituto Nacional de la Nutrición (National Institute of Nutrition; INN). 1990. "Resultados de la Encuesta Nacional de Alimentación y Nutrición 1989." Mexico City: INN.

Johnston, B. F., Cassio Luiselli, Celso Cartas and Roger Norton, eds. 1987. *U.S.-Mexico Relations: Agricultural and Rural Development.* Stanford: Stanford University Press.

Josling, Tim. 1992. "NAFTA and Agriculture: A Review of the Economic Impacts." Unpublished manuscript.

La Jornada. Mexico City daily newspaper.

López, Pilar. 1990. "La Unión de Ejidos Lázaro Cárdenas: El estancamiento de un proyecto económico y la proyección política de su líder." Unpublished manuscript. Mexico City.

———. 1990. "La producción del maíz en la zona sur de Nayarit." Unpublished manuscript. Mexico City.

Luiselli, Cassio. 1987. "The Way to Food Self-Sufficiency in Mexico and Its Implications for Agricultural Relations with the United States." In Johnston et al. 1987.

Lustig, Nora. 1990. "Economic Crisis. Adjustment and Living Standards in Mexico: 1982-1985." *World Development* 18(10).

———. 1992. *Mexico: The Remaking of the Economy.* Washington, D.C.: The Brookings Institution.

Martin del Campo, Antonio. 1988. "La política económica reciente y la agricultura." Pp. 143-96 in *Las sociedades rurales hoy*, edited by Jorge Zepeda Patterson. Zamora, Micoacán: El Colegio de Michoacán/Conacyt.

Martínez Vázquez, Sergio. N.d. "El movimiento maicero en Chiapas. 1986-1990." Unpublished manuscript.

Masera, Omar. 1990. *Crisis y mecanización de la agricultura campesina.* Mexico City: El Colegio de México.

Maydón Garza, Marín. 1988. "El crédito agropecuario en tiempos de inflación." *Comercio Exterior* 38(7): 593-605.

Medellín, Sergio. 1988. *Arboricultura y silvicultura tradicional de una comunidad totonaca de la costa.* Master's thesis. Xalapa, Veracruz: National Institute of Biotic and Natural Resources (INREB).

Méndez, Luis, Miguel Angel Romero, and Agusto Bolivar. 1992. "Solidaridad se institucionaliza." *El Cotidiano* 49:60-71.

Monsiváis, Carlos. 1987. *Entrada Libre: Crónicas de una sociedad que se organiza.* Mexico City: Editorial Era.

Montañez Villafaña, Carlos. 1988. "Los condicionantes de la política agropecuaria." *Comercio Exterior* 38(8):679-85.

Montañez, Carlos and Arturo Warman. 1985. *Los productores de maíz en México: Restricciones y alternativas.* Mexico City: Centro de Ecodesarrollo.

Mountjoy, Daniel C. 1988. *Peasant Occupational Strategies in Response to the Mexican Economic Crisis.* Master of Arts paper. Center for Latin American Studies, Stanford University.

Muñoz, Maurilio. 1963. "Mixteca Náhuatl-Tlapaneca." In *Memorias del INI*, Vol IX. Mexico City: INI.

Myhre, David. 1993. "The Unseen Instrument of Agricultural Restructuring in Mexico: The Growth, Crisis and Erosion of the Official Credit System." Paper prepared for the Instituto Latinoamericano de Estudios Transnacinales (ILET), Mexico City.

Myren, Delbert T. 1969. *The Puebla Project 1967-1969: A Progress Report on a Program to Increase Yields of Corn among Small Producers.* El Batan: CIMMYT.

Nolasco, Margarita. 1980. "El sistema urbano de los paises subdesarrollados: El caso de Coatzalcoalcos-Minatitlán." In *Conflicto entre ciudades y campo en América Latina*, edited by Ivan Restrepo. Mexico City: Nueva Imagen.

Obregón, R. 1989. *Contribución al estudio del sistema de producción agrícola "tlacolole" en el municipio de Alcozauca, Guerrero.* Thesis. Autonomous University of Chapingo (UACH). Chapingo, Mexico.

Orozco Alvarado, Javier. 1990. "La situación agrícola en Jalisco en el contexto del neoliberalismo económico." *Reflejos* 2(8).

Ortiz, Benjamín. 1988. "En el Totonacapan, ganadería contra autosuficiencia alimentaria." *Revista Extensión* No. 28:9-12. Universidad Veracruzana, Xalapa, Veracruz.

Oswald, Ursula. 1990. "Crisis y sobrevivencia en Morelos." Paper presented at the UNRISD/Centro Tepoztlán Seminar on Corn and the Economic Crisis in Mexico. January. Tepoztlán, Morelos.

Pastor, R. F. 1987. *Campesinos y reformas: La Mixteca, 1700-1856.* Mexico City: El Colegio de México.

Puig, Henri. 1976. *Vegetación de la Huasteca.* French Archeological and Ethnological Mission to Mexico. Mexico City.

Quintana, Victor. 1988. "Ni mojados ni maquileros: Campesinos." Manuscript.

    1991. "El año en que la modernización no alcanzó." *Cuadernos Agrarios*, nueva época, No. 1:134-39.

Reyes Osorio, Sergio et al. 1974. *Estructura agraria y desarrollo agrícola en México*. Mexico City: Fondo de Cultura Económica.

Robinson, Sherman. 1986. "Multisectorial Models of Developing Countries: A Survey." Working Paper No. 401, Agricultural and Natural Resource Division, University of California, Berkeley.

Rodríguez, Evelyn. 1987. *Cambio y continuidad en el uso de los recursos naturales entre los totnacas de la costa del Golfo*. Thesis. Facultad de Antropología, Universidad Veracruzana, Xalapa, Veracruz.

Rogers, Everett M., in collaboration with Lynne Svenning. 1969. *Modernization among Peasants: The Impact of Communication*. New York: Holt, Reinhart, and Winston.

Rojo, Paz. "Entrevista al señor Paz Rojo. 1985. Secretario de Organización de la Alianza Campesina del Noroeste de Chihuahua." *El Día,* January 19.

Ros, Jaime and Nora Lustig. 1987. *Stabilization and Adjustment Policies and Programs*. Country Study 7 -- Mexico. Helsinki: WIDER.

Ros, Jaime. and G. Rodriguez. 1986. "Estudio sobre la crisis financiera, las políticas de ajuste y el desarrollo agrícola en México." Mimeograph. Mexico City: Joint Agriculture Division, CEPAL/FAO.

Runsten, David. 1991. "Some Potential Impacts of a U.S.-Mexico Free Trade Agreement on Agricultural Labor." *Rural California Report* 3(1).

    1992. "Transaction Costs in Mexican Fruit and Vegetable Contracting: Implications for Asociación en Participación." Paper prepared for the conference "The Transformation of Mexican Agriculture: Opportunities, Dilemmas and Implications for California" at the University of California, Berkeley. December.

Salcedo, Salomón, José Alberto García, and Myriam Sagarnaga. 1993. "Política agrícola y maíz en México: Hacia el libre comercio norteamericano." *Comercio Exterior* 43(4):302-10.

Salinas de Gortari, Carlos. 1992. *Cuarto Informe de Gobierno, Anexo*. Mexico City: Poder Ejecutivo Federal.

Salinas de Gortari, Raúl. 1990. "El campo mexicano ante el reto de la modernización." *Comercio Exterior* 40(9):816-29.

SARH. 1990. "Programa Nacional de Modernización para el Campo, 1990-1994" ["National Program for the Modernization of the Countryside, 1990-1994"]. *Comercio Exterior* 40(10):987-1008.

    1992. Propuesta de Programa Integral de Apoyos a Productos Básicos. November. Mexico City: SARH.

    1993. *Procampo. Vamos al grano para progresar*. Mexico City: SARH.

SARH/INCA-RURAL (National Institute of Rural Training). 1989. Letters of agreeement dated January 6.

Schatan, Claudia. 1987. "Efectos de las políticas micro y macroeconómicas sobre el sector agropecuario y la seguridad alimentaria en México." Unpublished manuscript.

Schejtman, Alejandro. 1982. *Economia campesina y agricultura emr)resarial: Tipologia de product ores del agro mexicano.* Mexico City: Siglo XXI Editores/CEPAL, Mexico.

Tercer Encuentro Nacional de Organizaciones Económicas Campesinas. 1993. *Conclusiones de productores de granos básicos y oleaginosas* August. Hermosillo, Sonora.

Toledo, Victor and N. Barrera. 1986. *Ecología y desarrollo rural en Pátzcuaro. Un modelo para el análisis interdisciplinario de comunidades campesinas.* Mexico City: Instituto de Biología, UNAM.

Tudela, Fernando et al. 1989. *La modernización forzada del trópico: El caso de Tabasco.* Mexico City: El Colegio de México/UNRISD/IFIAS/CINVESTAV.

Unomásuno. A Mexico City daily newspaper.

Warman, Arturo. 1988. *La historia de un bastardo: Maíz y capitalismo.* Mexico City: Fondo de Cultura Económica/Instituto de Investigaciones Sociales (UNAM).

Warman, Arturo and Carlos Montañez. 1982. *El cultivo de maíz en Mexico: Diversidad, limitaciones y alternativas.* Mexico City: Centro de Ecodesarrollo.

Zapata Martelo, Emma. 1990. "Un intento de leer el papel de la mujer en la crisis de la agricultura de subsistencia." Paper presented at the UNRISD/Centro Tepoztlán Seminar on Corn and the Economic Crisis in Mexico. January. Tepoztlán, Morelos.

THE EJIDO REFORM RESEARCH PROJECT
CENTER FOR U.S.-MEXICAN STUDIES
UNIVERSITY OF CALIFORNIA, SAN DIEGO

In December, 1991, Article 27 of the Mexican Constitution was reformed to permit - but not to require - the privatization of previously inalienable, communally-controlled ejido land. The ejido reform - in association with related constitutional amendments, revamped agrarian codes, and redesigned agricultural policies - changes key aspects of land tenure, state-campesino relations, and establishes the framework for how rural Mexicans participate in the national and international economies.

With financial support from the Ford Foundation and from the Tinker Foundation, the Center for U.S.-Mexican Studies has assembled a multidisciplinary research team to collect key data and to produce basic interpretations that will further medium-and long-term research on the epoch-making changes now underway in the Mexican countryside. More than thirty researchers from Mexican, U.S., and Canadian research institutions are members of the project, which began in July, 1992. By combining the talents of a diverse and highly-qualified body of researchers, complemented by students training to be the next generation of much-needed agrarian scholars, the project will result in information and analysis useful to persons interested in understanding the paths of change in rural Mexico.

The series, **The Transformation of Rural Mexico**, draws on the contributions of project members, as well as of other researchers, to offer policymakers, agricultural leaders, and scholars timely information on the emerging shape of the Mexican countryside in the form of papers, short monographs and books. At the conclusion of the project, an edited volume presenting major research findings will be published.

To obtain more information about the Ejido Reform Research Project, including descriptions of available and forthcoming publications, upcoming activities, and guidelines for the project's 1995 competition for small grants supporting graduate student field research in rural Mexico, please write to: David Myhre, Coordinator, Ejido Reform Research Project, Center for U.S.-Mexican Studies, U.C.-San Diego 0510, La Jolla CA 92093-0510 (FAX: 619-534-6447).

AVAILABLE TITLES

Productores del Sector Social Rural en México
SARH-CEPAL. $15.00 Order Code: DP-01 (In Spanish)
Economic Restructuring and Rural Subsistence in Mexico: Corn and the Crisis of the 1980s
Cynthia Hewitt de Alcántara, editor. $18.00 Order Code: DP-02
The End of Agrarian Reform in Mexico: Past Lessons, Future Prospects
Billie R. DeWalt, Martha W. Rees, with Arthur D. Murphy. $10.00 Order Code: DP-03
Rural Reform in Mexico: The View from the Comarca Lagunera in 1993
Raúl Salinas de Gortari and José Luis Solís González. $8.00 Order Code: DP-04
Rebellion in Chiapas: Rural Reforms, Campesino Radicalism, and the Limits to Salinismo
Neil Harvey, with additional essays by Luis Hernández Navarro and Jeffrey W. Rubin. $7.00 Order Code: DP-05
Viva Zapata!: Generation, Gender, and Historical Consciousness in the Reception of Ejido Reform in Oaxaca
Lynn Stephen. $7.00 Order Code: DP-06.